Lecture Notes in Computer Science 5127

Commenced Publication in 1973
Founding and Former Series Editors:
Gerhard Goos, Juris Hartmanis, and Jan van Leeuwen

David Hausheer

Jürgen Schönwälder (Eds.)

Resilient Networks and Services

Second International Conference on Autonomous
Infrastructure, Management and Security, AIMS 2008
Bremen, Germany, July 1-3, 2008
Proceedings

 Springer

Volume Editors

David Hausheer
University of Zurich, UZH
Department of Informatics, IFI
Communication Systems Group, CSG
Binzmühlestrasse 14, 8050 Zurich, Switzerland
E-mail: hausheer@ifi.uzh.ch

Jürgen Schönwälder
Jacobs University Bremen
School of Engineering and Science
Electrical Engineering and Computer Science
Campus Ring 1, 28759 Bremen, Germany
E-mail: j.schoenwaelder@jacobs-university.de

Library of Congress Control Number: 2008930170

CR Subject Classification (1998): C.2, D.4.4, H.3, H.4

LNCS Sublibrary: SL 5 – Computer Communication Networks
and Telecommunications

ISSN   0302-9743
ISBN-10   3-540-70586-4 Springer Berlin Heidelberg New York
ISBN-13   978-3-540-70586-4 Springer Berlin Heidelberg New York

Springer is a part of Springer Science+Business Media

springer.com

© IFIP International Federation for Information Processing 2008
Printed in Germany

Typesetting: Camera-ready by author, data conversion by Scientific Publishing Services, Chennai, India
Printed on acid-free paper   SPIN: 12324514   06/3180   5 4 3 2 1 0

Preface

This volume of the *Lecture Notes in Computer Science* series contains the papers accepted for presentation at the Second International Conference on Autonomous Infrastructure, Management and Security (AIMS 2008). The conference took place in Bremen, Germany, hosted by the Jacobs University Bremen. AIMS 2008 was organized and supported by the EC IST-EMANICS Network of Excellence (#26854) in cooperation with ACM SIGAPP and ACM SIGMIS and co-sponsored by IFIP WG 6.6 and Jacobs University Bremen.

This year's AIMS 2008 constituted the second edition of a single-track and standalone conference on management and security aspects of distributed and autonomous systems, which took place initially in Oslo, Norway in June 2007.

The first objective of the AIMS conference series is to stimulate the exchange of ideas in a cross-disciplinary forum where there is sufficient time for discussion of novel ideas. A second objective is to provide a forum for doctoral students to discuss their research ideas in a wider audience and to receive training to help make their research careers successful. To this end, AIMS includes a PhD workshop and a tutorial program that is offered as part of the main conference program.

The theme of the Second AIMS conference was "Resilient Networks and Services" with a specific focus on novel technologies that can provide resilience in a scalable, economic, secure, and autonomic way. The research papers included in the AIMS proceedings discuss topics such as autonomy, incentives and trust, overlays and virtualization, load balancing and fault recovery, traffic engineering and analysis, and convergent behavior of distributed systems.

For the main conference program, we received a total number of 33 submissions from 15 countries (according to the affiliation of the first author). All submissions were initially checked using an automated tool to identify text fragments that can be found in already published papers. The Chairs of the Technical Program Committee (TPC) then went over all papers to identify papers that should not enter the review process, e.g., because the topic was out of scope or the paper length was inappropriate, or the paper contained a large amount of already published data. The remaining 25 papers were assigned to TPC members for review. The majority of papers received four independent reviews and no paper had less than three reviews. At the end of the review phase, authors were given access to the reviews and invited to write a rebuttal, while the TPC members were invited to discuss their reviews online. Based on the reviews, the rebuttals, and the online TPC discussions, the TPC Chairs selected 13 full papers for presentation at the AIMS conference. We note here that overall the submissions were of good quality and the number of clear reject papers or out of scope papers was remarkably small. Additionally, a number of four work-in-progress papers, which are not included in these proceedings, were presented as posters during the conference.

The AIMS PhD workshop is a venue for doctoral students to present and discuss their research ideas, as well as, and most importantly, obtain feedback from the audience about their investigation carried out so far. This year, the workshop was organized in two technical sessions where selected PhD investigations were presented and discussed. The PhD papers included in this volume describe the current state of such investigations, including their research problem statements, investigation approaches, and outlines of the results achieved so far. For AIMS 2008, 12 papers were submitted to the workshop. Each of them was assigned for review to three members of the PhD workshop TPC, composed of experienced researchers in the field. After the review phase, the PhD Workshop Chairs together with the PhD workshop TPC identified eight papers to be included in these proceedings and to be presented during the conference.

We would like to thank the many people who helped make AIMS 2008 such a high-quality and successful event. Our thanks first go to the PhD Workshop Chairs Lisandro Granville and Aiko Pras and to the Tutorial and Keynote Chair Arosha Bandara for all their efforts in constructing the technical program. In addition, we would like to acknowledge the great review work performed by the members of the TPCs and the additional reviewers. Another special thanks goes to all authors who submitted their contributions to AIMS 2008. Furthermore, we would like to express our thanks to the submission system handler, who performed an excellent job. Finally, we would like to extend our thanks to the Springer team, namely, Alfred Hofmann and Anna Kramer, for the smooth cooperation on finalizing these proceedings. Last but not least special thanks go to the local organization handled by Renate Knappe, Ha Manh Tran, and Iyad Tumar, and to Jacobs University for hosting the AIMS 2008 conference on their fascinating campus.

April 2008

David Hausheer
Jürgen Schönwälder

Organization

AIMS 2008 was organized by the EC IST-EMANICS Network of Excellence (#26854) in cooperation with ACM SIGAPP and ACM SIGMIS and co-sponsored by IFIP WG 6.6 and Jacobs University Bremen.

General Chair

Jürgen Schönwälder   Jacobs University Bremen, Germany

Program Chairs

David Hausheer   University of Zurich, Switzerland
Jürgen Schönwälder   Jacobs University Bremen, Germany

PhD Workshop Chairs

Lisandro Granville   UFRGS, Brazil
Aiko Pras   University of Twente, The Netherlands

Tutorial/Keynote Chair

Arosha Bandara   The Open University, UK

Steering Committee

Arosha Bandara   The Open University, UK
Mark Burgess   Oslo University College, Norway
Olivier Festor   INRIA, France
David Hausheer   University of Zurich, Switzerland
Aiko Pras   University of Twente, The Netherlands
Jürgen Schönwälder   Jacobs University Bremen, Germany
Rolf Stadler   KTH, Sweden

Technical Program Committee

Panayotis Antoniadis   Pierre and Marie Curie University, France
Arosha Bandara   The Open University, UK

Jan Bergstra	University of Amsterdam, The Netherlands
Mark Burgess	Oslo University College, Norway
Georg Carle	Univeristy of Tübingen, Germany
Isabelle Chrisment	Nancy University, France
Alva L. Couch	Tufts University, USA
Costas A. Courcoubetis	Athens University of Economics and Business, Greece
Vasilios Darlagiannis	EPFL, Switzerland
Hermann de Meer	University of Passau, Germany
Zoran Despotovic	DoCoMo Euro-Labs, Germany
Gabi Dreo Rodosek	Universität der Bundeswehr München, Germany
Olivier Festor	INRIA, France
Thomas Fuhrmann	University of Karlsruhe, Germany
Lisandro Granville	UFRGS, Brazil
Heinz-Gerd Hegering	Leibniz Supercomputing Center, Germany
James Won-Ki Hong	POSTECH, Korea
Alexander Keller	IBM, USA
Jorge Lobo	IBM Research, USA
Emil Lupu	Imperial College London, UK
Hanan Lutfiyya	University of Western Ontario, Canada
David A. Maltz	Microsoft Research, USA
Martin May	ETH Zurich, Switzerland
George Pavlou	University College London, UK
Aiko Pras	University of Twente, The Netherlands
Bruno Quoitin	Universite Catholique de Louvain, Belgium
Danny Raz	Technion, Israel
Helmut Reiser	Leibniz Supercomputing Center, Germany
Giancarlo Ruffo	Università di Torino, Italy
Joan Serrat	UPC, Spain
Radu State	INRIA, France
Burkhard Stiller	University of Zurich, Switzerland
Maarten van Steen	VU University Amsterdam, The Netherlands
Kurt Tutschku	NICT, Japan
Marcel Waldvogel	University of Konstanz, Germany
Felix Wu	University of California at Davis, USA

PhD Workshop Committee

Gabi Dreo Rodosek	Universität der Bundeswehr München, Germany
Olivier Festor	INRIA, France
Hanan Lutfiyya	University of Western Ontario, Canada
Joan Serrat	UPC, Spain
Rolf Stadler	KTH, Sweden
Burkhard Stiller	University of Zurich, Switzerland

Local Organization

Renate Knappe   Jacobs University Bremen, Germany
Ha Manh Tran   Jacobs University Bremen, Germany
Iyad Tumar   Jacobs University Bremen, Germany

Reviewers

Detailed reviews for papers submitted to AIMS 2008 were made by all of our reviewers, which correspond to the full Program Committee members as stated above and those reviewers listed below. Therefore, it is of great pleasure to the Program Co-chairs to thank all those reviewers for their important work.

Ali Fessi   University of Tübingen, Germany
Marc Fouquet   University of Tübingen, Germany
Georgios Karagiannis   University of Twente, The Netherlands
Franck Legendre   ETH Zurich, Switzerland
Marco Milanesio   Università di Torino, Italy
Rossano Schifanella   Università di Torino, Italy

Table of Contents

A Role-Based Infrastructure for the Management of Dynamic Communities

Alberto Schaeffer-Filho[1], Emil Lupu[1], Morris Sloman[1],
Sye-Loong Keoh[1], Jorge Lobo[2], and Seraphin Calo[2]

[1] Department of Computing, Imperial College London
180 Queen's Gate, SW7 2AZ, London, England
{aschaeff, e.c.lupu, m.sloman, slk}@doc.ic.ac.uk
[2] IBM T. J. Watson Research Center
19 Skyline Drive, Hawthorne, NY, 10532
{jlobo, scalo}@us.ibm.com

Abstract. This paper defines an operational framework for specifying
and establishing secure collaborations between autonomous entities that
need to interact and depend on each other in order to accomplish their
goals, in the context of mobile *ad-hoc* networks. We call such collaborations *mission-oriented dynamic communities*. We propose an abstract
model for policy-based collaboration that relies on a set of task-oriented
roles. Nodes are discovered dynamically and assigned to one or more
roles, and then enforce the policies associated with these roles according to the description of the community. In this paper we focus on the
roles that are needed to provide management and security functions for
dynamic communities.

1 Introduction

This paper seeks to address the problem of specifying and establishing a secure collaboration between autonomous entities that depend on each other and
need to interact in order to accomplish their goals. We call such collaborations
mission-oriented dynamic communities. Dynamic communities of autonomous
entities, such as unmanned autonomous vehicles or robots in general, can be
used to perform tasks that are dangerous or even impossible for humans. Such
communities can be deployed in emergency operations after floods or earth-
quakes where teams of agents coming from different organizations are assembled
for a mission; for reconnaissance of areas where hazardous chemicals or explo-
sives may be present; or search and rescue missions involving teams of unmanned
vehicles and rescue personnel. In these examples, the collaboration between the
autonomous entities is crucial to accomplish the intended goals. Our objective is
to dynamically create a secure collaboration between initially untrusted nodes
without manually pre-configuring all nodes for their desired functions. Instead,
a community must autonomously evolve and manage itself without human intervention. Thus, the main challenge is to devise a flexible infrastructure for

D. Hausheer and J. Schönwälder (Eds.): AIMS 2008, LNCS 5127, pp. 1–14, 2008.

community specification and management that can cater for such various requirements of many different applications.

Our approach is based on previous work on doctrines [1], which has been extended to cater for both management and application *roles*. In particular we focus on security management within the community. A community specifies a dynamic collection of roles to which nodes are assigned dynamically when discovered or as the mission context changes. Roles define two classes of policies, obligations and authorizations [2], that specify how the roles interact with each other in the scope of the community, as well as the services and resources that they allow other roles to access. Role assignment may be subject to *constraints* defined in the community specification that guarantee the integrity of the community. The doctrine approach concentrated management functions into a single coordinator node, whereas we explicitly identify a set of security management roles and their policies, and we split the management tasks across distributed collaborating nodes that are assigned to these roles. Our approach is flexible in that new roles can be easily defined for different management functions, depending on the risk context or the security requirements associated with each mission-oriented community. We also propose a methodology using policies to define flexible protocols for role interactions based on finite state machines which can be easily adapted to specific application requirements.

This paper caters for three important aspects regarding the community management: firstly, how our approach devolves management roles to community members by dynamically loading management tasks across distributed nodes; secondly, how to build a secure collaboration relying on a set of basic security mechanisms, which may be easily extended to address new security requirements; thirdly, how our infrastructure scales-down and can be deployed in resources with limited computational power and memory, typical of search and rescue applications (collaborations of autonomous robots or rescue personnel carrying small computing devices in the field).

The implementation of the framework defined here uses the infrastructure provided by *Self-Managed Cells* (SMCs) and the Ponder2 policy framework, which were developed at Imperial College [3], [4]. We use a scenario of a reconnaissance community of *unmanned autonomous vehicles* (UAVs), which form a mobile *ad-hoc* network. Typical examples of UAVs in this community are video surveillance and information aggregation vehicles that need to collaborate in order to achieve their goals [5], [6]. With respect to our past work, this paper extends [1] with: an enhanced role model for security management, an implementation on Gumstix and Koala robots rather than in a simulation, overhead/evaluation measurements, a formalization of community behavior and revisions based on Ponder2 rather than Ponder. Additionally, this paper also explores the uses of the middleware described in [3], [4].

The paper is structured as follows: Section 2 describes our role-based community model. Section 3 presents the security requirements and how protocols for management and security of communities can be specified using policies. Section 4 describes our prototype and Section 5 outlines the related work. Finally, Section 6 presents the concluding remarks.

2   Role-Based Community Model

A community specification describes a set of task-oriented *roles* that need to collaborate in order to achieve their goals. The specification contains a number of *policies* that must be enforced by different entities, according to their roles in the community. Nodes are assigned to roles in order to perform specific tasks in the community, based on their credentials and capabilities. The community specification also defines a set of *constraints* relating to role assignments. Policies are of two types: *obligation* and *authorization* policies.

Obligation policies are of the form:

$$on < event > do$$
$$if < conditions > then$$
$$< target >< action >;$$

Obligations cater for the adaptive behavior of nodes. They specify what management actions (also referred to as *methods*) must be performed in response to events, provided a set of conditions is satisfied. The event is a term of the form $e(a1,...,an)$, where e is the name of the event and $a1,...,an$ are the names of its attributes. The condition is a boolean expression that may check local properties of the nodes and the attributes of the event. The target is the name of a role where the action will be executed and so the target must support an implementation of the action. The action is a term of the form $a(a1,...,am)$, where a is the name of the action and $a1,...,am$ are the names of its attributes.[1] The attributes of an event may be used for evaluating the condition (to decide whether to invoke the action or not), or they may be passed as arguments to the action itself. Implicitly the role to which this policy belongs is the *subject* of the obligation i.e. the entity enforcing the policy, and the action is invoked on a *target* role. Note the target may be the same as the subject i.e. a role may perform actions on itself.

Authorization policies are of the form:

$$auth[+/-] < subject > \longrightarrow if < condition > then$$
$$< target >< action >;$$

These policies are access control rules that specify what actions a *subject* is allowed (positive authorization) or forbidden (negative authorization) to invoke on a *target*. The subject and the target are role names. The action and the condition are defined like in obligations. Authorization decisions could be made by one or more specific roles in the community, but our current implementation is based on the target making decisions and enforcing the policy as we assume target nodes wish to protect the resources they provide to the community.

---

[1] To simplify notation an obligation policy can have a list of target-action pairs, all evaluated when the event is true and the condition holds.

Let R be a set of roles, A a set of authorization policies and O a set of obligation policies. For any role r in R, r is defined in (O, A) as the collection of obligation policies in O and authorization policies in A such that the subject in the obligation policies is r and the target in the authorization policies is also r.

A community may also specify a set of *constraints* expressing additional conditions on role assignments. We currently support two types of constraints: *cardinality* and *separation of duty* constraints. Cardinality constraints (CC) are defined as a relation between a role and a minimum and a maximum number of instances that the role can have in the community. Hence:

$$CC \subseteq R \times \mathbb{N} \times \mathbb{N}$$

Where $\mathbb{N}$ denotes the set of natural numbers, and for any tuple $(r, n, m) \in CC, n \leq m$, and r cannot appear in more than one tuple in CC.

Separation of duty constraints (SC) [7] are defined by a relation which specifies that a node cannot be assigned to a set of roles at the same time (e.g. the same node may not perform roles for *"handling hazardous chemicals"* and for *"supplies delivery"* simultaneously). Hence:

$$SC \subseteq \wp(R)$$

Where $\wp(R)$ denotes the power set of R. A set s in SC indicates that no node in the community can be assigned to all the roles in s simultaneously.

The set of constraints C of a community is defined by the union of its cardinality constraints and separation of duty constraints, $CC \cup SC$. Finally, a community description i is defined by the set of roles R, the sets of policies O and A, and the set of constraints C:

$$Community_i = < R, O, A, C >$$

The abstract model representing a community is illustrated in Fig. 1. Although there is some similarity with the RBAC model [8], our roles are not just limited to

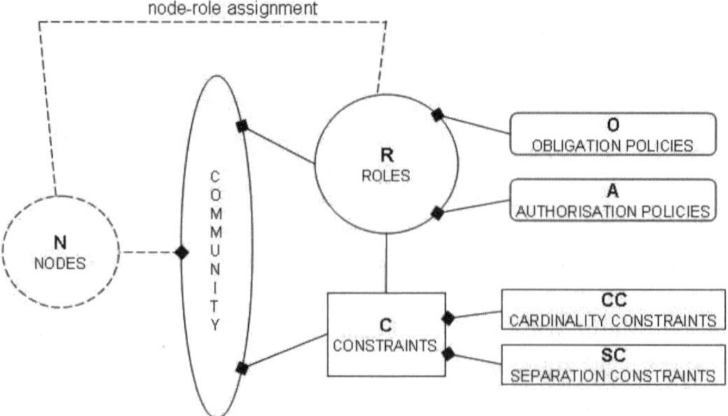

Fig. 1. Dynamic community (solid lines represent the community specification and dashed lines represent the dynamic assignment of new nodes to this community)

defining authorizations in terms of privileges, but they also cater for obligations. We do not support role inheritance in our community model because of runtime penalties it may incur in a distributed environment and also because such inheritance would not apply to the obligations which are also part of the roles [9].

Nodes are dynamically assigned to one or more roles defined in the community specification. As described in the next section, this assignment is usually undertaken by a *coordinator* role and most flexibly defined by a set of policies determining to which role a newly discovered entity should be assigned based on its capabilities. In order to characterize the assignment of nodes to roles, we rely on the abstraction of *interfaces*. An *interface itf* is defined by a tuple $< Cap, Met, Eve >$, representing the sets of capability descriptions Cap associated with this interface, and also the sets of methods Met and events Eve that it offers.

- Met : the collection $\{Met_k : 1 \leq k \leq o\}$ represents a set of method names offered by this interface.
- Eve : the collection $\{Eve_l : 1 \leq l \leq p\}$ represents a set of event names offered by this interface.
- Cap : the collection $\{Cap_i : 1 \leq i \leq m\}$ represents a set of high-level capability names that this interface offers. Each capability Cap_i is associated with a subset of the collection $\{Met_k : 1 \leq k \leq o\}$ of methods and a subset of the collection $\{Eve_l : 1 \leq l \leq p\}$ of events.

While capabilities represent the functionality of an interface at an abstract level (e.g. *"video"*, *"storage"*), methods and events describe its functionality at the implementation level.

An interface definition may be associated with a role, thus identifying the functionality expected of a node before it can be assigned to that role or with a node itself, thus identifying the functionality provided by that node. The uses are also referred to as *expected interfaces* and *provided interfaces* respectively. A node can be assigned to a role if its provided interface *entails* the expected interface of the role. The *entailment operator* for interfaces is defined as follows: for any $itf_a < Cap_a, Met_a, Eve_a >$, $itf_b < Cap_b, Met_b, Eve_b >$, we say that itf_a entails itf_b, or $itf_a \models itf_b$, if:

$$(Cap_b \subseteq Cap_a) \wedge (Met_b \subseteq Met_a) \wedge (Eve_b \subseteq Eve_a)$$

Therefore, $itf_a \models itf_b$ if all the elements of itf_b are also present in itf_a. Informally, a node can be assigned to a role if its provided interface is more general than the role's expected interface.

3   Secure Community Management

This section describes how the community model presented in Section 2 can be applied for the management of secure components in a dynamic community. We start by outlining the security requirements and the community operations, and then introduce a methodology for the specification of management protocols in dynamic communities.

3.1 Security Requirements and Management Roles

Security management in dynamic communities requires supporting the functions of *authentication, membership management* and *access control*. In addition, a set of management procedures is required for the *coordination* of communities. These are essential mechanisms because they ensure that all members are authenticated before joining the community, that the community keeps track of all participants and their roles (and can detect failures), that access control restrictions apply to all resources and services offered by nodes, and that the vital management procedures for community maintenance are performed. We describe in this section how the basic security management requirements for communities are fulfilled.

The *coordinator* role specifies the overall management of the community and groups tasks related to community bootstrapping and assignment of new members to roles, as well as the validation of constraints. Initially, the coordinator role is responsible for broadcasting messages advertising the community to nearby nodes. It enforces policies that govern the preferred assignment strategy of nodes to roles based on their capabilities (but which remains subject to the node's interface satisfying the assignment condition described in Section 2). Whenever a node is assigned to a role, the policies associated with that role are loaded into the node. The coordinator checks whether the minimum requirements for the community are met and whether separation of duty constraints are satisfied. If the coordinator detects that the constraints are not being met, it may try to re-assign roles in the community. If this is not possible the coordinator may decide to dissolve the community. At bootstrap, the node that instantiates the community specification is automatically assigned to the coordinator role. In addition, at this point the coordinator node may be also assigned to other critical management roles (e.g. *authenticator* role): however, the coordinator may delegate one or more of these roles as the community evolves and new members join it.

The *authenticator* role validates the identity and attributes of nodes that wish to join the community. A typical approach for authentication is based on the use of public-key certificates and we assume that only nodes possessing certificates signed by trusted CAs are able to join a community. To this end, public-keys of the certification authorities (CAs) that are relevant to the community may be pre-loaded in the community specification. This avoids the need to contact a CA and is necessary in deployed environments where access to a network infrastructure may be intermittent or non existent. Our initial implementation is based on a PKI solution and uses *X.509 digital certificates*. Non-PKI based approaches are currently also being investigated.

The *membership manager* role keeps track of the members in the community. The community must deal with nodes which move out of communication range, run out of battery or disconnect. If a member does not signal its presence within a given time period, it is considered to have left or become disconnected and the membership manager informs the other members that a node has left. This causes the constraints of the community to be reevaluated by the coordinator, as the departure of a member may violate the cardinality constraints.

Finally, *access control* is our last basic security requirement. Our current implementation distributes the access control enforcement amongst all (target) roles to allow them to protect their resources and permit access to specific subject roles (see Section 2). However, if an entity is not able to enforce its own access control policies, it may outsource these control decisions to a specific role in the community or to its own trusted agent. Note that the community is not limited to these management roles; new roles can be specified to perform additional security or management procedures as required.

3.2 Community Management Overview

When receiving the community broadcast sent by the *coordinator*, a node presents its *X.509 digital certificate* to the community's *authenticator*, which then performs the node validation. The node also validates the authenticator's credentials and the community description and decides whether to join the community or not. If mutual authentication is successful, potential roles for assignment are selected by the *coordinator*, according to the node's capabilities: policies specify the preferable assignment strategy by listing one or more *"required"* capabilities for each role. These are matched against the node's capabilities. The matching is performed by selecting the roles whose list of required capabilities is contained in the node's list of actual capabilities. Among these roles, only those satisfying the cardinality and separation of duty constraints are selected, and the node is finally assigned to these roles by the *coordinator*.

The assignment process includes transferring to the node the obligation and authorization policies that are part of a role specification, event definitions needed by those policies, and a subset of the domain structure of the coordinator is copied to the node: this contains a list of all roles defined by the community (which can be seen as placeholders) and the members currently assigned to each role (i.e., nodes associated with each placeholder).

The consistency of the membership database is kept using a soft-state strategy, where nodes that do not periodically renew their entry with the *membership manager* are automatically removed, using the algorithm described in [1]. Notice, however, that this algorithm is solely performed by the *membership manager* role. There is obviously a trade-off on how frequently nodes should revalidate their soft-state and how often updates in the membership list should be propagated by the *membership manager* to the other members. For this reason, these actions are modeled by policies which can be easily changed to adapt updating rates to different community requirements.

3.3 A Methodology for Modeling Community Management

The interaction between the roles in the community is defined in terms of the obligation policies each (subject) role enforces. These policies specify actions that must be performed in response to events, and such actions can be seen as steps in the protocol that defines the interaction between roles. We can model such interactions in a community by defining a *finite state machine* (FSM), where arrows represent the generation of events and states are actions that represent

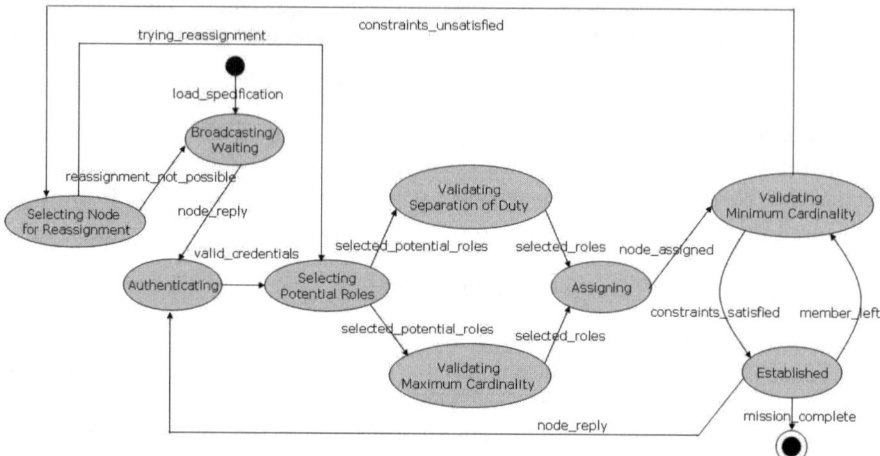

Fig. 2. Modeling community management

protocol steps. We only focus on modeling interactions between management roles, but the same approach can be used for application-specific interactions.

The FSM in Fig. 2 exemplifies an interaction protocol in a community that supports the three management roles previously described: coordinator, authenticator and membership manager. The protocol specifies that after the community specification is loaded into the coordinator, the community broadcasts its presence and waits for node replies. A reply triggers the authentication step; if the node is successfully authenticated, the potential roles for assignment are selected; then, constraints are checked and the node is assigned to the roles that satisfy both maximum cardinality and separation of duty constraints, provided the node possesses the required capabilities for the roles. At this point, if the minimum cardinality constraints are satisfied, the community changes to the state *"established"*, otherwise it remains in a *"broadcasting/waiting"* state. The protocol may have other steps, but our intended contribution is not in terms of defining a specific management protocol, but to illustrate the methodology for modeling community interactions: each step in the protocol can be seen as an action (or set of actions) performed by a policy triggered by the event that corresponds to the incoming arrow – if a step also generates the event required to trigger the policy which specifies the next step, we can *"chain"* the steps of the protocol.

We are therefore specifying the community management in terms of policies that perform steps in the protocol. This is similar to the approach used in PDL [10], where internal events are used to link the execution of policies. However, in PDL only local events were considered, whereas here events can be sent to remote nodes performing a given role. This flexibility is clearer if we consider the addition of entirely new management roles to the community. These can be used then to enhance the protocol, by adding new management steps to it in terms of additional obligation policies.

4   Implementation and Evaluation

The work on dynamic communities was implemented in Java, relying on the infrastructure provided by *Self-Managed Cells* (SMCs) [3], which uses the Ponder2[2] policy framework. An SMC consists of hardware and software components forming an autonomous administrative domain which supports both *obligation* and *authorization* policies. Policies can be added, removed, enabled and disabled to change the behavior of an SMC without interrupting its functioning. We assume the nodes assigned to roles within a community are SMCs.

The evaluation described in this section intends to show how our infrastructure for community management scales-down and can be deployed in resources with limited computational power and memory, which are likely to be found in search and rescue applications such as collaborations of autonomous robots or rescue personnel carrying small computing devices in the field. We deployed our prototype in two classes of lightweight, constrained devices: Gumstix[3] and Koala robots[4] (Fig. 3). The Gumstix has a 400 MHz Intel XScale PXA255 processor with 16 MB flash memory and 64 MB SDRAM, running Linux and Wi-Fi enabled. The Koala robot has a Motorola 68331, 22 MHz onboard processor, 1 MB ROM and 1 MB RAM. The robot is extended with a KoreBot module which has a 400 MHz ARM PXA255 processor, 64 MB SDRAM and 32 MB flash memory, running Linux and also Wi-Fi enabled. In addition, the robot has 16 infrared proximity sensors around its body, and a video camera. Both run the lightweight JamVM[5].

Either a Gumstix, which is a very portable device, or a robot can discover other Gumstix or robots, assign them to roles, and deploy the policies pertaining to the role on them. New members are authenticated using *X.509 digital certificates* before a policy-based decision on their admission to the community and role assignment is made. Assignment policies, enforced by the *coordinator* role,

Fig. 3. Gumstix (left) and Koala robot with video capability (right)

---

[2] http://www.ponder2.net
[3] http://www.gumstix.com
[4] http://www.k-team.com
[5] http://jamvm.sourceforge.net

$obliCoord := root/factory/ecapolicy\ create.$
$obliCoord\ event : root/event/nodeAuthenticated.$
$obliCoord\ condition : [: cap\ |\ interface\ hasCapabilities : "video"\ from : cap].$
$obliCoord\ action : [: name : address\ |\ role/coordinator\ assign : name$
$\qquad\qquad from : address\ to : "surveyor"\ community : reconnaissance].$

Fig. 4. Policy specifying assignment rule for nodes possessing video capability

are used to specify preferences for the assignment of nodes to roles. Membership is also managed. Members of the community must periodically signal their presence with the *membership manager* and should a node become disconnected from the community (e.g. a robot runs out of battery) its role can be re-assigned to one of the existing devices, provided it has the capabilities to fulfil that role.

We show in Fig. 4 an obligation policy, to illustrate the kind of policies loaded across SMCs participating in a community. The policy is a typical assignment policy, specifying that nodes possessing the capability *"video"* must be preferably assigned to the role *surveyor* (and would normally belong to the *coordinator* role specification).

A discussion on the Ponder2 syntax is out of the scope of this paper, but essentially this snippet creates an *event-condition-action* policy (*ecapolicy*) named *obliCoord*, which is triggered by an event of the type *nodeAuthenticated*. The condition verifies if *"video"* is among the set of capabilities *"cap"* provided as argument of the event. If the condition evaluates to true, the action to be executed is the assignment (action *assign*) of the node whose *name* and *address* were provided as parameters of the event to the role *surveyor* with respect to the object *reconnaissance* (which is an instance of *Community*). The target of the *assign* action is the *coordinator* role.

The size of the bytecodes required for running the prototype, including Ponder2 and necessary libraries, is 710 KB. The size of a typical policy written in Ponder2 syntax is about 620 bytes (but this obviously depends on the complexity of the policy). The size of a typical community specification (with 5 roles, each role specifying 5 policies) written in Ponder2 is about 20.4 KB (but it is also subject to the complexity of the policies, number of policies, and number of roles in the specification). In terms of memory usage during runtime, we observed that a Gumstix running the *coordinator* role, and keeping the community specification loaded in memory, required 15 MB for the Ponder2 process and 9224 KB for the *rmiregistry* process[6] (*RMI* is one of the communication protocols supported by SMCs). On the other hand, a Koala robot running an application role (containing 5 policies) required 8384 KB for the Ponder2 process and 4492 KB for the *rmiregistry* process. Increasing the number of policies loaded in the robot from 5 to 10 caused a negligible overhead in terms of memory consumption. The small

---

[6] By comparison, an empty JamVM and rmiregistry uses about 3200 KB and 5900 KB respectively, and a JamVM running an empty Ponder2 instance and rmiregistry uses about 8200 KB and 5900 KB respectively.

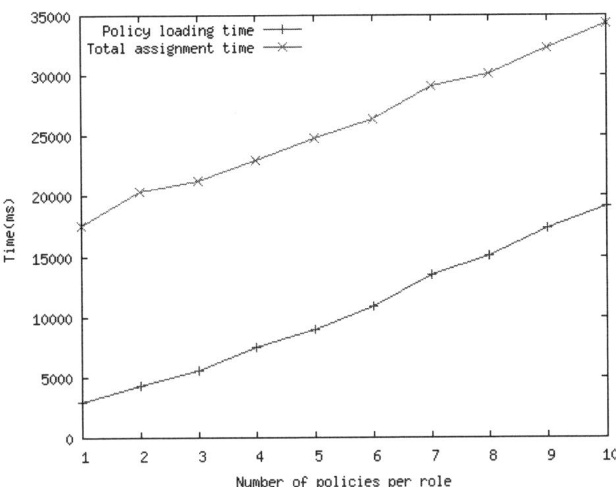

Fig. 5. Total assignment time *versus* policy loading and deployment time

footprint needed for our role management infrastructure highlights that other devices with a similar configuration and capacity could also have been used.

The graph in Fig. 5 depicts some initial performance measurements running our prototype on devices with very constrained computational power. The tests consisted in measuring the time taken for a Gumstix running the *coordinator* role to assign a nearly discovered Koala robot to another role, containing a variable number of policies. We have measured both the time taken to transfer and deploy only the policies, as well as the whole assignment process The latter involves the transfer of the policies, the transfer of additional community information such as event definitions, the creation of role placeholders in the remote node, sending an event informing that a new node has joined the community, and the attribution of the discovered node to the role in question by the *coordinator*.

Our results show that for roles with a small number of policies the total cost of assignment is dominated by the cost of tasks not related to policy transfer, but as we increase the number of policies per role, this fixed cost tends to become negligible in comparison to the cost of loading and deploying policies (which increases linearly). This suggests that the prototype is able to support more complex roles where the only significant cost is the policy transfer, because the residual component of the assignment time remains constant. We also observed that most of this time (about 97% on average) is spent on RMI serialization and network delay when transferring data from the Gumstix to the robot, and only a small part corresponds to the time that is actually spent by the robot to instantiate the policies. We expect that Ponder2's ability of supporting alternative communication protocols will mitigate this overhead. The evaluation of other aspects of the community strategy, in particular the cost of role replacement when a node fails, remains to be done as future work.

5   Related Work

Although related work exists in the area of ad-hoc communities, we are not aware of any that similarly addresses structural community issues based on dynamic roles and assignment policies. The industrial work on autonomic computing, led primarily by IBM [11] but also addressed by Motorola [12] and HP [13], usually tends to focus on network management of large clusters and web servers. Self-managed cells are suitable for more dynamic and mobile pervasive settings, e.g. communities of ad-hoc unmanned autonomous vehicles. The control-loop performed by SMCs is much simpler than the control-loop used by those projects, as it does not depend on planning techniques or ontologies in order to support self-management. Mobile UNITY [14] provides a notation system for expressing the coordination among mobile unities of computation. It focuses on the formalization of coordination schemas, and not on the management of communities.

Research on policies has been active for several years, especially regarding policies for network and systems management. Examples include PCIM [15], PDL [16] and PMAC [17]. Although they use similar event-condition-action rules for encoding adaptation, these approaches are targeted for management of large-scale and networked systems, and do not scale-down for managing small devices.

Finally, the management of dynamic communities may be enhanced with the inclusion of additional security and management mechanisms: threshold cryptography [18] for preventing a compromised authenticator from accepting rogue members and intrusion detection [19] for monitoring potential risks and attacks are some of the options, but their inclusion in our dynamic communities still requires further investigation. Our focus however is not on developing such mechanisms but instead on the management infrastructure they require.

6   Discussion and Concluding Remarks

As well as application-specific roles, a community infrastructure must define a flexible framework for the management of the community itself. This is most flexibly achieved by: *(a)* identifying roles corresponding to the community management functions, *(b)* defining the community operation in a higher level FSM based model, and *(c)* dividing and deploying the management steps as dynamically replaceable policies.

Our strategy of *splitting* the management tasks in several different roles, which will be then assigned to different nodes, caters for the distributed management of a community. Typically, in search and rescue missions, the *coordinator* is assigned based on chain of command and on capabilities. It may constitute a single point of failure, however a community is not under threat if the coordinator fails – the community is stable and continues to operate, but new members cannot join until a new coordinator is assigned. This is mitigated by *assigning a replacement node to the role*. Replicating the coordinator (or any management role) would require replica consensus and would significantly increase messaging (with power consumption and security implications), and therefore the role replacement strategy is preferable. Our model caters for an extensible infrastructure for management of dynamic communities, where new roles can be added, according to the management and security requirements of each mission-oriented dynamic community.

The work presented in this paper significantly extends our past results and shows how Ponder2 and Self-Managed Cells offer a flexible infrastructure for self-management and autonomy in such MANETs. The overall implementation overhead shows that our prototype scales well and can be deployed in constrained resources with limited computational power and memory, which are likely to be found in mobile ad-hoc communities.

To apply our model in larger scale scenarios, we will require the ability to cater for communities that interact with other communities. For example, we can think of *hierarchical composition* of communities, where a rescue team has as one of its members a medical team, which is a community itself. The inner community would encapsulate its management and the outer would not be concerned with the details of the management in the inner community. This architecture of hierarchical communities allows the management to scale-up, with self-managed, encapsulated communities, but future work still has to investigate the abstractions required to support cross-community interactions.

Acknowledgments

Research was sponsored by the U.S. Army Research Laboratory and the U.K. Ministry of Defence and was accomplished under Agreement Number W911NF-06-3-0001. The views and conclusions contained in this document are those of the author(s) and should not be interpreted as representing the official policies, either expressed or implied, of the U.S. Army Research Laboratory, the U.S. Government, the U.K. Ministry of Defence or the U.K. Government. The U.S. and U.K. Governments are authorized to reproduce and distribute reprints for Government purposes notwithstanding any copyright notation here on. We also acknowledge financial support in part from the EC IST EMANICS Network of Excellence (#26854). Finally, the authors wish to thank Eskindir Asmare for his contributions in defining the reconnaissance scenario for UAVs used in this paper.

References

1. Keoh, S.L., Lupu, E., Sloman, M.: Peace: A policy-based establishment of ad-hoc communities. In: Proc. of the 20th Annual Computer Security Applications Conference (ACSAC), Washington, DC, pp. 386–395. IEEE Computer Society, Los Alamitos (2004)
2. Sloman, M., Lupu, E.: Security and management policy specification. IEEE Network 16(2), 10–19 (2002)
3. Lupu, E., Dulay, N., Sloman, M., Sventek, J., Heeps, S., Strowes, S., Twidle, K., Keoh, S.L., Schaeffer-Filho, A.: AMUSE: autonomic management of ubiquitous systems for e-health. J. Concurrency and Computation: Practice and Experience (May 2007)

4. Schaeffer-Filho, A., Lupu, E., Dulay, N., Keoh, S.L., Twidle, K., Sloman, M., Heeps, S., Strowes, S., Sventek, J.: Towards supporting interactions between self-managed cells. In: 1st International Conference on Self-Adaptive and Self-Organizing Systems (SASO), Boston, USA, pp. 224–233. IEEE Computer Society, Los Alamitos (2007)
5. Asmare, E., Dulay, N., Lupu, E., Sloman, M., Calo, S., Lobo, J.: Secure dynamic community establishment in coalitions. In: MILCOM, Orlando, FL (2007)
6. Asmare, E., Dulay, N., Kim, H., Lupu, E., Sloman, M.: A management architecture and mission specification for unmanned autonomous vehicles. In: 1st SEAS DTC Technical Conference, Edinburgh, Scotland (2006)
7. Clark, D.D., Wilson, D.R.: A comparison of commercial and military computer security policies. In: IEEE Symposium on Security and Privacy (1987)
8. Sandhu, R.: Rationale for the rbac96 family of access control models. In: RBAC 1995: Proceedings of the first ACM Workshop on Role-based access control, p. 9. ACM Press, New York (1996)
9. Lupu, E., Sloman, M.: A policy based role object model. In: Proc. 1st Int. Enterprise Distributed Object Computing Workshop, Gold Coast, Queensland, Australia, pp. 36–47. IEEE, Los Alamitos (1997)
10. Bhatia, R., Lobo, J., Kohli, M.: Policy evaluation for network management. In: INFOCOM, Tel-Aviv, Israel, pp. 1107–1116. IEEE CS-Press, Los Alamitos (2000)
11. Kephart, J.O., Chess, D.M.: The vision of autonomic computing. IEEE Computer 36(1), 41–50 (2003)
12. Strassner, J., Agoulmine, N., Lehtihet, E.: Focale a novel autonomic networking architecture. In: Latin American Autonomic Computing Symposium, Campo Grande, MS, Brazil (July 2006)
13. HP: Hp utility data center: Enabling enhanced datacenter agility (May 2003), http://www.hp.com/large/globalsolutions/ae/pdfs/udcenabling.pdf
14. Roman, G.C., Payton, J.: Mobile unity schemas for agent coordination (March 2003)
15. Moore, B., Ellesson, E., Strassner, J., Westerinen, A.: Policy core information model, version 1 specification. request for comments 3060, network working group (2001), http://www.ietf.org/rfc/rfc3060.txt
16. Lobo, J., Bhatia, R., Naqvi, S.: A policy description language. In: Proceedings of the 16th National Conference on Artificial Intelligence, Orlando, FL, July 1999, pp. 291–298 (1999)
17. Agrawal, D., Calo, S., Giles, J., Lee, K.W., Verma, D.: Policy management for networked systems and applications. In: Proceedings of the 9th IFIP IEEE International Symposium on Integrated Network Management, Nice, France, pp. 455–468. IEEE CS-Press, Los Alamitos (2005)
18. Zhou, L., Haas, Z.: Securing ad hoc networks. Technical report, Cornell University, Ithaca, NY, USA (1999)
19. Lunt, T.F.: A survey of intrusion detection techniques. Computers and Security 12(4), 405–418 (1993)

PSH: A Private and Shared History-Based Incentive Mechanism

Thomas Bocek[1], Wang Kun[2], Fabio Victora Hecht[1], David Hausheer[1],
and Burkhard Stiller[1,3]

[1] Department of Informatics IFI, University of Zurich, Switzerland
{bocek,hecht,hausheer,stiller}@ifi.uzh.ch
[2] Research Institute of Telecommunication Transmission RITT, China
Telecommunication Technology Labs, China
wangkun@chinattl.com
[3] Computer Engineering and Networks Laboratory TIK, ETH Zurich, Switzerland

Abstract. Fully decentralized peer-to-peer (P2P) systems do not have
a central control mechanism. Thus, different forms of control mechanisms are required to deal with selfish peers. One type of selfish behavior
is the consumption of resources without providing sufficient resources.
Therefore, incentive schemes encourage peers to share resources while
punishing selfish peers. A well-known example of an incentive scheme
is Tit-for-Tat (TFT), as used in BitTorrent. With this scheme, a peer
can only consume as much resources as it provides. TFT is resilient to
collusion due to relying on private histories only. However, TFT can only
be applied to peers with direct reciprocity.

This paper presents a private and shared history (PSH) based incentive mechanism, which supports transitive relations (indirect reciprocity). Furthermore, it is resilient to collusion and it combines private
and shared histories in an efficient manner. The PSH approach uses a
shared history for identifying transitive relations. Those relations are verified using private histories. Simulations show that the PSH mechanism
has a higher transaction success ratio than TFT.

1 Introduction

Peer-to-peer (P2P) systems have numerous advantages over centralized systems. Load balancing, robustness, scalability, and fault tolerance are properties
that a P2P system can offer. However, challenges in P2P systems include free-
riders [1], malicious peers, Sybil attacks [4], self-interest [13], and other forms
of attacks [11]. Incentive mechanisms are used to address those challenges and
encourage peers to act cooperatively.

A simple incentive scheme is Tit-for-tat (TFT) as used in BitTorrent [2]. In
this scheme, a peer can only consume as much resources as it provides. The TFT
mechanism keeps, for each peer, a history of past resource exchanges or transactions. This history is private, that is, it contains only first-hand information; consequently, peers have a limited view on transactions to peers with direct reciprocity.

D. Hausheer and J. Schönwälder (Eds.): AIMS 2008, LNCS 5127, pp. 15–27, 2008.

Thus, private history is suitable for symmetric resource interest [5], for example in a file-sharing system with many popular files. With a TFT mechanism based on shared history, transaction information is shared and accessible by other peers, with the result that indirect reciprocity is detectable. Thus, TFT based on shared history (transitive TFT) is suitable for asymmetric resource interest. However, shared history approaches are prone to false reports and collusion [5].

This paper proposes a new incentive mechanism which is a combination of private *and* shared history. While shared history is used to propagate resource exchange information, private history is applied to verify its correctness. This approach is termed private shared history incentive mechanism (PSH). Additionally, PSH uses an efficient mechanism to propagate history by including it in resource request and response messages.

The evaluation of PSH requires two steps. First, to show that the mechanism works as expected in general. Second, to test this mechanism in a distributed environment such as PlanetLab. This paper presents the first step. PSH incentive mechanism simulations show that this approach has a transaction success ratio of up to 73% higher than TFT. Message count is, in average, 46% higher. Message size is 288% larger, in average.

There are several possible applications of PSH. In file-sharing systems with many unpopular files, there are few direct relations between peers for which TFT does not work well. In this case, PSH shows its strength. Additionally, PSH can be applied for trading resources such as computing power, memory capacity, or bandwidth in a computational Grid. In such a Grid, it is rarely the case that Grid nodes have symmetric resource interests, since those resources shared in a Grid are typically non-replicable and exclusive, i.e. resource usage diminishes the total amount of available resources [6]. PSH enables a Grid node to contribute resources to the Grid in idle times, and to consume additional resources from other Grid nodes during peak times.

The remainder of this paper is structured as follows. Section 2 discusses related work while Section 3 introduces the design of the incentive scheme. Section 4 provides the implementation details and presents results, while Section 5 draws conclusions.

2   Related Work

Incentive schemes can be divided into two groups: (1) trust-based and (2) trade-based incentive schemes [12]. With a trust-based incentive scheme, peers are encouraged to act in a certain way to gain as much trust as possible. With a trade-based incentive scheme, resources are traded and peers are encouraged to provide as much resources as they consume. This can be based on direct reciprocity as in TFT, or indirect reciprocity as in transitive TFT.

2.1   Trust-Based Incentive Schemes

Kamvar et al. [8] propose a global unique trust value based on a peer's history. The EigenTrust algorithm can effectively identify malicious peers and isolate them. The authors have showed in simulations that their approach can reduce the number of peers providing inauthentic files.

Lian et al. [9] propose multi-level TFT to achieve robust incentives. This approach is a balance between EigenTrust and TFT. The authors have implemented and tested their approach in the Maze [18] system. Multi-level TFT introduces limited indirect trust levels, to reduce the trust metric size. As in EigenTrust, multi-level TFT aggregates transitive trust values. The evaluation shows that a two-level matrix performs better than relying on private history only, while efficiently dealing with malicious peers.

Another enhancement of EigenTrust is described in [3]. The authors compared EigenTrust with the following different extensions: inverse EigenTrust, truncated PageRank, bit propagation, and badness based on BadRank. Simulations showed that EigenTrust with badness based on BadRank performs always better than EigenTrust alone with respect to authentic downloads.

A similar approach to EigenTrust is described in [10]. The authors propose a voting reputation system, in which opinions of other peers are considered. Those peers can vote on a peer's reputation. A highly reputable peer vote has a higher value. However, this approach is prone to whitewashing, and a high cost for initial joining is a side effect.

PeerTrust [16] compares the trustworthiness of peers using a new trust metric. This metric uses three important trust parameters: feedback, number of transactions, and the credibility of the feedback. The authors showed in simulations the feasibility of their approach.

2.2 Trade-Based Incentive Schemes

Trade-based incentive schemes, such as KARMA [15] and the mechanism used by PPay [17] introduce a broker role. PeerMint [7] uses multiple remote peers to store and aggregate accounting information in a trustworthy and scalable way. It applies a structured P2P overlay network to map accounts onto a redundant set of peers and organizes them in an efficient and scalable manner. The scheme uses session mediation peers to maintain and aggregate session information about transactions between peers. This minimizes the possibility of collusion. However, malicious peers acting as a brokers or mediators are an open issue.

Feldman et al. [5] proposed to use the MaxFlow algorithm for collusion free data propagation. The authors suggest to modify the MaxFlow algorithm to evaluate paths in constant time. However, not all paths will be found (indirect reciprocity).

Ngan et al. [14] present an architecture to enforce fair sharing of storage resources, which is robust against collusion. The architecture uses auditing and usage records, which are publicly available. A peer can be randomly audited by any other peer. The authors show in simulations that the overhead of auditing is small and scales in large networks, and that peers have an incentive to provide correct data.

Table 1. Related work comparison

Algorithm	Aggregation	Transitive exchange	Collusion resistance	Local data
PSH	no	yes	yes	yes
Eigentrust	yes	yes	no	yes
ML-TFT	yes	yes	no	yes
Feldman et al.	no	yes	yes	no
Ngan et al.	no	no	yes	yes

2.3   Comparison of Incentive Schemes

Table 1 shows a comparison of related work. Since PeerMint, KARMA and PPay require a broker, and PeerTrust focus on metrics, they are not included in this table. Unlike multi-level TFT, PSH does not aggregate the propagated values. PSH verifies each information directly on a peer, thus detecting collusion. The path finding algorithm presented by Feldman et al. requires many contacts with other peers, while PSH requires few contacts because transaction data is locally available, as this data is propagated with each request. The work presented by Ngan et al. uses auditing to verify resource information, while PSH tries to find a transitive resource exchange path.

3   Design

PSH uses shared history to find peers with indirect reciprocity and private history to verify the reciprocity for those peers.

3.1   Requirements

Although PSH uses shared history, the mechanism shall be collusion resistant. In addition, data propagation must be scalable, robust, and fault tolerant. To allow an initial transaction, a peer may consume resources until a credit limit is reached. The credit limit must be low enough to discourage peers from creating new identities (white-washing). A last requirement is the workload to be placed on the requesting peer, preventing DoS attacks. If load is placed mostly on the answering peer, too many requests may cause an overload.

3.2   Assumptions

It is assumed that peers have asymmetric resource interests, i.e. a peer that provides resources to another peer has no interest in the resources that peer has to offer. Furthermore, each peer's public key is assumed to be known or able to be requested. Since signatures are verified directly on the respective peer, no trusted third party is required.

3.3   Algorithm

PSH behaves like TFT if two peers are about to exchange resources and previous transaction information is present in the other's private history. If it is

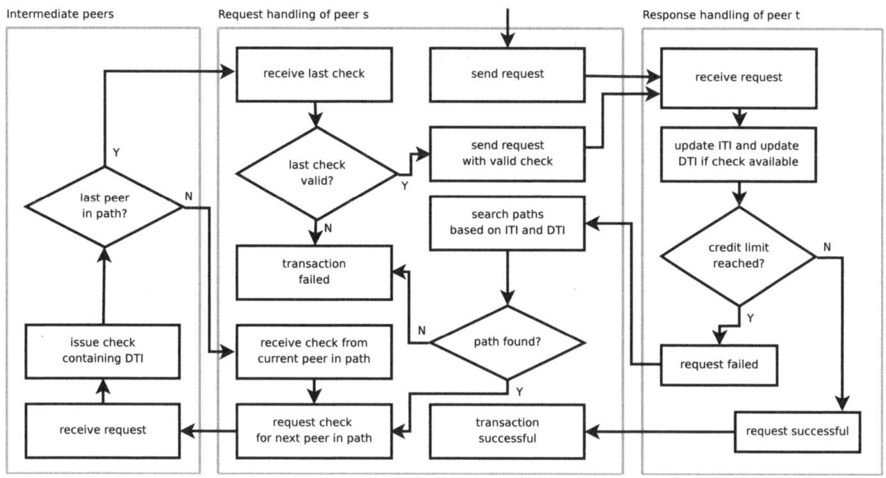

Fig. 1. General PSH incentive mechanism

not present, PSH looks for a path, that is, a linked list of peers with transitive history information, from the source peer to the target peer. Each of those peers in the path is requested to issue a check, that means, to transfer their signed credit balance between the source and the next in the path or the target.

Figure 1 shows the general architecture of the request / response handling in PSH. Arrows between grey boxes indicate a TCP or UDP connection. The figure shows that the workload is mainly on the requesting peer, because path searching is done on the requesting peer.

In Figure 1, peer s sends a resource request to peer t. If the request succeeds, then both private histories from peer s and t are updated as in TFT. If it fails, peer s searches for a path. If a path cannot be found, the request fails. If the path cannot be traversed, the request fails as well. If the path can be traversed and a valid check can be returned, peer s asks peer t again with this valid check.

3.4   Shared History Data Propagation

Each peer stores two tables of history information, a direct transaction information (DTI) table and an indirect transaction information (ITI) table. A DTI table contains information based on direct reciprocity (private history). An ITI table is based on indirect reciprocity (shared history). A DTI entry for peer x and peer y $DTI_x(y)$ is defined as the amount of exchanged resources. For a successful resource transaction from peer x to peer y, the former stores $DTI_x(y)$, while peer y stores $DTI_y(x)$, where $DTI_x(y) = -DTI_y(x)$. Along with each request and response message, a subset of DTI entries with the highest timestamp is exchanged to avoid creating new connections. The ITI table contains accumulated DTI from other peers, e.g., peer x has $ITI_y(z) = 3$, which means peer x knows about transactions between peer y and peer z. The ITI and DTI

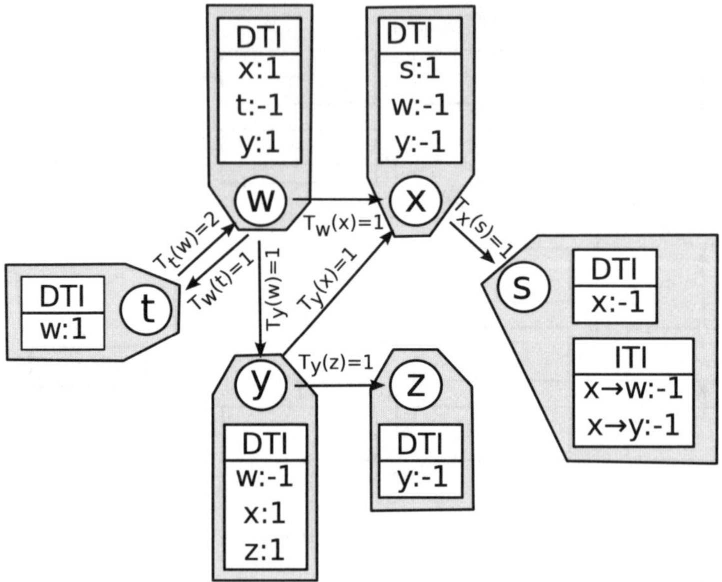

Fig. 2. Initial states of peer t, w, x, y, z, and s, showing DTI and ITI tables

tables are used to find a path from a given source to a target. If such a path exists, then indirect reciprocity can be inferred.

Since many paths may exist, the size of a complete ITI table has polynomial complexity $O(n^2)$, where n is the total number of peers in the system. A reduction of complexity can be achieved by evaluating a limited path length L instead of $|n|$, where $L < n$. Further complexity reduction can be achieved by expiring transactions in the ITI table using a time decay function $f_{decay}(transaction)$. Therefore, not all existing paths are found.

A transaction between two peers x and y is defined as $T_x(y) = z$, z being the transaction value. Each transaction contains a timestamp. Figure 2 shows example values of DTI and ITI in a state in which transactions T have already happened. In this example, peer s is the source and peer t is the target. For better readability, the ITI table is only displayed for peer s.

3.5 Private History Verification

Once a path has been found using the shared history, the verification process starts. This process queries every intermediate peer on that path $P(s, x, \ldots, t)$, where s is the source, t is the target and $x, \ldots$ are intermediate peers, to issue a check. An intermediate peer receives a request containing the source, the predecessor and successor peers. The intermediate peer checks and accounts the balance of the predecessor and successor peers, with the effect that the intermediate peer transfers its debts from the predecessor to the source. The intermediate peer sends a signed check with the new balance to the source peer. Each

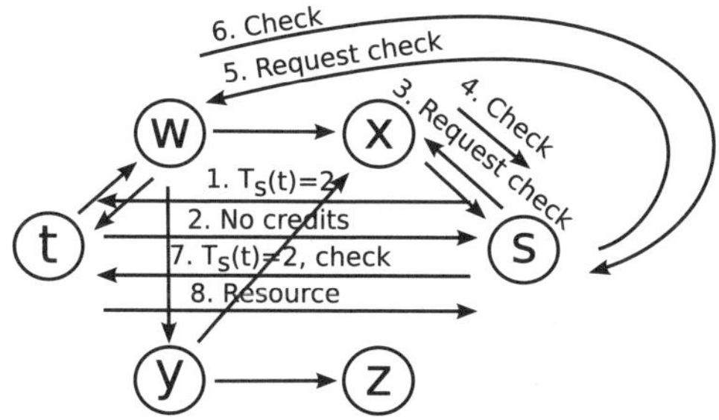

Fig. 3. Example: Peer s requests resources form peer t

intermediate peer is requested sequentially to send a check to the requesting peer until the successor peer is the target peer. If an intermediate peer fails to send a check, *e.g.*, because of an imbalance due to old history data, then the path is invalid.

In Figure 3, peer s requests a resource with value 2 from peer t (1), assuming the initial state in Figure 2. Since the credit limit has been set to 1, peer t reports (2) that this exceeds the credit limit. Peer s evaluates its DTI and ITI tables. The ITI table of peer s contains the DTI from peer x (cf. Figure 2). The negative response for the request contains the DTI of peer t, so peer s updates its ITI accordingly in (2). Then, peer s searches a path using the ITI and DTI tables using breadth-first search and finds $s \rightarrow x \rightarrow w \rightarrow t$.

In Figure 3 peer s requests from peer x (3) a check. Peer x settles and updates its DTIs for peer w and peer s to $DTI_x(s) = 0$ and $DTI_x(w) = 0$. The check that is sent back (4) contains a signed message with $ST_w(s) = 1$, where ST stands for settled transaction. Peer s contacts peer w (5) with this check and asks peer w to settle and update its DTIs for peer t and peer x, which results in $DTI_w(x) = 0$ and $DTI_w(s) = 0$, respectively. Then a check $ST_t(s) = 1$ is sent back (6). Peer s requests resources from peer t (7) and provides the check from peer w. Peer t settles and updates its DTI to $DTI_t(s) = 1$ and $DTI_t(w) = 0$. The request for a resource with value 2 is granted (8). After this transaction, peer t updates its DTI table with $DTI_t(s) = -1$.

4   Implementation and Simulation

PSH has been implemented and tested using Java 1.6. Message communication between peers is asynchronous. For short messages UDP is used, otherwise TCP.

4.1   Implementation

The time decay function $f_{decay}(transaction)$ is implemented as a queue with up to 100 entries to keep memory usage low. This means that the DTI and ITI tables contain up to 100 transaction entries each. The oldest entry will be removed if this limit is exceeded. An entry contains credit amount and node address. The transferred subset of DTI values is limited to 6 as a compromise between message size and data propagation.

Two versions of PSH have been simulated and compared to TFT: PSH as described in Section 3, and PSH with a reduced number of message transfers (PSH_r), both with $L = 3$. The reduction has been achieved by sending a subset of the DTI only if a request failed. PSH_r does not retry to send the request after a failed transaction, while PSH retries up to 3 times. A retry in PSH can be successful if a path can be found and verified. A retry in TFT would always fail because a peer only updates its history after a successful transaction. In contrast, PSH may update its history with a check from another peer and a retry may be successful.

4.2   Simulation

All simulations have been performed with 100 peers that share resources. Every peer has always exactly one resource, and requests 10 times a randomly chosen resource. Each simulation is run 10 times; averaged results are displayed. The simulation is repeated with the number of unique resources in the system varying from 1 to 100. In a system with only one unique resource, every peer requests

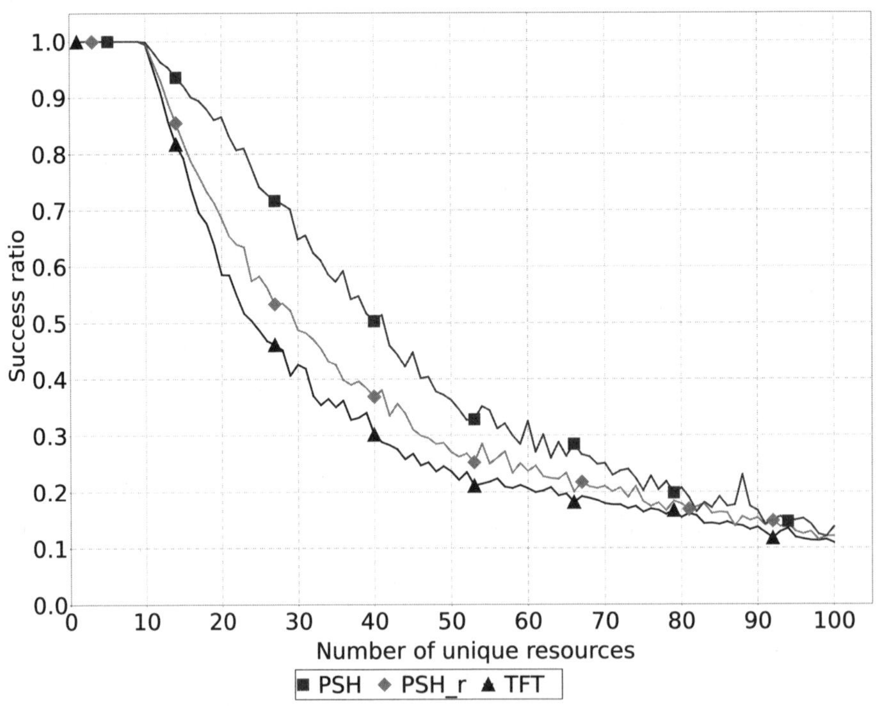

Fig. 4. Transaction success ratio for PSH, PSH(r), and TFT

the same resource, thus the interest is symmetric. With 100 unique resources on 100 nodes, there is a high probability that interest is asymmetric.

The success ratio is defined as $s/(f + s)$, where s is the number of successful transactions and f is the number of failed transactions. As shown in Figure 4, the success ratio of PSH is always higher than TFT, particularly when the number of unique resources is around 32. The higher success ratio is due to the shared history data. PSH_r is at an intermediate position, performing better than TFT, but worse than PSH, since the algorithm does not retry transactions.

The message count represents the total number of messages per transaction sent through the network. The total message size shows the total amount of bytes sent over the network. The message count and size include resource request and response messages, and for PSH additionally check request and reply messages.

In Figure 5, the message count for TFT is constant at 2 messages per transaction, since a transaction consists of a request and a reply message. In PSH, besides resource requests, peers also exchange checks, therefore, the number of messages is higher — up to twice as many as TFT, peaking on 32 unique resources. An important factor that contributes to this high number is the PSH retry behavior. Since PSH_r does not perform retries, its number of messages are, on average, only 2.22% above TFT, at maximum 6.4%.

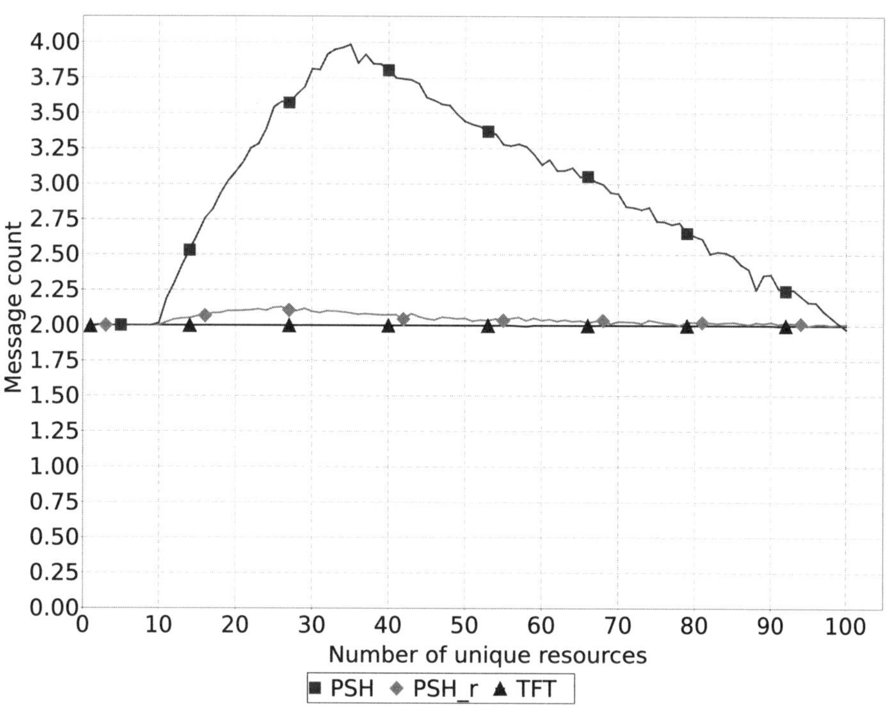

Fig. 5. Message count of PSH, PSH(r), and TFT per transaction

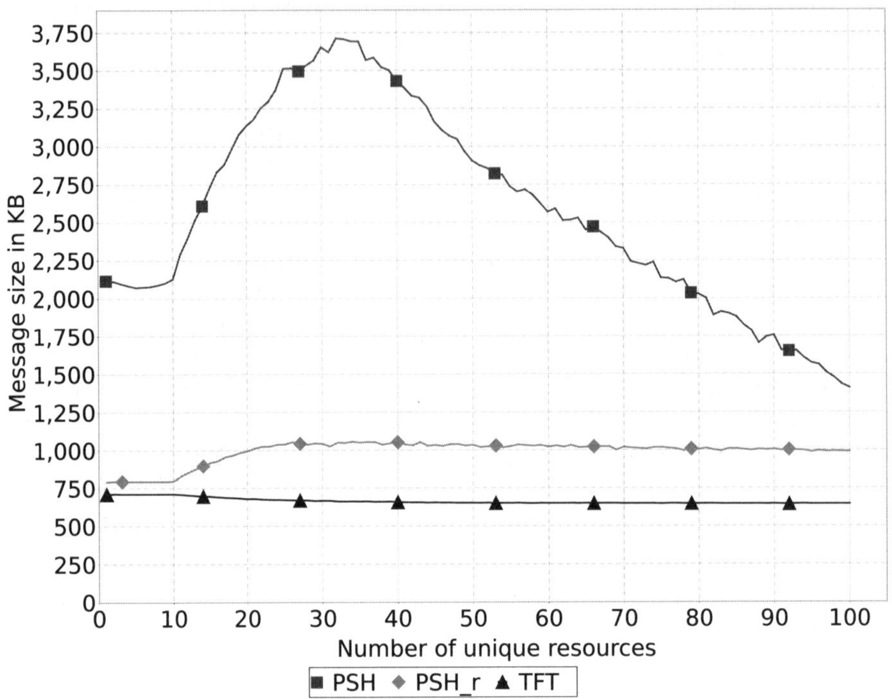

Fig. 6. Total message size of PSH, PSH(r), and TFT

In Figure 6, the message size is higher for PSH and PSH_r than for TFT due to two factors: (1) the message count is larger, and (2) messages contain also history information. The message size of PSH_r is smaller than PSH because of fewer history information.

Both Figures 5 and 6 show a similar behavior for PSH. First message size and count increases. This is due to the fact that the number of unique resources decreases. This leads to a decrease of the success ratio, which leads to message retries, with up to 3 retries. At the peak level, for about 33 unique resources (32 in our particular simulation), one resource is kept by approximately 3 peers. From that point on less than 3 peers have the same resource, thus, PSH sends fewer retry messages and the message size and count decreases.

5   Summary, Discussion, Conclusion, and Future Work

This paper presents PSH, a transitive TFT incentive mechanism, which has a higher transaction success ratio than TFT for peers with indirect reciprocity. Simulations show the trade-off between a higher success ratio and a higher message size and count. PSH has a success ratio that is up to 73% higher than TFT. The message size is up to 5.6 times higher and the message count up to 2 times higher. However, with PSH modifications such as PSH_r, the success ratio can be increased, when compared to TFT, with only a small overhead with respect to message size (49% larger than TFT in average) and count (2.2% larger than TFT in average).

5.1 Discussion

A subset of history information is propagated together with request and response messages. Thus, if a peer does not interact with any other peer, history information does not flow and already stored information becomes inaccurate. A path that relies on inaccurate data will fail. In such cases, PSH retries the request, which result in a higher message size and count. To avoid this problem, a proper time decay function is applied.

A check from a peer has to be signed and thus, the public key has to be transferred first. Besides the message overhead, signing a message is a CPU intensive task. Thus, PSH is not suitable for micro-trading, i.e. trading many small resources in short time.

5.2 Conclusion

PSH works better than TFT in systems with many different resources, i.e. in systems with an asymmetry of interest. This paper shows that there is potential to improve TFT by introducing PSH. The cost of a higher transaction success ratio is an increased message size. If a high transaction rate is more important than bandwidth constraints, then PSH should be preferred over TFT.

5.3 Future Work

The PSH mechanism could also be used for trust and reputation management. As the collected history information is locally available, the trust value can be calculated for each request and additional variables could be considered in the trust calculation.

The PSH mechanism has been thoroughly tested and simulated. While this first step of the evaluation shows that the mechanism works as expected, for the second step of the evaluation, further measurements in a distributed environment such as PlanetLab with more than 100 nodes are needed, in order to show that PSH is robust, fault and delay tolerant, and scalable. Future work will measure how PSH works with collusion and false reports, while varying the number of retries and the credit limit.

Acknowledgement

This work has been performed partially in the framework of the EU IST Project EC-GIN (FP6-2006-IST-045256) as well as of the EU IST NoE EMANICS

(FP6-2004-IST-026854). The authors acknowledge valuable feedback from their colleagues and project partners.

References

1. Adar, E., Huberman, B.A.: Free Riding on Gnutella. First Monday, Internet Journal 5(10) (October 2000)
2. Cohen, B.: Incentives Build Robustness in BitTorrent. In: Workshop on Economics of Peer-to-Peer Systems, Berkeley, CA, USA (June 2003)
3. Donato, D., Paniccia, M., Selis, M., Castillo, C., Cortese, G., Leonardi, S.: New Metrics for Reputation Management in P2P Networks. Technical report, Banff, Alberta, Canada (May 2007)
4. Douceur, J.R.: The sybil attack. In: IPTPS 2001: Revised Papers from the First International Workshop on Peer-to-Peer Systems, London, UK, pp. 251–260. Springer, Heidelberg (2002)
5. Feldman, M., Lai, K., Stoica, I., Chuang, J.: Robust Incentive Techniques for Peer-to-Peer Networks. In: EC 2004: Proceedings of the 5th ACM conference on Electronic commerce, pp. 102–111. ACM Press, New York (2004)
6. Hausheer, D.: PeerMart: Secure Decentralized Pricing and Accounting for Peer-to-Peer Systems, Number 16200. Shaker Verlag, Aachen, Germany (2006)
7. Hausheer, D., Stiller, B.: PeerMint: Decentralized and Secure Accounting for Peer-to-Peer Applications. In: IFIP Networking Conference, Ontario, Canada, May 2005, pp. 40–52 (2005)
8. Kamvar, S.D., Schlosser, M.T., Garcia-Molina, H.: The Eigentrust algorithm for reputation management in P2P networks. In: WWW 2003: Proceedings of the 12th international conference on World Wide Web, pp. 640–651. ACM Press, New York (2003)
9. Lian, Q., Peng, Y., Yang, M., Zhang, Z., Dai, Y., Li, X.: Robust Incentives via Multi-level Tit-for-tat. In: 5th Int. Workshop on Peer-to-Peer Systems (IPTPS), Santa Barbara, CA, USA (February 2006)
10. Marti, S., Molina, H.G.: Limited Reputation Sharing in P2P Systems. In: 5th ACM Conference on Electronic Commerce (EC 2004), pp. 91–101. ACM Press, New York (2004)
11. Nielson, S.J., Crosby, S., Wallach, D.S.: A Taxonomy of Rational Attacks. In: Castro, M., van Renesse, R. (eds.) IPTPS 2005. LNCS, vol. 3640. Springer, Heidelberg (2005)
12. Obreiter, P., Nimis, J.: A Taxonomy of Incentive Patterns - The Design Space of Incentives for Cooperation. In: Moro, G., Sartori, C., Singh, M.P. (eds.) AP2PC 2003. LNCS (LNAI), vol. 2872. Springer, Heidelberg (2004)
13. Shneidman, J., Parkes, D.C.: Rationality and Self-Interest in Peer to Peer Networks. In: Kaashoek, M.F., Stoica, I. (eds.) IPTPS 2003. LNCS, vol. 2735. Springer, Heidelberg (2003)
14. Wallach, D.S., Ngan, T.-W., Druschel, P.: Enforcing Fair Sharing of Peer-to-Peer Resources. In: 2nd International Workshop on Peer-to-Peer Systems (IPTPS), Berkeley, California (February 2003)
15. Vishnumurthy, V., Chandrakumar, S., Sirer, E.: KARMA: A Secure Economic Framework for Peer-to-Peer Resource Sharing. In: Workshop on Economics of Peer-to-Peer Systems, Berkeley, CA, USA (June 2003)

16. Xiong, L., Liu, L.: Peertrust: supporting reputation-based trust for peer-to-peer electronic communities. IEEE Transactions on Knowledge and Data Engineering 16(7), 843–857 (2004)
17. Yang, B., Garcia-Molina, H.: PPay: Micropayments for Peer-to-Peer Systems. In: CCS 2003: Proceedings of the 10th ACM conference on Computer and communications security, pp. 300–310. ACM Press, New York (2003)
18. Yang, M., Chen, H., Zhao, B.Y., Dai, Y., Zhang, Z.: Deployment of a large-scale peer-to-peer social network, Boston, MA, USA (June 2004)

Cooperation under Scarcity: The Sharer's Dilemma

Michael Rogers[1] and Saleem Bhatti[2]

[1] University College London, London WC1E 6BT, UK
m.rogers@cs.ucl.ac.uk
[2] University of St. Andrews, Fife KY16 9SS, UK
saleem@cs.st-andrews.ac.uk

Abstract. Many researchers have used game theory to study the problem of encouraging cooperation in peer-to-peer and mobile *ad hoc* networks, where resources are provided collectively by the users. Previous work has modelled the problem as either a multi-player social dilemma or a network of two-player prisoner's dilemmas, but neither of these approaches captures a crucial aspect of the problem, namely *scarcity*: when resources are limited, players must not only consider how to establish and sustain cooperation with each opponent, but how to allocate resources among their opponents in order to maximise the total cooperation received.

This paper presents a new game theoretic model of cooperation under scarcity, *the sharer's dilemma*, and a simple *expected utility strategy* that is shown to perform well against a wide range of opponents. The expected utility strategy can easily be applied to file sharing networks to create an incentive for users to contribute resources.

1   Introduction

Any system with infrastructure that is provided collectively by the users faces the problem of encouraging users to contribute resources as well as consuming them. In other words, users must cooperate with one another. Cooperation in peer-to-peer and mobile *ad hoc* networks has received a great deal of attention from researchers in recent years, and many incentive mechanisms to encourage cooperation have been proposed. However, in this paper we will argue that such mechanisms have so far lacked a suitable theoretical foundation: some use *ad hoc* methods that may be vulnerable to manipulation by selfish users, while others are based on game theoretic models that fail to capture the problem of allocating scarce resources among neighbours. We develop a new game theoretic model of this problem and show that a strategy based on strict utility-maximisation creates an incentive for selfish users to cooperate.

The next section of this paper reviews existing models of cooperation in networks, including the prisoner's dilemma and multi-player dilemmas. Section 3 introduces our new model, the sharer's dilemma, and describes the expected utility strategy. Section 4 presents the results of simulations comparing a number of strategies. We discuss the limitations of our findings in section 5, and conclude the paper in section 6 with some directions for future work.

D. Hausheer and J. Schönwälder (Eds.): AIMS 2008, LNCS 5127, pp. 28–39, 2008.

2 Game Theoretic Models of Cooperation

If a communication network is viewed as a group of self-interested individuals interacting according to rules specified by the protocol designer, then *game theory* provides
tools for modelling the behaviour of rational participants, and *mechanism design* can
be used to create protocols that reward cooperation, encouraging rational participants
to behave in ways that benefit the network [1,2,3].

It might seem reductive to regard the participants in a communication network as simple egoists – even economists no longer believe that people are motivated purely by self-
interest [4,5,6] – but here we are concerned with the *behaviour of nodes* rather than the
intentions of users: game theory is not appropriate for modelling all human interactions,
but it is well suited to modelling those interactions in which humans delegate routine
decisions to software, reducing complex social considerations to a choice between pro-
grammatic 'strategies'. Even if most participants have the best interests of the network
at heart, game theory allows us to assess the network's vulnerability to exploitation by a
selfish minority. Mechanisms that prevent free riding may also be able to prevent denial-
of-service attacks in which malicious users exhaust the resources provided by others.

2.1 The Prisoner's Dilemma

Simple games can embody surprisingly complex problems, and perhaps no simple game
has received more attention than *the prisoner's dilemma*, a single-round game for two
players, each of whom chooses between two actions, *cooperation* and *defection*, and
receives a payoff that depends on the choices of both players: T is the 'temptation'
payoff for unilateral defection, R is the 'reward' payoff for mutual cooperation, P is
the 'punishment' payoff for mutual defection, and S is the 'sucker' payoff for unilateral
cooperation [7].

The dilemma arises because $T > R > P > S$, which means a rational player
will defect regardless of her opponent's choice. The players cannot escape the dilemma
by communicating about their intentions, because a rational player will claim that she
intends to cooperate, but will then defect. Thus rational players always defect, leading
to a suboptimal payoff $P < R$ for both players.

The prisoner's dilemma has been used to model a wide range of situations in nature
and society where the benefit of cooperation is greater than the cost. Wahl and Nowak [8]
describe the prisoner's dilemma in terms of the cost of cooperating, c, and the benefit of
receiving cooperation, b. The restriction $b > c > 0$ leads to the payoff structure described
above. Roberts and Sherratt [9] describe the dilemma using a single parameter, $k = b/c$.

Public goods problems, social dilemmas [10] and reciprocal altruism [11] find natural expression in the form $b > c > 0$, but not all prisoner's dilemmas can be expressed
in this way: for example, many studies use the payoffs $T = 5, R = 3, P = 1, S = 0$.
In this paper we will only consider dilemmas that arise from the costs and benefits of
cooperating and can therefore be expressed in the form $b > c > 0$.

2.2 The Shadow of the Future

Although rational players always defect in the single-round prisoner's dilemma, it may
be possible to establish cooperation if the game is repeated for more than one round.

Players who expect to interact for many rounds must consider the long-term effects of their short-term decisions: automatic defection is no longer necessarily the best strategy, because players have the chance to recognise cooperative opponents and gain a higher payoff through mutual cooperation (although each player will still be tempted to defect once her opponent has started to cooperate).

Simple strategies for the repeated prisoner's dilemma include Tit For Tat, which cooperates in the first round and thereafter copies its opponent's action from the previous round [12]; Win Stay Lose Shift, which cooperates in the first round and thereafter repeats its previous action if it receives cooperation, or switches to the other action if it suffers defection [13]; and Stochastic Tit For Tat, which cooperates with a probability equal to the fraction of rounds in which the opponent has cooperated [14]. All of these strategies create an incentive for rational opponents to cooperate, while minimising losses against uncooperative opponents.

2.3 Multi-player Dilemmas

When a dilemma involves more than two players, the model must specify which actions affect which players. If each player chooses one action that affects all her opponents, the situation is a *social dilemma* [10]; encouraging cooperation is harder than in two-player games, because it is not possible to cooperate with cooperators while defecting against defectors [15,16].

In a *networked social dilemma*, each player chooses one action that affects her neighbours in a spatial lattice or other network [17,18,19,20]. Cooperation can succeed if cooperative players' interactions with other cooperators sufficiently outnumber their interactions with defectors.

Finally, if each player can choose a different action for each opponent, the situation can be modelled as a *network of two-player games*. Several networked variants of the prisoner's dilemma have been developed [21,22,23,24], all based on the assumption that a player's choices and payoffs in her pairwise games are independent. However, if the payoffs represent the costs and benefits of cooperating, we may ask whether the assumption of pairwise independence is always realistic: there may be situations in which a player has limited resources for cooperation, but can allocate them freely among her pairwise interactions. In such cases no two-player strategy indicates how best to allocate her scarce resources.

We argue that many of the situations modelled as networked dilemmas fit this pattern: players can allocate their resources unevenly, cooperating more with some opponents than with others. Hunters sharing food, animals grooming one another, and network nodes uploading files are all faced with opportunities to strengthen or weaken cooperative relationships by choosing how much to share, and with whom.

3 The Sharer's Dilemma

To explore the problem of allocating resources in networked dilemmas we propose a simple extension to the prisoner's dilemma, incorporating scarcity into the game by limiting the number of times a player can cooperate in each round. We call this new game *the sharer's dilemma*. The prisoner's dilemma can be viewed as a special case in which the limit is high enough that cooperation with every opponent is possible in every round.

As with the prisoner's dilemma, many variants of the game are possible, but here we will only consider the simplest case: in each round, a player can either cooperate with one of her opponents or defect against them all. While simple, this starting point captures the essential problem of cooperation under scarcity: when resources are limited, the problem is not only how to establish and sustain cooperation with each opponent, but how to prioritise opponents in order to maximise the total cooperation received.

Strategies from the prisoner's dilemma can be adapted to the sharer's dilemma by specifying how to choose between neighbours when more than one neighbour is eligible for cooperation.

3.1 The Expected Utility Strategy

If a player expects that cooperating with an opponent will result in a higher level of cooperation in return, she can weigh the expected benefit of her opponent's reciprocation against the cost of cooperating, and compare the incentives offered by different opponents. This idea is the basis of our *expected utility strategy* for the sharer's dilemma.

A player using the expected utility strategy estimates the benefit of cooperating with each opponent, under the assumption that all the benefit received from the opponent so far is a result of reciprocation – in other words the cooperation received can be attributed to the cooperation given. The benefit of all the cooperation received in previous rounds divided by the cost of all the cooperation given in previous rounds is the *expected benefit per unit of cost* of cooperating in the current round. A player maximises her expected benefit by cooperating with whichever opponent will provide the greatest benefit in return.

When comparing her opponents in this way, a player does not need to know the cost or benefit of cooperation from the opponent's point of view – she only needs to estimate the cost to herself of cooperating, and the benefit to herself of the resulting reciprocation, so costs and benefits may be subjective.

If it is possible to measure costs and benefits in the same units then the cost of earning reciprocation can be subtracted from the expected benefit, and a player may defect if the cost of cooperating exceeds the expected benefit. However, even if costs and benefits are not commensurable, a player can still use the expected utility strategy to maximise her benefit by earning the most reciprocation per unit of cost.

Like any cooperative strategy, the expected utility strategy faces the problem of *bootstrapping*: when two players first meet, one or both of them must risk cooperating without knowing how much reciprocation (if any) will result. In the prisoner's dilemma, Tit For Tat and Win Stay Lose Shift take the simple approach of always cooperating in the first round, but this may not be possible in the sharer's dilemma due to the limit on the amount of cooperation per round. The expected utility strategy could assign a high expected benefit to first-time interactions, but this might be vulnerable to exploitation by *whitewashers* who can continually change identities [25];

alternatively, the benefit could be estimated using the average benefit of previous first-time interactions [26].

Uncertainty about the duration of the game can be incorporated into the strategy by applying a *discount factor* to future payoffs, reducing the expected benefit of reciprocation if games tend to be short-lived [25]. The discount factor need not be the same for all opponents; if old players can be expected to outlive new players, as in many peer-to-peer networks [27,28,29], then it may be appropriate to use a heavier discount factor for new opponents.

4 Simulations

This section describes simulations to compare various strategies for the sharer's dilemma. Our model is a population of n players connected uniformly at random so that each player has d neighbours on average. In each round of the game, each player either cooperates with one of her neighbours, increasing the neighbour's payoff by b, or defects, increasing her own payoff by c. The players make their choices in a random order each round.[1]

We simulate two strategies adapted from the prisoner's dilemma: the first, Tit For Tat (TFT), cooperates with a randomly chosen neighbour that cooperated with it in the previous round, or defects if no neighbours cooperated. The second, Stochastic Tit For Tat (STFT), cooperates with one randomly chosen neighbour, choosing each neighbour with a probability proportional to the fraction of rounds in which the neighbour has cooperated. To bootstrap cooperation, TFT and STFT treat new neighbours as if they cooperated in the previous round.

We also simulate a strategy based on BitTorrent's incentive mechanism, which uses reciprocation to encourage peers in a file sharing network to upload [30]. Each peer maintains an *active set* of connections, with all other connections 'choked' (nothing is uploaded). The peer updates its active set periodically, unchoking those connections that have recently provided the best download speeds, so neighbours that upload more quickly are more likely to be unchoked. To bootstrap cooperation, the active set also includes one randomly chosen connection.

To model this behaviour in the sharer's dilemma, the BitTorrent (BT) strategy cooperates in each round with a randomly chosen member of its active set, which contains one randomly chosen neighbour and the s other neighbours that have provided the most cooperation in recent rounds. A new active set is chosen every r rounds, using an exponential moving average to measure the cooperation received from each neighbour.[2]

Finally, we simulate the expected utility (EXU) strategy described in the previous section, which cooperates with whichever neighbour has provided the highest benefit/cost ratio in previous rounds, unless the highest ratio is less than 1 (meaning that the cost exceeds the benefit), in which case EXU defects. Cooperating with a neighbour lowers its benefit/cost ratio, while receiving cooperation raises its ratio. To bootstrap

---

[1] In all the simulations presented here, $n = 1,000$, $d = 10$ and $c = 1$. Three different values of b are simulated, as explained in the text.

[2] The results presented here use $s = 1$ and $r = 5$, which appear to give the best payoff for the BT strategy in this setting.

cooperation, EXU assigns new neighbours a benefit of b and a cost of c, as if they have cooperated once and received cooperation once.

4.1   Fixed Population Proportions

Each simulation consists of 20 independent runs of 2,000 rounds each. At the end of each round a randomly chosen player is removed and replaced with a new player using the same strategy, who is connected to d randomly chosen neighbours. To allow the initial conditions to fade, no measurements are taken during the first half of the run. The payoff received by each strategy is averaged over the second half of the run.

In the first set of simulations the population contains equal proportions of the four reactive strategies described above and the simple strategies Always Cooperate (AC) and Always Defect (AD). We vary the strength of the dilemma by simulating three different values of b, the benefit of cooperation; the cost $c = 1$ is held constant. The first frame of Figure 1 shows the payoff received by each strategy for $b = 1.5$, $b = 2.5$ and $b = 3.5$. When b is close to c, AD narrowly outperforms all the reactive strategies except EXU. Increasing b favours the cooperative strategies at the expense of AD. For all values of b, EXU receives the highest payoff.

We also evaluate each reactive strategy separately against AC and AD, as shown in the small frames of Figure 1. Each population contains equal proportions of AC, AD and the strategy being tested. Once again the outcome depends on the value of b. For $b = 1.5$, none of the reactive strategies does better than AD, although EXU comes close. However, as b increases, all the reactive strategies except TFT do better than AD.

The poor performance of TFT can be ascribed to its short memory: even in a perfectly cooperative population, the probability of receiving cooperation from a given neighbour in a given round is only $1/d$. TFT only considers the previous round, so it is often unable to distinguish between cooperators and defectors. The other reactive strategies evaluate their neighbours over longer periods.

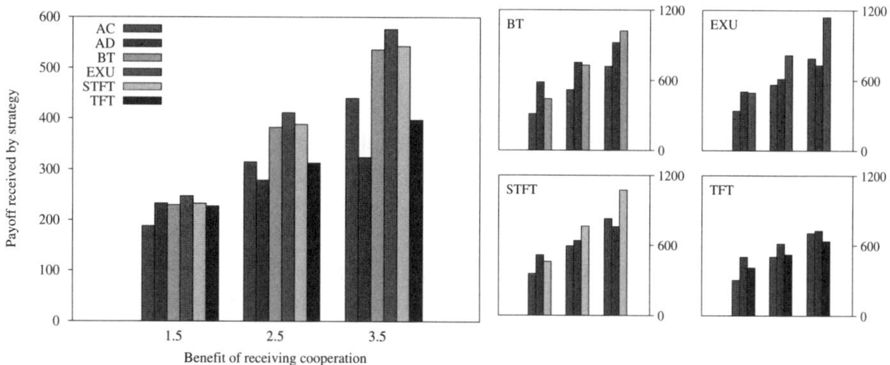

Fig. 1. Fixed population proportions. The payoff received by each strategy as a function of b, the benefit of receiving cooperation, averaged over 20 runs. The large figure shows a population containing all six strategies; the small figures show populations containing AC, AD and each of the four reactive strategies.

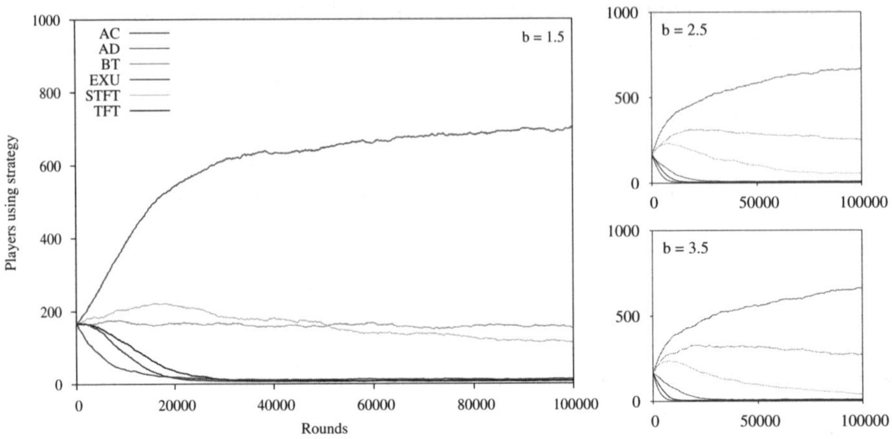

Fig. 2. Evolution of the population. The number of players using each strategy as a function of the number of rounds, averaged over 50 runs, for $b = 1.5$ (left), $b = 2.5$ (top right) and $b = 3.5$ (bottom right).

All the results shown in Figure 1 are significant at the 99% level using the two-tailed Mann-Whitney U test.[3]

4.2   Evolutionary Simulations

To further investigate how each strategy fares in a mixed population, we now allow the population proportions to evolve. As before, at the end of each round a single player is chosen uniformly at random and replaced with a new player, but now the new player's strategy is chosen using the *roulette wheel method*: the probability of the new player adopting each strategy is proportional to the total payoff received by that strategy in the previous round. Thus the mixture of strategies in the population evolves according to the payoffs received: a player's payoff can be interpreted as her *reproductive fitness* [31].

To prevent any strategy from becoming extinct, if the strategy of the player being replaced is used by five or fewer players, the new player always adopts the endangered strategy. This allows strategies that are unsuccessful under certain conditions to re-emerge later in the game, and prevents strategies from being eliminated by random drift.

Figure 2 shows the evolution of the population for $b = 1.5$, $b = 2.5$ and $b = 3.5$, averaged over 50 independent runs of 100,000 rounds each. AC is quickly pushed to the edge of extinction: by cooperating equally with all its neighbours, it wastes resources on AD that could have been used to earn reciprocation from reactive neighbours. TFT has

---

[3] Student's t test is not suitable for making comparisons between strategies because the samples are not independently and randomly drawn from normally distributed populations. The Mann-Whitney U test was chosen because it makes fewer assumptions about the population distribution.

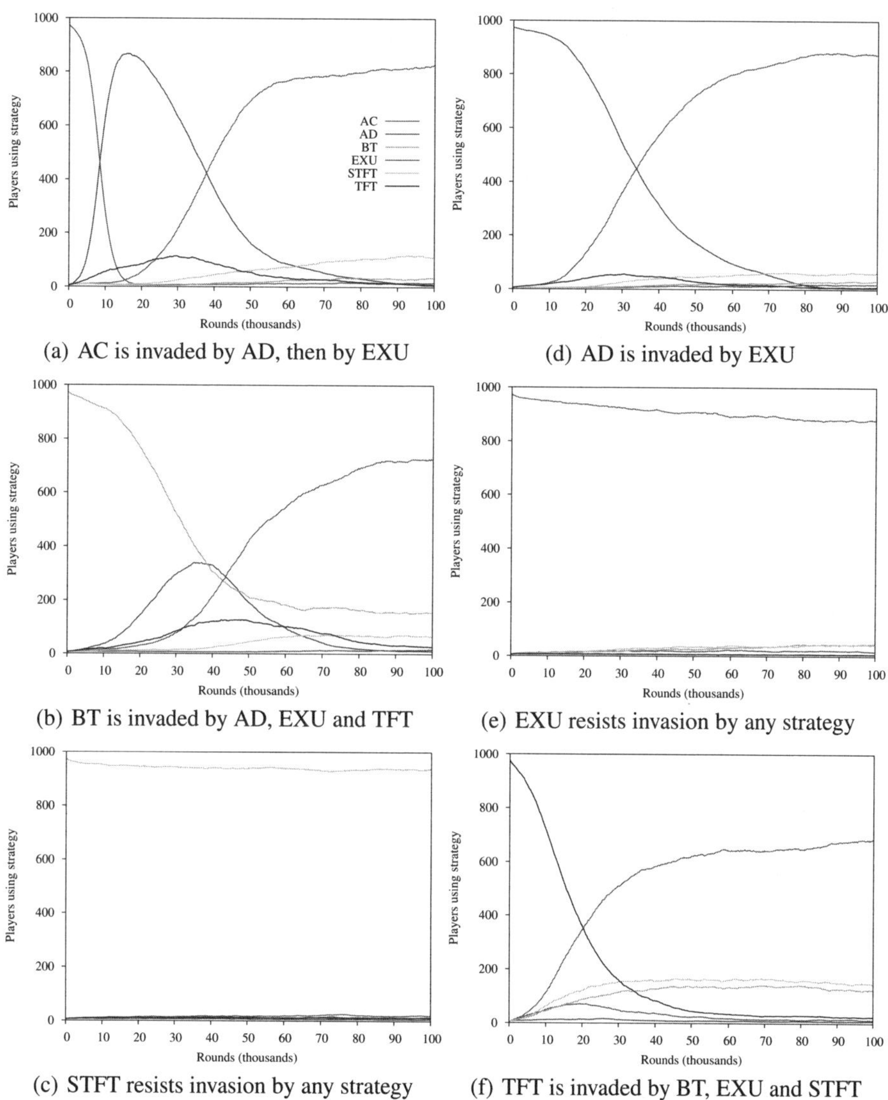

(a) AC is invaded by AD, then by EXU

(d) AD is invaded by EXU

(b) BT is invaded by AD, EXU and TFT

(e) EXU resists invasion by any strategy

(c) STFT resists invasion by any strategy

(f) TFT is invaded by BT, EXU and STFT

Fig. 3. Invasion simulations. The number of players using each strategy as a function of the number of rounds, averaged over 50 runs, for $b = 1.5$. EXU can invade any strategy except STFT; EXU and STFT both resist invasion.

trouble distinguishing between cooperators and defectors due to its short memory, and it too is quickly defeated.[4] Once AC has been eliminated, the other reactive strategies all outperform AD. It might seem paradoxical that any strategy would benefit from the

---

[4] This is not a weakness of the Tit For Tat strategy as such, but only of our method of adapting it to the sharer's dilemma. STFT, which is also based on the Tit For Tat strategy from the prisoner's dilemma, does not have the same weakness.

elimination of altruists, but in evolutionary simulations it is relative payoffs, rather than absolute payoffs, that are decisive: the defeat of AC makes the environment harsher for the reactive strategies, but harsher still for AD, which receives most of its cooperation from AC.

Despite their selfishness, BT, EXU and STFT succeed in establishing almost full cooperation: after 20,000 rounds the fraction of players cooperating in each round is always above 95%. As in the simulations with fixed population proportions, EXU outperforms all the other strategies for all values of b.

To test the significance of the results we use the two-tailed Mann-Whitney U test to compare the number of players using each strategy at the end of the 50 runs. All the differences between strategies are significant at the 99% level, with the exception of AD and TFT, which are not significantly different when $b = 1.5$ or $b = 2.5$.

4.3   Invasion Simulations

The previous sections have shown that the expected utility strategy performs well when played by a substantial fraction of the population, but we would also like to know whether it is suitable for use in populations dominated by other strategies. To find out, we simulate the evolution of six populations, each containing 975 players of one strategy and five players of each of the other strategies. As before, no strategy is allowed to drop below five players. The results are averaged over 50 runs of 100,000 rounds each.

The results for $b = 1.5$ are shown in Figure 3. EXU is able to invade any strategy except STFT. This is a strong result – clusters of Tit For Tat players can invade other strategies in networked variants of the prisoner's dilemma [12], but in our simulations there are no clusters: new players are connected to every existing player with equal probability.

STFT and EXU can each resist invasion by any other strategy. In 50 longer runs of 1 million rounds each, EXU stabilises at 80% of the population when it starts as the dominant strategy, while STFT stabilises at 90% when it is initially dominant. This shows that each strategy does better against itself than it does against the other, making both strategies *evolutionarily stable*, at least among the strategies considered here [31].

5   Discussion

This paper is only a preliminary exploration of the sharer's dilemma – many interesting aspects of the game remain to be investigated. For example, we have assumed that all players possess equal resources for cooperation, but the dynamics of cooperation may change when some players have more resources than others. Piatek *et al.* [32] have shown that when high-capacity BitTorrent nodes are able to participate in multiple swarms they benefit from allocating their resources between swarms, to the detriment of the low-capacity nodes in each swarm. The sharer's dilemma gives us a theoretical framework for investigating whether such issues apply to cooperation under scarcity in general. We can simulate variation in capacity by updating the players at different rates, with high-capacity players making their choices more frequently than low-capacity players, allowing them to cooperate more often in a given period of time.

In the simulations presented here we have also assumed that all players assign the same subjective cost to cooperating and the same subjective benefit to receiving cooperation. This restriction is not required by the model, and we would like to explore the effect of variation within the population: for example, free riding might be an appealing strategy to players who consider the cost of cooperating to be high, while altruism might appeal to those who consider the cost to be low. However, when players can receive different payoffs from the same outcomes, it becomes difficult to compare the success of different strategies in a meaningful way, and the use of evolutionary simulations becomes problematic; we will need to consider new ways of comparing strategies before we can explore subjective payoffs.

A third simplifying assumption concerns network structure: we have only considered random graphs where a new player is connected to each existing player with equal probability. This rules out the formation of clusters, for example, which might help to establish cooperation in otherwise hostile networks; on the other hand, if players are able to choose their neighbours, defectors might be able to exploit the first-time cooperation of reactive strategies. The structure and dynamics of the network are clearly relevant to the outcome of the game, so when using the sharer's dilemma to model any scenario we will need to make sure that we are modelling the network, as well as the individual players, realistically.

6   Conclusions and Future Work

We have seen that a simple extension to a well-known game can provide a new perspective on the problem of cooperation in networks: incorporating scarcity into the prisoner's dilemma reframes the problem of cooperation as a problem of prioritisation and suggests new strategies based on maximising expected utility. The sharer's dilemma provides a game theoretic model for many situations in nature and society where the benefit of cooperation is higher than the cost, and where resources for cooperation are scarce.

It is easy to see how the strategies described in this paper could be applied to peer-to-peer file sharing networks such as BitTorrent; our simulations, though simplified, show that the expected utility strategy performs well in a mixed population of other strategies, indicating that it may be possible to deploy it incrementally in existing networks.

We are also interested in the possibility of using the expected utility strategy in multi-hop networks, such as peer-to-peer overlays and mobile *ad hoc* networks, to create an incentive for nodes to forward messages. However, this will require a more complex utility model that can incorporate actions whose outcome depends on the choices of other nodes. We are currently investigating the use of Savage's concept of *subjective expected utility* to choose between actions with uncertain outcomes [33].

References

1. Gibbons, R.: Game Theory for Applied Economists. Princeton University Press, Princeton (1992)
2. Feigenbaum, J., Shenker, S.: Distributed algorithmic mechanism design: Recent results and future directions. In: Proceedings of the 6th International Workshop on Discrete Algorithms and Methods for Mobile Computing and Communications, pp. 1–13 (2002)

3. Shneidman, J., Parkes, D.: Rationality and self-interest in peer to peer networks. In: Kaashoek, M., Stoica, I. (eds.) IPTPS 2003. LNCS, vol. 2735, pp. 139–148. Springer, Heidelberg (2003)

4. Bolton, G., Ockenfels, A.: ERC: A theory of equity, reciprocity, and competition. American Economic Review 90(1), 166–193 (2000)

5. Fehr, E., Schmidt, K.: A theory of fairness, competition and cooperation. Working Paper 4, Institute for Empirical Research in Economics, University of Zurich (April 1999)

6. Fehr, E., Gachter, S.: Altruistic punishment in humans. Nature 415(6868), 137–140 (2002)

7. Kuhn, S.: Prisoner's dilemma. In: Zalta, E. (ed.) The Stanford Encyclopedia of Philosophy (2003), http://plato.stanford.edu/archives/fall2003/entries/prisoner-dilemma/

8. Wahl, L., Nowak, M.: The continuous prisoner's dilemma: I. linear reactive strategies. Journal of Theoretical Biology 200, 307–321 (1999)

9. Roberts, G., Sherratt, T.: Development of cooperative relationships through increasing investment. Nature 394(6689), 175–179 (1998)

10. Dawes, R.: Social dilemmas. Annual Review of Psychology 31, 169–193 (1980)

11. Trivers, R.: The evolution of reciprocal altruism. Quarterly Review of Biology 46(1), 35–57 (1971)

12. Axelrod, R.: The Evolution of Cooperation. Basic Books, New York (1984)

13. Nowak, M., Sigmund, K.: The alternating prisoner's dilemma. Journal of Theoretical Biology 168(2), 219–226 (1994)

14. Nowak, M., Sigmund, K.: Oscillations in the evolution of reciprocity. Journal of Theoretical Biology 137(1), 21–26 (1989)

15. Félegyházi, M., Hubaux, J., Buttyán, L.: Equilibrium analysis of packet forwarding strategies in wireless ad hoc networks - the dynamic case. Technical Report IC/2003/68, EPFL (November 2003)

16. Félegyházi, M., Hubaux, J., Buttyán, L.: Nash equilibria of packet forwarding strategies in wireless ad hoc networks. IEEE Transactions on Mobile Computing 5(5), 463–476 (2006)

17. Nowak, M., May, R.: Evolutionary games and spatial chaos. Nature 359(6398), 826–829 (1992)

18. Nowak, M., Bonhoeffer, S., May, R.: Spatial games and the maintenance of cooperation. Proceedings of the National Academy of Sciences USA 91, 4877–4881 (1994)

19. Epstein, J.: Zones of cooperation in the demographic prisoner's dilemma (1997), Santa Fe Institute Working Paper 97-12-094

20. Ohtsuki, H., Hauert, C., Lieberman, E., Nowak, M.: A simple rule for the evolution of cooperation on graphs and social networks. Nature 441, 502–505 (2006)

21. Grim, P.: The greater generosity of the spatialized prisoner's dilemma. Journal of Theoretical Biology 173(4), 353–359 (1995)

22. Cohen, M., Riolo, R., Axelrod, R.: The role of social structure in the maintenance of cooperative regimes. Rationality and Society 13, 5–32 (2001)

23. Axelrod, R., Riolo, R., Cohen, M.: Beyond geography: Cooperation with persistent links in the absence of clustered neighborhoods. Personal and Social Psychology Review 6(4), 341–346 (2002)

24. Nowak, M., Sigmund, K.: Evolutionary dynamics of biological games. Science 303, 793–799 (2004)

25. Feldman, M., Chuang, J.: The evolution of cooperation under cheap pseudonyms. In: 7th International IEEE Conference on E-Commerce Technology, Munich, Germany (July 2005)

26. Lai, K., Feldman, M., Stoica, I., Chuang, J.: Incentives for cooperation in peer-to-peer networks. In: Workshop on Economics of Peer-to-Peer Systems, Berkeley, CA, USA (June 2003)

27. Stutzbach, D., Rejaie, R., Sen, S.: Characterizing unstructured overlay topologies in modern P2P file-sharing systems. In: Internet Measurement Conference (IMC 2005), Berkeley, CA, USA (October 2005)
28. Bustamante, F., Qiao, Y.: Friendships that last: Peer lifespan and its role in P2P protocols. In: 8th International Workshop on Web Content Caching and Distribution, Hawthorne, NY, USA (September-October 2003)
29. Guha, S., Daswani, N., Jain, R.: An experimental study of the Skype peer-to-peer VoIP system. In: Proceedings of the 5th International Workshop on Peer-to-Peer Systems (IPTPS 2006), Santa Barbara, CA, USA, pp. 1–6 (February 2006)
30. Cohen, B.: Incentives build robustness in BitTorrent. In: Workshop on Economics of Peer-to-Peer Systems, Berkeley, CA, USA (June 2003)
31. Smith, J.M.: Evolution and the Theory of Games. Cambridge University Press, Cambridge (1982)
32. Piatek, M., Isdal, T., Anderson, T., Krishnamurthy, A., Venkataramani, A.: Do incentives build robustness in BitTorrent? In: Proceedings of the 4th USENIX Symposium on Networked Systems Design and Implementation (NSDI 2007), Cambridge, MA, USA, pp. 1–14 (April 2007)
33. Savage, L.: The Foundations of Statistics. Wiley, Chichester (1954)

A Distributed Certification System for Structured P2P Networks

François Lesueur, Ludovic Mé, and Valérie Viet Triem Tong

SUPELEC, SSIR Group (EA 4039)
Avenue de la Boulaie - CS 47601 - 35576 Cesson-Sévigné cedex - France
`firstname.lastname@supelec.fr`

Abstract. In this paper, we present a novel distributed certification system in which signing a certificate needs the collaboration of a fixed ratio of the nodes, hence a varying number of nodes. This number is dynamically adjusted to enforce the ratio in a fully distributed way, which is mandatory for decentralized varying-size P2P networks. A certificate allows then to link the key pair of a node to some rights granted to it.

Keywords: P2P, Security, Distributed Certification.

1 Introduction

P2P networks have been widely used for the last few years as they allow the design of low cost and high availability systems. These large networks are based on a fully distributed architecture, in which every user has an equivalent role.

There are two types of P2P networks: unstructured ones and structured ones. In unstructured P2P networks (Gnutella [1]), requests are broadcasted or routed through random walks. In structured ones (Chord [2]), requests are routed using generated routing tables. We consider here structured P2P networks security.

Since security techniques used in traditional centralized systems rely on trusted entities, directly using such techniques would break the P2P basics. It is thus crucial to provide fully distributed security mechanisms for P2P networks.

In this paper, we present a novel distributed certification mechanism. This certification mechanism fully distributes a Certification Authority: signing a certificate needs the collaboration of $t\%$ of the nodes. Then, considering such a certificate valid is similar to trusting $t\%$ of the nodes would not collude to create a false certificate. This mechanism relies on agreements by a static ratio of the nodes (and hence a dynamic number of nodes) and not by a static number of nodes as in [3]. Moreover, this adaptation is done in a fully distributed way, as opposed to [4]. A certificate contains the public key of its owner and any rights that may be needed by this owner (access rights, name ownership, ...). As far as we know, this is the first approach proposing a dynamic threshold in a large and distributed environment.

We also briefly present three applications for this distributed certification, mitigating the sybil attack [5], excluding misbehaving nodes and providing intelligible names for P2P Voice over IP rather than cryptographic key hashes.

D. Hausheer and J. Schönwälder (Eds.): AIMS 2008, LNCS 5127, pp. 40–52, 2008.

In Section 1, we present some related work. Then, in Section 2, we present our distributed certification system. In Section 3, we discuss the security of our system against attackers. In Section 4, we present experimental results. In Section 5, we present the suggested applications. Finally, we conclude and propose some future work.

2   Related Work

We first introduce structured P2P networks and we then present previous work on distributed certification.

2.1   Structured P2P Networks

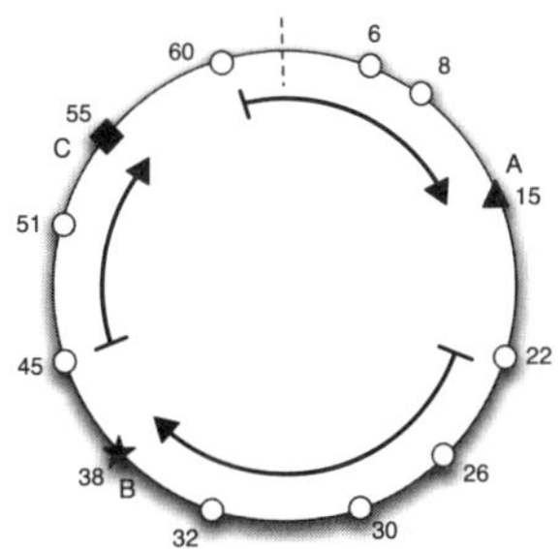

Fig. 1. Simplified representation of Chord with identifiers going from 0 to $2^6 - 1 = 63$. ▲, ♦ and ★ are nodes (PC) and ○ are resources (files). Node A, which $nodeId$ is 15, is responsible for resources 60, 6 and 8.

Structured P2P networks provide a virtual space called *overlay*. Each node (PC) is uniquely identified by a $nodeId \in \mathcal{K}ey\mathcal{I}ds$; in the same way, each *resource* (file, ...) is uniquely identified by a key identifier $keyId$, $keyId \in \mathcal{K}ey\mathcal{I}ds$ (for a file, the key is usually its SHA1 fingerprint). Nodes and resources thus share the same identifier space $\mathcal{K}ey\mathcal{I}ds$, which is finite but supposed large enough (often 2^{160} elements due to the size of SHA1 fingerprints). Each node is responsible for the management of a part of the resources and the overlay provides routing facilities with a logarithmic cost for a node to access a specific identifier.

In Chord for instance, the identifiers space is represented as a ring going from 0 to $2^{160} - 1$ and each node is responsible for all the resources between it and its preceding node in the overlay. This organization is illustrated in Figure 1.

2.2   Distributed Certification

We first present threshold cryptography which is the basis of previous work on distributed certification as well as of our proposition. We then study previous work on distributed certification in peer groups.

Threshold Cryptography. In threshold cryptography, based on Shamir secret sharing [6], the enciphering of a message can only be achieved through the collaboration of a given number of entities. Threshold cryptography consists in splitting a secret key and distributing the resulting shares on different entities. We present here threshold cryptography based on [7].

(t, n)-threshold cryptography allows for enciphering a message with any t shares chosen among those issued to n entities, each entity usually owning one distinct share. t and n are predefined constants, set up at the initialization. If nobody knows the secret key, this key is better protected from misbehaving people. t shares are needed to encipher a message, but $t - 1$ shares hold *no* information on the secret key. An attacker must thus obtain t shares of the secret key to be able to recover the full key.

When some entity wants to obtain the signature of some data d, it asks t other entities to sign d with their own share. The signature of d by the secret key is then a combination of the t partial signatures. For instance, if the signature function f is homomorphic, i.e., $f(x+y) = f(x) \times f(y)$ (the RSA function is homomorphic), the combination of the partial signatures is simply their multiplication. Only the partial signatures are public and not the key shares. Such threshold cryptography schemes have been previously used to provide distributed certification.

Distributed Certification in Peer Groups. Distributing a certification process can be achieved through threshold cryptography. In [3], Kong *et al.* propose a distributed certification based on the cooperation of t nodes, t being a fixed number of nodes during the whole life of the system. The choice of t is a problem since $t = 3$ might for instance be a correct value for a network composed of 10 nodes but is clearly too small when the same network has grown to 1000 nodes: t should be a ratio of the number of nodes.

In [4], Saxena *et al.* propose to adapt the threshold t *dynamically* using algorithms proposed by Frankel *et al.* in [8]. A server manages a counter of the network size and detects the need for changing the threshold. Besides scaling and robustness problems in threshold changing algorithms, the reliance on a server is opposed to P2P bases and lowers the availability of the network. None of these schemes is thus sufficient for distributing certification in a P2P network.

In this paper, we propose a novel distributed certification scheme. In this scheme, the threshold is dynamically adjusted in a fully distributed way, which is mandatory for decentralized varying-size networks such as P2P ones.

3   A Distributed Certification System

In this section, we present our distributed certification mechanism in a structured P2P network. First, we describe the principle of the proposed certification system. Then, we present the sharing of the secret key used to distribute the certification process. Finally, we explain the distributed certification algorithm.

3.1   Principle

The network is characterized by an RSA public/secret key pair (P, S): P is publicly known and S is shared among the nodes (no node knows S). This key pair is generated by founding members using a distributed algorithm as Boneh and Franklin proposed in [9]. Certificates follow the X.509 format and contain in particular the public key of their owners and some rights granted to these owners. They are signed with S through a novel threshold cryptography scheme.

Each solicited node of the P2P network decides locally if it should participate in the certification process. Such decisions are based on local observations, security policy or proofs included in the certification request (see Section 6). Obtaining a valid certificate requires the agreement and cooperation of a fixed *ratio* t of the members of the network. Then, trusting the validity of this certificate is equivalent to trusting that such a ratio of node would not collude to lie.

In the following, we make the assumption that there is no successful Sybil Attack [5] in the network, i.e., each person has only one connected node and its identifier is truly random. We discuss in Section 6.1 a self-healing node admission control, rejecting sybil nodes using our distributed certification operated by already accepted ones (which are thus non-sybil).

3.2 Sharing the Network Secret Key

The sharing of the network secret key is based on the homomorphic property of the RSA enciphering function. Generally, if $S = (e, m)$ denotes the RSA network secret key, we can pick s *shares* $e_1, \ldots, e_s$ such that $e = \sum_{i=1}^{s} e_i$ and then for any data d:

$$d^e[m] = d^{\sum_{i=1}^{s} e_i}[m] = \left(\prod_{i=1}^{s} d^{e_i}[m] \right)[m]$$

In other words, the RSA signature of d with S, which is $d^e[m]$, is equal to the product of the signatures with each share modulo m, m being publicly known since it appears in the network public key $P = (d, m)$.

If the security policy of the network defines that a certification has to be controlled by a ratio t of the nodes ($t \in [0, 1]$) and if n is the size of the network, then the secret key must be split in $s = t \times n$ shares. To provide a share to each member, each share e_i is then replicated on $g = \frac{1}{t}$ members composing a *sharing group*, each member knowing the list of his group. In order to sign a certificate, each share has to be involved and so a ratio t of the nodes must cooperate.

When the network grows (resp. shrinks), the number s of shares must grow (resp. shrink) in order to maintain $s = t \times n$, since t is a static ratio. However, each share should still be replicated on $g = \frac{1}{t}$ members, which is independent of the network size n. So, a sharing group can detect without knowing n (and hence without a central counter) if it is too small or too large.

When nodes join (resp. leave) the network, if a sharing group detects it is too large (resp. too small) to maintain $s = t \times n$, i.e., this group is composed of more (resp. less) than $\frac{1}{t}$ members, it splits and generates a new share (resp. merges with another group and discards one share). To create two shares e_{i0} and e_{i1} from a single share e_i, e_{i0} and e_{i1} must simply be chosen such that $e_{i0} + e_{i1} = e_i$ and e_i must be discarded. To prevent an attacker from keeping e_i and thus having a larger share than others, e_i is rendered useless by mixing e_{i0} and e_{i1} with two other randomly chosen shares e_x and e_y: a chosen random value Δ_0 (resp. Δ_1) is added to e_{i0} (resp. e_{i1}) and subtracted from e_x (resp. e_y).

After this operation, the sum of shares is still e but e_i is not part of the sharing anymore. Creating one share from two shares is exactly the opposite operation of splitting. These operations only involve members of the concerned sharing groups and not the whole network.

However, only creating two sharing groups from one (resp. one from two) does not allow to have each group composed of exactly $\frac{1}{t}$ members. In fact, we define two bounds g_{min} and g_{max} for merging and splitting sharing groups, which are respectively the minimum and maximum size of a sharing group. We thus have $\frac{1}{g_{max}} < t < \frac{1}{g_{min}}$ and we expect s to roughly equal $t \times n$. Finally, when a sharing group grows to g_{max} members, it is split in two groups of size $g_{new} = \frac{g_{max}}{2}$. If g_{new} was lower than g_{min}, then these two groups would both have to join another group right after having split, so we must have $g_{max} > 2 \times g_{min}$.

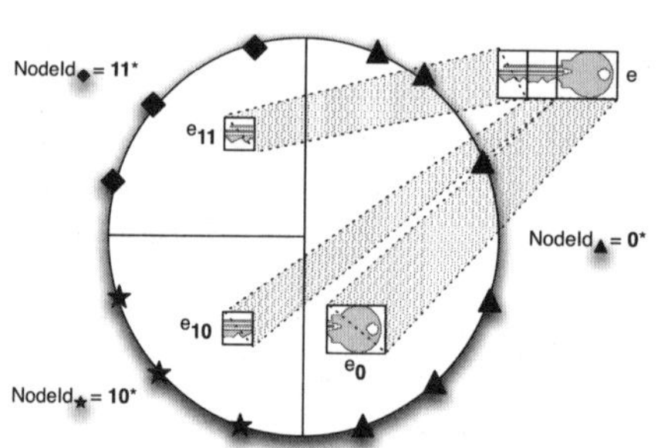

Fig. 2. Distribution of three shares e_0, e_{10} and e_{11} with $e = e_0 + e_{10} + e_{11}$. Each node knows the list of members of his sharing group.

Each share is uniquely identified by a binary *shareId* and is known by nodes which identifiers are such that $nodeId = shareId*$ in binary form (i.e., *shareId* is a binary prefix of *nodeId*). Each node knows only one share and nobody knows S entirely. Splitting a group knowing e_i (resp. merging two groups knowing e_{i0} and e_{i1}) creates two groups knowing respectively e_{i0} and e_{i1} (resp. one group knowing e_i).

In Figure 2, there are three shares e_0, e_{10} and e_{11}. Nodes which identifiers begin with 0 know e_0, those with 10 know e_{10} and those with 11 know e_{11}. To get some data signed with S, one must obtain and multiply this data signed with e_0, e_{10} and e_{11}, and thus need the cooperation of three nodes which identifiers begin respectively with 0, 10 and 11.

3.3   Distributed Certification Process

We first present an efficient certification algorithm and we then calculate the probability of success of this algorithm in presence of attackers.

Certification Algorithm. Given the sharing illustrated in Figure 2, we now explain the associated distributed certification process. This explanation is illustrated in Figure 3, on which the node A wants to obtain a certificate for a request Req. It has to obtain the cooperation of one node of each sharing group to obtain the signature $Req^e[m]$. This certification is realized in two steps.

The first step is to deploy a covering tree on the sharing groups. The node A requests two nodes whose binary identifiers begin respectively with 0 and 1: A is itself eligible for 0 and finds C to handle the *shareId* 1. Since A owns the share e_0, A stops here; C does not handle the share e_1 (which does not exist) so it forwards the request to two nodes B and C whose binary identifiers begin respectively with 10 and 11. B (resp. C) owns e_{10} (resp. e_{11}) so both nodes stop here (Figure 3(a)).

The second step is to create the certificate. B and C partially sign with e_{10} and e_{11} and send their results $Req^{e_{10}}[m]$ and $Req^{e_{11}}[m]$ to C (Figure 3(b)). C multiplies these two partial signatures, obtains $Req^{e_1}[m] = Req^{e_{10}+e_{11}}[m]$ and sends it back to A. A partially signs with e_0 to obtain $Req^{e_0}[m]$ (Figure 3(c)) and finally multiplies the partial signatures with e_0 and e_1, obtaining $Req^e[m]$ which is the signature of Req with $S = (e, m)$ (Figure 3(d)).

Since the public key corresponding to each share is unknown and partial signatures are thus unverifiable, each node involved in the certification can corrupt the signature. Misbehaving nodes can produce wrong exponentiations with owned share or wrong multiplications. We propose to ask $nbAsks$ nodes instead of one for a partial signature, following the hypothesis that there are less misbehaving nodes than well behaving ones. Asking several nodes, one can decide and return the most likely partial signature.

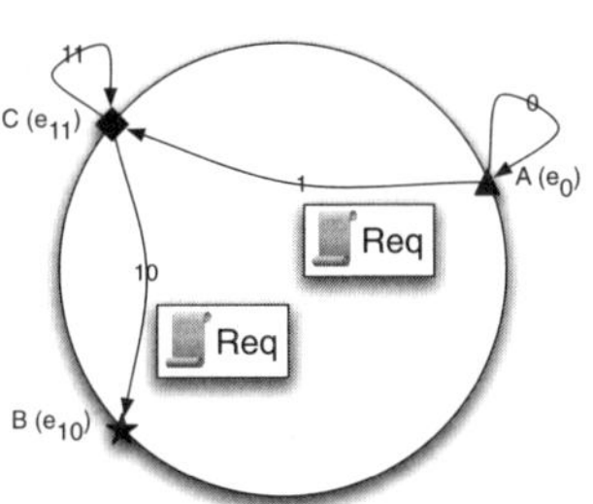

(a) A sends Req to other nodes

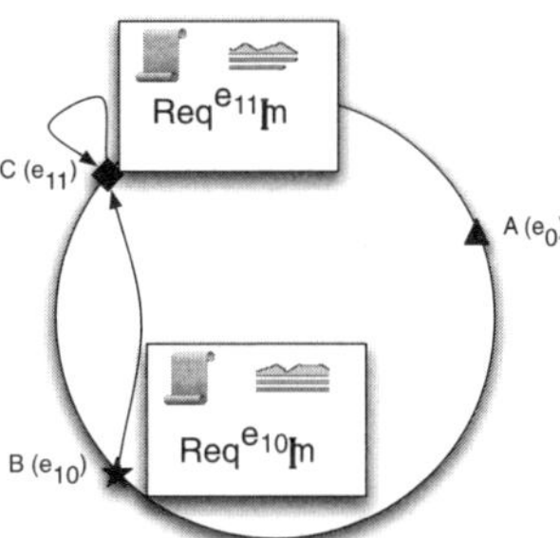

(b) B and C partially sign

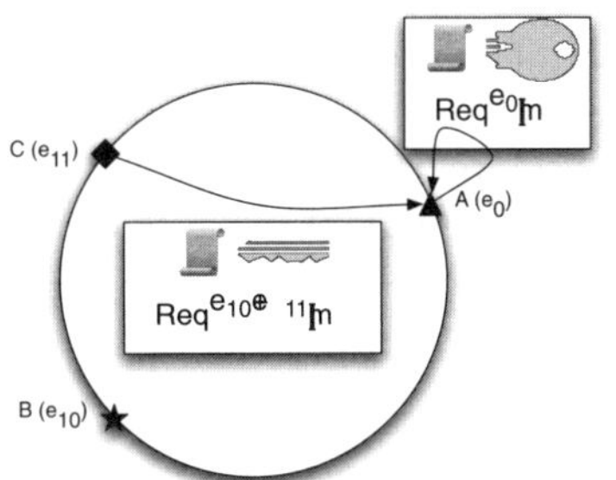

(c) C multiplies the two partial signatures and A partially signs

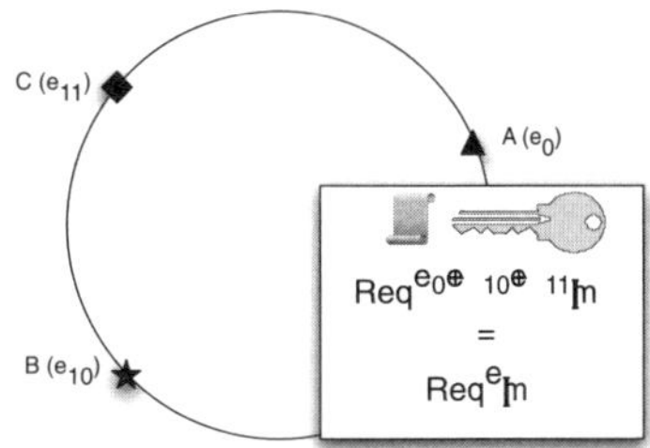

(d) A obtains the signature of Req with $S = (e, m)$

Fig. 3. Certification of Req with $S = (e, m)$. Shares do not transit.

Probability of Success of the Certification Algorithm. We calculate here the probability of success of a legitimate certification in the case where every honest node accepts to participate in the certification and every attacker tries to corrupt this process. Let $k \in [0,1]$ be the rate of attackers in the network. Each request for a partial signature is sent to $nbAsks$ nodes, $nbAsks$ odd, and the used result is the value returned by more than half of the nodes (we suppose the worst case where attackers collude to return the same incorrect partial signature).

Let us consider the tree representing the recursive calls to partially sign with a given $shareId$. The leafs of this tree correspond to the shares of the secret key which identifiers are prefixed by the given $shareId$. The internal nodes of this tree correspond to the share identifiers that are not present in the network and which provoke two recursive calls with longer identifiers, so this tree is binary. Each node of this tree coincide with one or several P2P members (if $nbAsks > 1$) asked for the corresponding $shareId$. We define the probability of success of a partial signature recursively on the height of the tree representing its recursive calls: $P(h)$ is the probability for a partial signature to succeed in a tree of height h (note that it includes the probability that the root node is honest).

If $h = 0$ (leaf), the certification succeeds if and only if this node is honest: $P(0) = 1 - k$. If $h > 0$, the certification succeeds if and only if the root node is honest and the two recursive calls succeed. Since the root node is eligible for one of the calls, the probability of this node being honest and this first call succeeding is $P(h-1)$. The second call is sent to $nbAsks$ nodes and this partial certification succeeds if the majority of calls succeed. A call succeeds with the probability $P(h-1)$ and fails with $1 - P(h-1)$: i calls thus succeed with the probability $C^i_{nbAsks}P(h-1)^i(1-P(h-1))^{nbAsks-i}$. This second partial signature succeeds when more than half of the requests succeed, yielding a probability of $\sum_{i=\frac{nbAsks+1}{2}}^{nbAsks} C^i_{nbAsks}P(h-1)^i(1-P(h-1))^{nbAsks-i}$. Putting it all together gives

$$P(h) = P(h-1) \times \sum_{i=\frac{nbAsks+1}{2}}^{nbAsks} C^i_{nbAsks}P(h-1)^i(1-P(h-1))^{nbAsks-i}$$

To obtain the complete signature, the root of the tree is called on the empty share identifier and the leafs correspond thus to the s shares of the secret key present in the network. Since this tree is binary, its height is $h = log_2(s)$. If n is the number of nodes and g_{min} (resp. g_{max}) is the minimal (resp. maximal) size of a sharing group, then the average number of shares is $s = \frac{2n}{g_{min}+g_{max}}$. The probability of success of the certification is thus $P(log_2(\frac{2n}{g_{min}+g_{max}}))$. We can conclude that the bigger the network is, the harder the certifications are. This probability is graphed in Section 5.

4   Security Analysis

In this section, we discuss the robustness of our system against attackers.

4.1   Obtaining a Fake Certificate

How to Obtain a Fake Certificate ? An attacker can create a fake certificate through obtaining the secret key of the network S. Since S is initially generated through a distributed algorithm, no member knows S at any moment. So, the attacker has to obtain every share to rebuild S, which means corrupting a node or inserting himself or an accomplice in every sharing group. Due to the large number of sharing groups (more than $\frac{n}{g_{max}} = \frac{n}{40}$ with the values proposed in Section 5), we think that corrupting a node in each group is quite hard. Inserting himself in each sharing group involves creating multiple identities which is a sybil attack (we made the assumption there is no such attack in Section 3.1). The only other possibility is a group of attackers getting every share and we thus calculate the probability of such a successful attack.

Probability for Colluding Attackers to get Every Share. Let k be the ratio of attackers. If a given sharing group is composed of g_i members, then the probability that there is no attacker in this group is $(1 - k)^{g_i}$. The probability that there is at least one attacker in this group is thus $1 - (1 - k)^{g_i}$.

Consider now a network composed of s sharing groups of resp. $g_1, \ldots, g_s$ members (hence the number of nodes is $\sum_{i=1}^{s} g_i$). Then the probability that there is an attacker in each sharing group is $\prod_{i=1}^{s} 1 - (1 - k)^{g_i}$. Since $1 - (1 - k)^{g_i} < 1$, this probability decreases when the number of shares s increases, i.e., when the network grows. Moreover, for a given network size, reducing the size of the groups g_i and hence increasing the number of shares s results in a lower probability of such an attack. This probability is graphed in Section 5.

4.2   Attacking an Honest Certification

How to Attack an Honest Certification ? An attacker can prevent a certification process through intercepting the certification request. This attack is prevented by requesting several nodes instead of one. An attacker can also try to make a share unavailable, through crashing all the nodes in a given sharing group or creating enough nodes or having enough accomplices to control all the nodes in such a group. We exclude here the case of crashing $g_{min} = 20$ nodes (value proposed in Section 5) and leave a potential countermeasure to future work. Creating enough nodes to control a full sharing group is a sybil attack, which is not handled here as stated in Section 3.1. The only other case is a group of attackers controlling all the nodes in a sharing group, which is discussed below.

Probability for Colluding Attackers to Control all the Nodes in a Sharing Group. Let k be the ratio of attackers. If a given sharing group is composed of g_i members, then the probability that there is only attackers in this group is k^{g_i}. The probability that there is at least one well-behaving node is thus $1 - k^{g_i}$.

Consider now a network composed of s sharing groups of resp. $g_1, \ldots, g_s$ members. Then the probability that there is at least one well-behaving node in each sharing group is $\prod_{i=1}^{s} 1 - k^{g_i}$. The probability that there is one group containing only attackers is thus the complementary probability $1 - \prod_{i=1}^{s} 1 - k^{g_i}$. Since $1 - k^{g_i} < 1$, this probability increases when the network grows. Moreover, for a given network size, reducing the size of the groups g_i and hence increasing the number of shares s results in a higher probability of such an attack. Given the probability presented in 4.1, the size of the groups implies thus a trade-off between these two possible attacks. This probability is graphed in Section 5.

5   Experimental Results

In this section, we present simulations results and compare them to theoretical results provided in Sections 3.3 and 4. We simulated our distributed certification system using *PeerSim* [10], an extensible P2P simulator. Parameters of our simulations are the number of nodes in the network, the percentage of attackers and the number of nodes *nbAsks* asked for each partial signature. Sharing groups are composed of $g_{min} = 20$ to $g_{max} = 40$ members, yielding $0.025 < t < 0.05$ (certification is only possible through the collaboration of 2.5 to 5% of the nodes).

In these simulations, we do not handle attacks on nodes. For instance, a *worm* attack could allow some attacker to take control of a large number of honest nodes. However, we think that protecting against such attacks is out of our current scope. Considered nodes are thus well-behaving or misbehaving depending only on the local user choice.

In Figure 4(a), we vary the number of nodes in the network with a constant percentage of attackers (10%, which is already a very large part since we do not consider worm attacks). As stated in Section 3.3, the larger the network is, the harder it is to achieve a successful certification. With 500 nodes, 20%

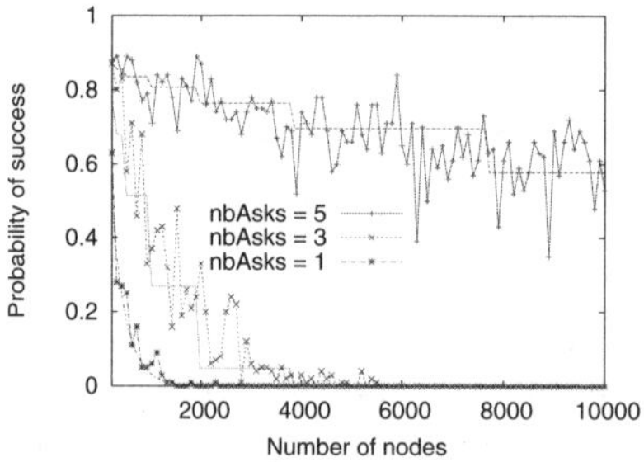

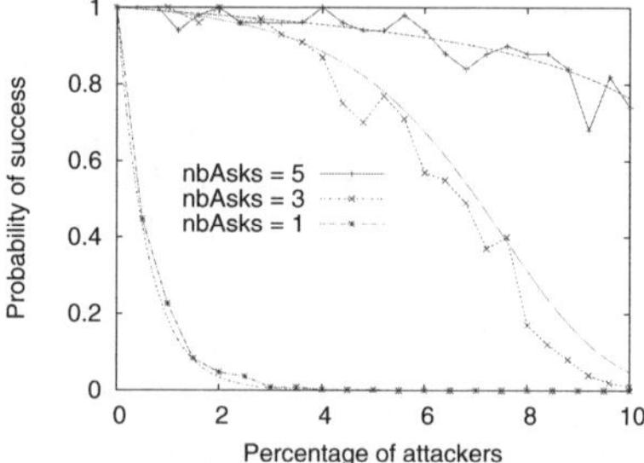

| (a) Percentage of success of the different algorithms in function of the number of nodes. Each experiment contains 10% of misbehaving nodes and each node asks 1, 3 or 5 other nodes for partial signatures. Corresponding theoretical curves are also drawn. | (b) Percentage of success of the different algorithms in function of the percentage of attackers. Each experiment contains 5000 nodes and each node asks 1, 3 or 5 other nodes for partial signatures. Corresponding theoretical curves are also drawn. |

Fig. 4. Certification results

of the certifications with $nbAsks = 1$ succeed. With more than 1500 nodes, no certification with $nbAsks = 1$ succeeds. Even if certification with $nbAsks = 5$ allows to handle more attackers, it is clear that it will be important to exclude attackers to maintain an efficient certification service.

In Figure 4(b), we vary the percentage of misbehaving nodes with a constant total number of nodes (5000, which is a median value of Figure 4(a)). With 1% of attackers, only 20% of certifications with $nbAsks = 1$ succeed. With more than 2% of attackers, this algorithm is not usable with $nbAsks = 1$. Certifications with $nbAsks = 3$ or $nbAsks = 5$ are able to tolerate much more attackers.

Figure 5(a) shows the probability for colluding attackers to obtain every share of the secret key in function of the percentage of attackers. The experimental curve with sharing groups composed of $g_{min} = 20$ to $g_{max} = 40$ members is bounded by the two theoretical curves where all groups are composed of 20 (resp. 40) nodes. In the worst case, 2.5% of the nodes ($\frac{1}{g_{max}} = 0.025$) should be able to obtain every share. However, obtaining every share requires not only to have more attackers than shares but also to specifically have an attacker in *each* sharing group. The theoretical probability of such an attack is in fact infinitesimal for less than 10% of attackers (theoretical curve with $g = 40$). Moreover, the experimental curve is much closer to the theoretical one with $g = 20$ than to the one with $g = 40$. This is due to the fact that, in the experiment, there are groups of different sizes between 20 and 40. It is then less probable for an attacker to get into those containing only 20 members: these small groups have a critical impact on this probability. Given that, the effective probability of such an attack is infinitesimal for less than 20% of attackers.

Figure 5(b) shows the probability for colluding attackers to be the only members of a sharing group and thus to be able to make this share unavailable. The experimental curve is also bounded by the two theoretical curves where

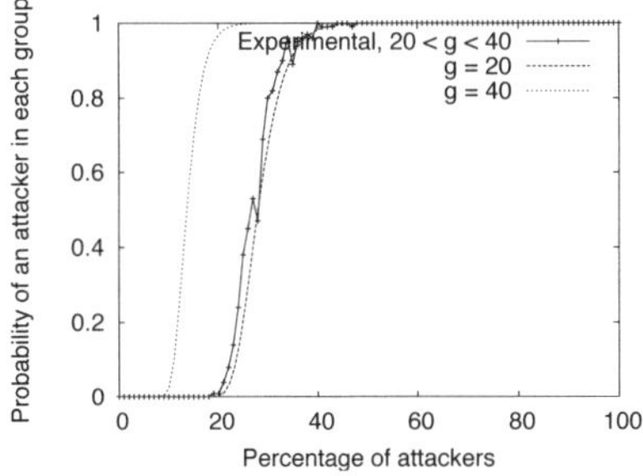

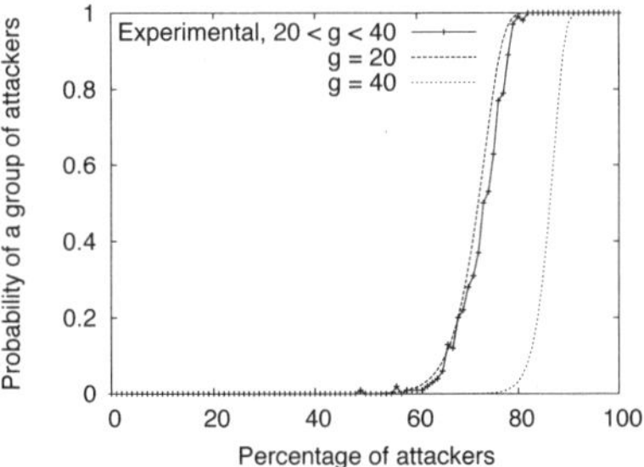

(a) Probability for colluding attackers to obtain every share of the secret key in function of the percentage of attackers. Corresponding theoretical curves are also drawn.

(b) Probability for colluding attackers to be the only members of a sharing group in function of the percentage of attackers. Corresponding theoretical curves are also drawn.

Fig. 5. Robustness results in a 10,000 nodes network

all groups are composed of 20 (resp. 40) nodes. It appears that the probability of such an attack is infinitesimal for less than 60% of attackers. For the same reasons as in the previous figure, the experimental curve is much closer to the theoretical one with $g = 20$ than to the one with $g = 40$.

6   Applications of Distributed Certification

In this section, we briefly introduce three applications of our distributed certification. These applications aim at preventing sybil attacks, excluding misbehaving nodes and finally providing a secure naming service.

6.1   Sybil Protection through Admission Control to the Network

In the sybil attack [5], an attacker creates many node identifiers and possibly picks a specific subset. With many node identifiers, an attacker can alter the overall performance of the network. Moreover, even with a few well-chosen identifiers, an attacker can isolate nodes or censor resources. First, he can isolate a victim node from the network and filter his requests by choosing precisely the node identifiers the victim node uses in its routing table: this victim node then sends all his requests to this attacker. Second, an attacker can take the control of a resource and of all its replicas by choosing identifiers close to the attacked resource identifier (if replication is done on nearby nodes). The problem is thus not only to limit the number of identifiers a user can create but also to enforce truly random identifiers.

Relying on friendship relations, *SybilGuard* [11] allows each node to decide whether another node is genuine or not and so limits the number of sybil nodes an attacker can create. However, the identifier of a node is the hash of its public key. An attacker can thus generate many key pairs and choose a specific one which hashes to an identifier in the desired part of the overlay: *SybilGuard* does not enforce random identifiers. We propose thus to combine our distributed certification with *SybilGuard*. To join the network, a new member must obtain a certificate containing his public key signed with the network secret key and thus needs the cooperation of a fixed ratio t of the nodes. Each of these nodes tests the new node with *SybilGuard* and cooperates only if the new node is detected as genuine: if the newcomer is detected as sybil, he does not obtain a certificate which prevents an attacker from creating many identifiers. Then, node identifiers are derived from the unpredictable signatures of the certificates. Each new member thus generates a key pair, registers his public key, and finally obtains his node identifier: a user cannot predict his identifier which ensures random ones. Accepted members are checked as non-sybil and the network is self-protected from sybil attacks.

6.2   Detection and Exclusion of Misbehaving Nodes

To prevent some adversarial behaviors in the P2P network, it is interesting to detect and exclude misbehaving nodes. For instance, in our certification algorithm, nodes ask several other nodes for the same partial signature and compare the results to cope with attackers returning fake partial signatures. Also, to obtain a resource, nodes may use redundant routing to prevent an attacker present on a route to this resource from forging a fake response. However, asking several nodes for a partial signature or using redundant routing generates overhead on the network. Excluding such attackers allows to reduce the number of nodes asked or redundant routes used for an identical success probability.

We propose thus to detect and exclude some types of misbehaving nodes. We make the assumption that the majority of the nodes are honest and we thus detect attackers which exhibit a minority behavior. Each node monitors some traffic and compares messages which should be the same. For instance, a minority partial signature or a minority response for a given resource requested through different routes is considered as an attack. If some traffic reveals an attack, then the victim sends the messages proving this attack to a ratio t of the nodes and these nodes revoke the membership certificate of the attacker with the network secret key (revocation is a special case of certification). This attacker is then globally excluded from the network.

6.3   Secure Naming of Resources

In [12], Bryan *et al.* propose to use a cheap and highly available P2P network as a VoIP directory. Each user inserts an entry in the P2P network mapping his name such as "John Smith" to his IP address. When a user wants to phone John Smith, he requests the resource identified by $h("John\ Smith")$ and obtains the IP address of John Smith. However, they do not propose any mechanism to prevent an attacker from intersecting such a request and replying a fake IP address. The only solution, to our best knowledge, is to call John Smith by a hash of his public key rather than by his name. This is not convenient to remember.

We propose that each new user obtains a certificate binding his user name to his public key, using distributed certification. Each node involved in this certification first checks if there is already a user with the same name by requesting this username in the DHT. Cache mechanisms of DHT should be able to manage this peak of identical requests. If and only if the name is free, then this node proceeds with the distributed certification: a certificate for a given name can only be obtained if this name is free. Then, a node wanting to phone "John Smith" requests the resource identified by $h("John\ Smith")$, obtains the certified public key of John Smith and his IP address, and can then challenge John Smith about his private key to authenticate him.

7   Conclusion and Future Work

We proposed here a distributed certification system for structured P2P networks. This mechanism provides the ability to leverage the local knowledge of a ratio t of the nodes to a global knowledge recognized by all the nodes in the network. Subsequent verifications of the certificates are simple checks on digital signatures.

We evaluated and validated this distributed certification in the presence of attackers through probabilities and simulations. We now plan on stressing a real implementation of our system under dynamics using the PlanetLab testbed.

We finally briefly presented three applications of distributed certification in structured P2P networks. These applications involve controlling the access of new nodes, excluding misbehaving nodes and providing a secure naming service. We now have to precise these applications and study interactions of the different steps.

Acknowledgments. The authors thank Orange Labs for partially funding this work and especially Hervé Debar for his involvement in the project and his advice and valuable comments.

References

1. Clip2: The gnutella protocol specification v0.4 (2000),
   `http://www9.limewire.com/developer/gnutella_protocol_0.4.pdf`
2. Stoica, I., Morris, R., Karger, D.R., Kaashoek, M.F., Balakrishnan, H.: Chord: A scalable peer-to-peer lookup service for internet applications. In: Proceedings of the ACM SIGCOMM Conference (SIGCOMM). Computer Communication Review, pp. 149–160. ACM Press, New York (2001)
3. Kong, J., Zerfos, P., Luo, H., Lu, S., Zhang, L.: Providing robust and ubiquitous security support for mobile ad hoc networks. In: Proceedings of the 9th IEEE International Conference on Network Protocols (ICNP). IEEE Computer Society, Los Alamitos (2001)
4. Saxena, N., Tsudik, G., Yi, J.H.: Experimenting with admission control in P2P. In: Proceedings of the International Workshop on Advanced Developments in System and Software Security (WADIS) (2003)
5. Douceur, J.R.: The sybil attack. In: Druschel, P., Kaashoek, M.F., Rowstron, A. (eds.) IPTPS 2002. LNCS, vol. 2429, pp. 251–260. Springer, Heidelberg (2002)
6. Shamir, A.: How to share a secret. Communications of the ACM 22(11) (1979)
7. Desmedt, Y.: Some recent research aspects of threshold cryptography. In: Okamoto, E. (ed.) ISW 1997. LNCS, vol. 1396, pp. 158–173. Springer, Heidelberg (1998)
8. Frankel, Y., Gemmell, P., MacKenzie, P.D., Yung, M.: Optimal-resilience proactive public-key cryptosystems. In: Proceedings of the 38th Annual IEEE Symposium on Foundations of Computer Science (FOCS). IEEE Computer Society, Los Alamitos (1997)
9. Boneh, Franklin,: Efficient Generation of Shared RSA Keys. In: Kaliski Jr., B.S. (ed.) CRYPTO 1997. LNCS, vol. 1294, pp. 425–439. Springer, Heidelberg (1997)
10. Jelasity, M., Jesi, G.P., Montresor, A., Voulgaris, S.: PeerSim P2P Simulator (2004), `http://peersim.sourceforge.net/`
11. Yu, H., Kaminsky, M., Gibbons, P.B., Flaxman, A.: Sybilguard: Defending against sybil attacks via social networks. In: Proceedings of the ACM SIGCOMM Conference (SIGCOMM), pp. 267–278. ACM Press, New York (2006)
12. Bryan, D.A., Lowekamp, B.B., Jennings, C.: SOSIMPLE: A serverless, standards-based, P2P SIP communication system. In: Proceedings of the International Workshop on Advanced Architectures and Algorithms for Internet Delivery and Applications (AAA-IDEA) (2005)

N2N: A Layer Two Peer-to-Peer VPN

Luca Deri[1] and Richard Andrews[2]

[1] ntop.org, Pisa, Italy
[2] Symstream Technologies, Melbourne, Australia
`{deri,andrews}@ntop.org`

Abstract. The Internet was originally designed as a flat data network delivering a multitude of protocols and services between equal peers. Currently, after an explosive growth fostered by enormous and heterogeneous economic interests, it has become a constrained network severely enforcing client-server communication where addressing plans, packet routing, security policies and users' reachability are almost entirely managed and limited by access providers. From the user's perspective, the Internet is not an open transport system, but rather a telephony-like communication medium for content consumption.

This paper describes the design and implementation of a new type of peer-to-peer virtual private network that can allow users to overcome some of these limitations. N2N users can create and manage their own secure and geographically distributed overlay network without the need for central administration, typical of most virtual private network systems.

Keywords: Virtual private network, peer-to-peer, network overlay.

1 Motivation and Scope of Work

Irony pervades many pages of history, and computing history is no exception. Once personal computing had won the market battle against mainframe-based computing, the commercial evolution of the Internet in the nineties stepped the computing world back to a substantially rigid client-server scheme. While it is true that the today's Internet serves as a good transport system for supplying a plethora of data interchange services, virtually all of them are delivered by a client-server model, whether they are centralised or distributed, pay-per-use or virtually free [1].

Direct, free and private interoperation between domestic Internet users - for example a direct file transfer or a point-to-point server-less message exchange - is generally prevented by the market-driven characteristics of typical corporate and domestic Internet access systems. These tend to mask the user's IP identity and limit peer accessibility:

- In many cases, end users do not have any control over their connection configuration, which is totally managed by Internet service providers (ISPs).
- ADSL, fibre or cable Internet users are generally hidden through chains of NAT [35] devices that may even start at the customer's premises with the ubiquitous home access gateway. In some cases, a domestic user connection has a private,

D. Hausheer and J. Schönwälder (Eds.): AIMS 2008, LNCS 5127, pp. 53–64, 2008.

i.e. non-public, IP address, which prevents an external peer initiating a direct IP session. This kind of access is generally acceptable to a domestic content consumer, given the client-server nature of most Internet services. In this scenario, a NAT-ed access appears indistinguishable in performance with respect to a "premium service" offering permanent, public IP assignment.

- Firewalls outside the user's control, greatly reduce the possibility of a user being contacted by a direct session initiated elsewhere. Furthermore these devices limit the protocols that can be used in a direct information transfer between geographically distributed peers.

All of these facts lead to the conclusion that for the vast majority of users, the Internet is a severely constrained IP transport system that hinders visibility and data exchange. Even when users are visible, dynamic addressing techniques and roaming issues prevent them from being consistently addressed by a unique name and having equal capabilities regardless of the access connection that they are using. The consequence is that the increasing success of social networks and communities is restricted to selected service models. Users can for instance exchange files only through a specialised application (e.g. Microsoft Messenger) instead of pushing files onto a user's public folders.

User experience is restricted to a consumer-provider model. Even user-to-user communications are defined within the bounds of users connecting to a common server. Partial solutions for the set of problems outlined above are already offered by many peer-to-peer (P2P) applications, but they approach the problem at the application level, rather than at network level. In general, these solutions rely upon distributed hash tables (DHTs) [2] for setting up a so-called network overlay among peers. This overlay network is in turn used as a communication means for specific, overlay-network-aware services typically file sharing and instant messaging.

P2P has become a truly disruptive approach that has changed the way the Internet is used: it has allowed users to create an application-based closed network in which data can be exchanged even with the limitations of the "closed" Internet such as firewalls, dynamic IPs and NAT [36]. Usually P2P is limited to a specific service (e.g. file sharing) rather than attacking the problem of generic IP communications through firewall restrictions. True IP users target an IP address and a service (e.g. http://www.google.com) for datagram exchange, while P2P users target an application token (e.g. song xyz or skype user abc). The fact that P2P applications are able to cross most firewalls is not perceived by their end-users as a security hole but rather as a desirable property. In fact people do not care about IP configuration, but they do care about permanent service availability regardless of the connection type (cable, wifi, phone) and physical location (e.g. at home, on the street or at work).

Unfortunately P2P has been used predominantly at the application level, and the above-listed beneficial properties of P2P protocols are limited to solving particular application-level problems. Based on these considerations, the authors decided to exploit P2P principles in order to interconnect network resources that otherwise would not be reachable due to network configuration and security restrictions [3].

N2N (network to network) is a novel layer-two over layer-three P2P virtual private network (VPN) application developed by the authors, which allows users to exploit properties typical of P2P applications at the network level instead of application level. This means that users can gain unrestricted IP visibility and be reachable with the same address regardless of their current network environment. In a nutshell, as OpenVPN moved SSL [11] from application (e.g. used to implement the https protocol) to network protocol, N2N moves P2P from application to network level.

2 The Design of N2N

A virtual private network [4] is a secure logical network that is tunnelled though another network. VPNs are often used for implementing secure point-to-point communications through the public Internet. Therefore they usually feature user authentication and content encryption. Network administrators use VPNs for securely and permanently connecting remote sites through the Internet without the need for expensive leased lines. Mobile users and telecommuters use VPNs to connect to their private office. The key elements of VPNs are (a) encryption (which protects sensitive data while travelling on the public Internet) and (b) encapsulation (which allows transport between cooperating tunnel end-points).

Permanent VPNs are often implemented at layer two with protocols such as 802.1q [5], and at layer three with BGP/MPLS [6] and are often static in terms of topology and peers. Semi-permanent VPNs such as those used by mobile users can be based on standard protocols such as PPTP [7] and L2TP over IPSEC [8] or de-facto products such as Cisco VPN and OpenVPN [9]. VPNs are implemented either using complex (to implement, administer and use) protocols such as IPSEC [10] or using SSL/TLS [11] that were originally designed to securely interconnect applications such as web servers with browsers.

Regardless of the VPN type, the key concept is that network administrators configure the VPN and users must use the setups specified by administrators in order to use it. VPN servers must be accessible by means of a public IP address such that the client can reach the VPN server. VPNs therefore form a star-topology with the service located at the publically reachable nexus. Server reachability can be an issue as many VPN systems use non-TCP/UDP protocol, or use privileged low (< 1024) ports (e.g. ISAKMP used by IPSEC uses port 500) that are often blocked by firewalls. This means that VPN clients can be unusable from many places like public hotspots, hotels and many GPRS connections. User mobility and remote access often do not work with a VPN model.

The above limitations of the current VPN systems have been the driving force for the authors for the design of N2N. In a nutshell we ask: "Is it possible to have decentralised, network-administrator-free, secure and permanent network access with a single/uniform address regardless of the current user's location, local IP address and network type?".

The authors designed N2N to give N2N users the ability to create dynamic private networks. As happens with community networks, users should be able to create their own overlay network which other users are invited to join. With VPN the network administrator chooses who may join the VPN and what interactions will be tolerated. N2N is somewhat similar to Hamachi [12], a popular application mostly used for creating private networks on which to play games. With N2N users can choose their IP address and the encryption keys, whereas with Hamachi this is not possible and all the security is delegated to Hamachi, making the whole solution weak from a security point of view.

The main design features of N2N are:

- N2N is an encrypted layer two private network using a P2P protocol. Each N2N node has a name and a common encryption key pre-shared among the users that have been invited to join the network (community).
- Encryption is performed at edge nodes using open ciphers with user-defined encryption keys. This differs from popular applications like Skype and Hamachi where the traffic is encrypted by the application with no control by the application user. Skype developers can decode Skype traffic [13], which gives users a false sense of security. This does not happen with N2N where only users holding the private keys can decrypt the traffic.
- Each N2N user can simultaneously belong to multiple communities. Users will have an encryption key, MAC and IP address for each N2N community.
- Like most P2P protocols, N2N has one or more supernodes and several edge nodes. Supernodes are used to introduce edge nodes and to cross symmetric NAT. N2N packets are encrypted/decrypted only by edge nodes and supernodes forward packets based on a clear-text packet header without inspecting the packet payload. This is a core differentiator of N2N.
- N2N can cross NAT and firewalls in the reverse traffic direction (i.e. from outside to inside) so N2N nodes become directly reachable from the community even if running on a private network.
- N2N communities are meant to be self-contained, but it is possible to route traffic across N2N communities. Packet forwarding through N2N is disabled by default, as this can be a security flaw. N2N users can enable it if necessary but doing so requires explicit user awareness.

The need to cross NAT and firewall devices motivated the use of P2P principles for interconnecting N2N nodes. During the design phase, the authors analysed several popular P2P protocols [14] ranging from proprietary (e.g. Skype SDK) to open (e.g. BitTorrent [15]) protocols. Unfortunately most protocols have been created for file sharing and are not suitable for N2N because PDUs (Protocol Data Units) have been designed to carry file information (e.g. name, length, type, attributes such as MP3 tags) and perform distributed file searches. Even though existing P2P protocols were not immediately usable for N2N without modification, some concepts already present in other P2P architectures [16] have been utilised as is explained in the following chapter. In addition to the properties listed so far, N2N presents further differences from other approaches [28] [29] [30]:

- Unlike most P2P overlay networks such as Chord [25] and Pastry [26] that are affected by the problem or locating objects/peers in a limited number of overlay hops, in N2N this is not a problem as, by design, peers are reachable either directly or in one hop when passing through the N2N community. This design choice has dramatically simplified peer lookup and membership information without requiring complex algorithms for information bookkeeping [27].
- N2N node membership is rather static. Nodes usually register with a N2N community and stick with it as long as the node is operational. In other networks such as Gnutella or Napster the membership change rate is much higher and can lead to issues as the network topology might need to be changed in order to handle new members.

- N2N nodes themselves do not store, cache, replicate or manage any content. This is because N2N connects network peers rather than content and consumers.
- The goal of N2N is not to share files but rather to allow peers to communicate generically in a secure way and to locate each other by consistent addressing regardless of their physical network location. Data sharing is accomplished by higher layer protocols as the Internet design intended.

3 N2N Architecture and Implementation

Edge nodes run on a host that can be placed in a private or public LAN. Supernodes are used to introduce edge nodes and relay packets to an edge behind symmetrical NAT (which prevents it from being directly reachable by peers). With symmetric NAT all requests from the same internal IP:port to a specific IP destination:port are mapped to an external IP:port. If the same internal host sends a request with the same source address and port to a different destination, a different external mapping is used. This prevents the arrival of packets from any other remote socket.

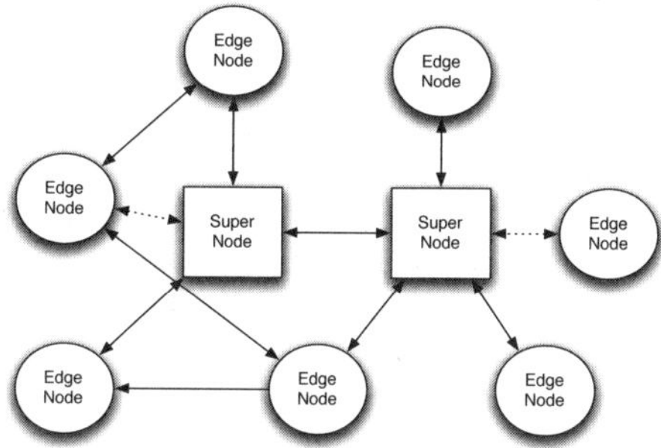

Fig. 1. N2N architecture

Edge nodes have a list of supernodes to which they register at startup. Supernodes temporarily store information about the edge nodes; such information needs to be periodically refreshed by the edge node. Edge nodes register to the first available supernode; registration to additional supernodes happens if the supernode to which the edge node is registered becomes unresponsive.

As N2N is a layer two VPN, edge nodes are identified uniquely by a 6 byte MAC address and a 16 byte community name. Edge nodes use TAP [17] devices that act as virtual ethernet devices implemented in the operating system kernel. In TAP devices, the ethernet driver is implemented in a user-space application. N2N provides such a driver implementation, which encapsulates encrypted ethernet frames within UDP packets as in Figure 2.

The kernel sees the TAP device as the path through which to send ethernet frames (based on LAN routing). UDP capsules arriving on the IP side are decrypted and the ethernet frames injected into the kernel as if they had arrived from an ethernet adapter. The use of TAP devices reduces the design of the architecture to familiar

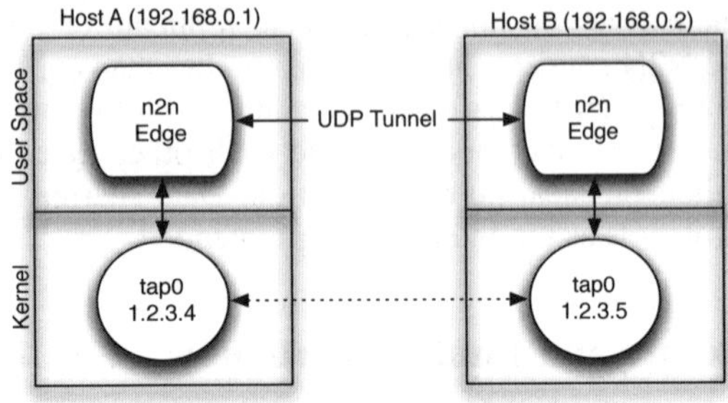

Fig. 2. N2N node communications

LAN concepts. The use of UDP encapsulation simplifies firewall and NAT traversal compared to other encapsulations such as GRE [18] that are often blocked by firewalls.

When an edge node is started, it registers with the first configured supernode and sends an acknowledged registration packet. If the acknowledgement is not received, the edge node retries then move on to another supernode. Registrations are sent periodically in order to refresh the edge registration and make sure that any firewalls between the edge and the supernode do not block the connection due to inactivity. This means the supernode can relay packets to the edge node as long as the firewall stays open. This is the technique used by N2N to traverse NAT in the reverse direction. Each supernode keeps a list of paths to each edge node keyed by {community, MAC}. N2N provides layer-2 broadcast via the supernodes, which act to forward broadcast and multicast packets to all edge nodes in the community. As edge nodes receive remote packets they also build a list of {MAC, UDP socket} for peers in the community, and send registration requests directly to the peers. Figure 3 shows how this can lead to a NAT traversal in the reverse traffic direction.

Peer registration provides a mechanism for edges to form direct connections thereby removing the supernode from the path. If the sender edge node receives an acknowledgement for a register message previously sent directly to a remote node, then the nodes can reach each other directly. If one of the peers is behind symmetric NAT, the act of sending a registration request directly to the other peer opens a return path through the firewall. If both peers are behind symmetric NAT, direct connectivity is not possible. As happens with ARP [21], dynamic peer registrations expire if not renewed. Note that:

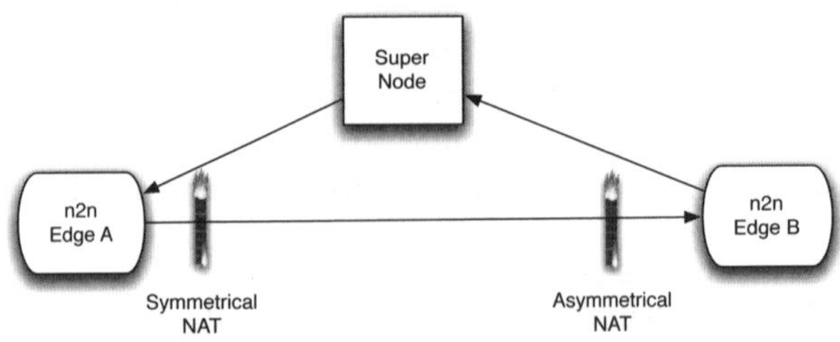

Fig. 3. N2N communications through NAT

- The N2N community name is conceptually similar to the 802.1q VLAN ID.
- Dynamic peer registration may fail, e.g. due to firewalling. In this case packets can use asymmetric routing, e.g. A to B via S but direct from B to A.

N2N uses Twofish [19] as its encryption algorithm. The authors chose this symmetric key block cipher as it is fast, unpatented and its source is uncopyrighted and licence-free. Each N2N community has a shared key that is used to encrypt/decrypt N2N packet payloads. If a supernode is compromised, injected traffic will be discarded as supernodes do not ever know community keys. layer-2 frames are also compressed using the Lempel-Ziv-Oberhumer (LZO) [20] algorithm that, like Twofish, is fast, efficient and available under the GNU GPL license. The N2N packet header is not compressed (nor encrypted) which allows supernodes to forward packets.

MAC address duplication within N2N can lead to the same problems that occur in ethernet networks so care must be taken to avoid conflicts. Edge nodes can have dynamic IP addresses by means of a DHCP server attached to an edge node in a community. As N2N TAP interfaces behave like real (e.g. ethernet) interfaces, it is also possible to run other services such as those defined by the IETF Zeroconf Working Group including, but not limited to, multicast DNS (mDNS) and DNS Service discovery [22]. Unlike most P2P systems, a node naming scheme [33] for locating peers is redundant in N2N.

4 N2N Evaluation and Testing

As N2N is a technology that is designed to interconnect heterogeneous computers, the authors ported it to three common platforms: Linux, MacOS X including BSD variants, and Windows. From the software point of view the code base is the same. Platform-specific code was needed for supporting the various TAP APIs. The authors acknowledge that the OpenVPN project has done a significant amount of work, so that today it is relatively simple to use TAP devices in a multivendor environment.

In the test setup, the supernode was installed on a Linux PC with a public IP address although this is not really necessary as long as the supernode UDP port is publically reachable. N2N nodes were placed behind several types of NAT/firewall devices, including symmetric NAT and multi-NAT (i.e. cascaded NAT devices) that are often used by ISPs. Edge nodes have been used on all above listed platforms in order to evaluate interoperability. As soon as the edge application starts, the node is part of the N2N community and can communicate with remote N2N peers. Several protocols were tested successfully, ranging from SSH to dynamic FTP.

As N2N uses TAP devices, it is possible to run popular tools such as tcpdump and wireshark on the TAP interfaces. Edge-to-supernode traffic is both encrypted and compressed, but traffic at the TAP interface is clear-text.

All existing IP-based applications can run on N2N without any change or recompilation. Even multicast works within N2N communities as long as the routing tables are correctly configured. Nevertheless the full power of N2N is unleashed when using community-based applications such as Retroshare [23] or I Hear You [24], the latter being a P2P VoIP application.

While N2N's throughput is similar to other VPN implementations such as OpenVPN and PPTP as they share the basic building blocks, its major advantages compared to those technologies are:

- The ability to create a private network without a central control point.
- Direct packet exchange, which increases network efficiency and reduces latency.
- Applications see N2N as just another ethernet LAN.
- The code base is extremely small with no dependencies on external libraries (e.g. OpenSSL) or proprietary software, so it can be embedded into small devices and appliances.

N2N is a major step ahead compared to application layer P2P networks because it is transparent and usable by all applications without any N2N awareness. If N2N had been implemented at a higher layer, it would have been usable only by applications aware of it; as happens with most P2P applications.

N2N may appear as a way to circumvent many management mechanisms for security and privacy, and allow subcultures to share information free of monitoring. In this respect N2N might appear more as a problem rather than a solution to connectivity issues. The authors have not designed N2N to be a tool for defending users against network surveillance, but rather as utilitarian network overlays through which information can flow directly, securely and reliably.

4.1 Comparing N2N and Mobile IP

Mobile IP [33] is a scheme to allow global dynamic routing of IP packets to a static IP address when the host holding the static address is mobile. This is done by a series of routing tricks involving NAT and tunneling. It requires a central holder of the static IP address to be present to relay all packets destined for the mobile host. The presence of a packet relay node presents scalability and reliability problems. The types of problems to expect can be found extrapolating the lessons learned from GPRS, where the GGSN forms a bottleneck to traffic and a single-point of failure. N2N by contrast drastically alleviates these problems for participating communities of hosts. When a member of an N2N community changes its public IP address, all other members begin utilising the new address on ARP refresh and direct peer-to-peer communication is transparently restored without the need for a packet relay node such as the home agent in Mobile IP. Mobile IP is designed for use with telco-provided services where the care-of IP address assigned to a roaming device is routable and not firewalled. As a result Mobile IP is of little value when the mobile host changes its IP address to that of a host on a LAN which is isolated from the public internet by a firewall. N2N by contrast will pierce the firewall and transparently provide peer-to-peer communications once more. For the symmetric NAT case, N2N reduces to a similar situation as Mobile IP where the supernode must act as a packet relay. The peer-to-peer nature of N2N should deliver far better interactive performance due to the drastically reduced round-trip time and the removal of a queueing point which exists at the home agent in Mobile IP. The shortening of the packet path reduces the average round-trip time as there are fewer hops to cover. The removal of the packet relay reduces the variance of round-trip time which - in Mobile IP - is influenced by momentary load associated with packet forwarding for other nodes.

Community in the N2N sense refers to a set of participating hosts which elect to be part of the community by maintaining registrations with the community supernodes. The uses of such communities are many. The pattern describes the internal communications of most small businesses, peer groups, affiliations, etc. N2N provides a LAN extension to a mobile community. No matter where a participating host roams to and what transport it uses, it remains a member of the N2N L2 network. Traditional road-warrior setups depend on client-server models with the mobile host being the client. Network security and resource access rely heavily on this model making it difficult to provide true peer-to-peer applications. Indeed the availability and uptake of true peer-to-peer applications may be hindered by the difficulty in providing such applications across network boundaries. N2N provides an enabling technology for true peer-to-peer IP communications models such as push-to-talk type conferencing, information synchronisation by push (rather than pull-from-server) or by broadcast.

Being a direct peer-to-peer technology N2N scales much better than solutions such as Mobile IP which rely on a single point of packet aggregation and forwarding [32]. The N2N model makes use of the supernodes only when required - typically at the time when a host must be contacted but its location is unknown. The supernode has minimal participation in packet delivery and as such is not a limiting factor on host-to-host round-trip time or throughput.

4.2 N2N Scalability

N2N has been designed to be simple and address connectivity limitations present in most networks as explained in the previous sections. By no means has N2N been designed to implement a large overlay networks where thousand of nodes can join for a few reasons:

- Large overlays create a significant traffic load on supernodes which can lead to performance degradation.
- In order to optimise the overlay and increase the number of supernodes, some edge nodes (e.g. those that are not behind a symmetrical NAT) should become a hybrid edge-supernode as happens with most P2P applications. Yet this would impact on node performance.
- Efficient supernode selection based on criteria like round trip time and available bandwidth is necessary for a large overlay. However this would significantly add complexity to the N2N code and produce extra node traffic in order to periodically calculate supernode section metrics.

That said, the authors are aware that the next N2N release should address some issues, including better scalability. In any case, this planned evolution will not upset the core N2N principles, which were designed to be simple, reliable, and usable for business activities.

4.3 Network Management and N2N

Most management protocols have not been designed to run across firewalls and NAT. However in some cases, network administrators are forced to use them in this scenario and often the solution is to setup the firewall with static access rules. This however is not a clean solution as it is rather simple to forge packets, in particular UDP-based protocols such as SNMP. However TCP-based used to administer remote hosts protocols such as VNC [34] and RDC (Remote Desktop Connection), are not suggested to run across firewalls as a protocol flaw could compromise the whole network.

Network management applications can take advantage of N2N for creating secure WAN management networks on which protocols can flow without having to take into account security and network constraints. Using different community names, administrators can add extra security by creating several overlays one for each group of homogeneous management resources, so that management traffic is further partitioned. Implementing the same partitioning scheme using traditional techniques such as VLAN or VPNs would have been much more difficult and in some cases (e.g. on WANs) probably not feasible at all.

5 Open Issues and Future Work

Although fully operational, the N2N development is not over. The authors are:

- Implementing N2N tunneling over other protocols such as HTTP and DNS in order to give users the ability to run N2N even on those partially open networks where only a few protocols such as email and web are allowed.
- Designing security mechanisms to avoid intruders and bugged edge nodes which could disable a community with node registration bombing.
- Enhancing supernode selection and registration algorithms, so that edge nodes dynamically select the fastest reachable supernode among the list of available supernodes [31].
- Evaluating the porting of N2N onto small devices such as Apple iPhone and Linux-based network devices including DreamBox and Android phones when available.

In a nutshell the plan is to allow N2N to run on:

- Most partially-open networks and give mobile users the ability to have secure access with a fixed N2N IP address, if configured, regardless of their location, e.g. at the airport lounge, in a hotel room or at the office.
- Hostile networks where attackers can try to break N2N community security.
- Embedded portable devices that can be used for letting users access their own private network from all applications in a secure way, without having to cope with the limitations of most networks that often allow only reduced Internet access.

6 Final Remarks

This paper has described a novel type of P2P VPN that enables the creation of secure, private networks regardless of the peer locations, network access type, or operating system. Unlike the current VPN generation, N2N is fully decentralised and uses supernodes only at start-up or whenever peers are behind symmetric NATs that prevent direct peer communication. Existing applications do not need to be changed in any way to exploit N2N. The ability to tunnel N2N traffic over protocols such as HTTP and DNS makes it a very useful technology for allowing users to overcome restrictions in many networks. N2N users can be partitioned into networks and have a permanent, unique N2N IP address regardless of the current address of the device running N2N. This makes N2N suitable for creating overlay networks of users sharing homogeneous information. Finally, traffic encryption at the edge and not by any controlling entity, enables users to securely exchange sensitive information with much less risk of being intercepted or observed by unwanted peers.

Acknowledgment and Code Availability

The authors would like to thank Simone Benvenuti, Carlo Rogialli and Maria Teresa Allegro for their help and suggestions during N2N development.

N2N is distributed under the GNU GPL 3 licence and is available at the ntop home page http://www.ntop.org/n2n/ and other mirrors on the Internet.

References

1. Fuggetta, A.: The Net is Flat, Cefriel Technical Report (2007),
   `http://alfonsofuggetta.org/mambo/images/stories/Documents/Papers/TheNetIsFlat.pdf`
2. Maymounkov, P., Mazières, D.: Kademilia: A Peer-to-peer Information System Based on XOR Metric. In: 1st Intl. Workshop on Peer-to-Peer Systems (2002)
3. Deri, L.: Empowering peer-to-peer services. In: EFNIW Workshop (2007)
4. Gleeson, B., et al.: IP Based Virtual Private Networks. RFC 2764 (2000)
5. McPherson, A., Dykes, B.: VLAN Aggregation for Efficient IP Address Allocation. RFC 3069 (2001)
6. Rosen, E., Rekhter, Y.: BGP/MPLS IP Virtual Private Networks. RFC 4364 (2006)
7. Hamzeh, K., et al.: Point-to-Point Tunneling Protocol (PPTP). RFC 2637 (1999)
8. Patel, B., et al.: Securing L2TP using IPsec. RFC 3193 (2001)
9. Hosner, C.: Open VPN and the SSL VPN Revolution. Sans Institute (2004)
10. Kent, S., et al.: Security Architecture for the Internet Protocol. RFC 2401 (1998)
11. Dierks, T., Allen, C.: The TLS Protocol. RFC 2246 (1999)
12. LogMe In, Hamachi Security – an Overview, White Paper (2007)
13. Skype Ltd, Skype Public API (2008), `https://developer.skype.com/`
14. Khan, K., Wierzbicki, A. (eds.): Foundation of Peer-to-Peer Computing, vol. 31(2) (2008), Special Issue, Elsevier Journal of Computer Communication

15. BitTorrent Protocol Specification (2008),
    http://www.bittorrent.org/protocol.html
16. Balakrishnan, H., et al.: Looking up data in P2P systems. Communications of the ACM (2003)
17. Krasnyansky, M.: Universal TUN/TAP Driver (2001),
    http://vtun.sourceforge.net/
18. Hanks, S., et al.: Generic Routing Encapsulation (GRE). RFC 1701 (1994)
19. Schneider, S., et al.: Twofish: A 128-Bit Block Cipher. Couterpane Labs (1998)
20. Oberhumer, M.: LZO Compression Library (2005)
21. Plummer, D.: An Ethernet Address Resolution Protocol. RFC 826 (1982)
22. Cheshire, S., Steinberg, D.: Zero Configuration Networking: The Definitive Guide. O'Reilly Media, Sebastopol (2005)
23. The Retroshare Team, Retroshare (2007),
    http://retroshare.sourceforge.net/
24. Trotta, M.: I Hear You (2008), http://ihu.sourceforge.net/
25. Stoica, I., et al.: Chord: A Scalable Peer-To-Peer Lookup Service for Internet Applications. In: Proceedings of ACM SIGCOMM (2001)
26. Rowstron, A., Druschel, P.: Pastry: Scalable, Decentralized Object Location, and Routing for Large-Scale Peer-to-peer Systems. In: Proc. of IFIP/ACM Middleware (2001)
27. Gupta, A., et al.: One Hop Lookups for Peer-to-Peer Overlays. In: Ninth Workshop on Hot Topics in Operating Systems (2003)
28. Wang, C., Li, B.: Peer-to-Peer Overlay Networks: A Survey, Technical Report, Dept. of Computer Science, HKUST (2003)
29. Keong Lua, E., et al.: A Survey and Comparison of Peer-to-Peer Overlay Network Schemes. IEEE Communications Surveys (2005)
30. Castro, M., et al.: Exploiting Network Proximity in Peer-to-peer Overlay Networks, Technical Report MSR-TR-2002-82, Microsoft Research (2002)
31. Jovanovic, M., et al.: Scalability Issues in Large Peer-to-peer Networks - A Case Study of Gnutella. Technical Report, Univ. of Cincinnati (2001)
32. Li, X., Plaxton, C.: On Name Resolution in Peer to Peer Networks. In: Proceedings of 2nd Intl. Workshop on Principles of Mobile Computing (2002)
33. Perkins, C.: IP Mobility Support. RFC 2202 (1996)
34. Richardson, T.: The RFC Protocol (2007),
    http://www.realvnc.com/docs/rfbproto.pdf
35. Touch, J.D.: Those pesky NATs. IEEE Internet Computing, 96 (July/August 2002)
36. Information Sciences Institute, TetherNet (2002),
    http://www.isi.edu/tethernet/

Secure Sharing of an ICT Infrastructure through Vinci

Fabrizio Baiardi[1] and Daniele Sgandurra[2]

[1] Polo G. Marconi, La Spezia
[2] Dipartimento di Informatica
Università di Pisa
{baiardi, daniele}@di.unipi.it

Abstract. *Virtual Interacting Network CommunIty* (Vinci) is a software architecture that exploits virtualization to share in a secure way an information and communication technology infrastructure among a set of users with distinct security levels and reliability requirements. To this purpose, Vinci decomposes users into *communities*, each consisting of a set of users, their applications, a set of services and of shared resources. Users with distinct privileges and applications with distinct trust levels belong to distinct communities. Each community is supported by a virtual network, i.e. a structured and highly parallel overlay that interconnects virtual machines (VMs), each built by instantiating one of a predefined set of VM templates. Some VMs of a virtual network run user applications, some protect shared resources, and some others control traffic among communities to discover malware or worms. Further VMs manage the infrastructure resources and configure the VMs at start-up. The adoption of several VM templates enables Vinci to minimize the complexity of each VM and increases the robustness of both the VMs and of the overall infrastructure. Moreover, the security policy that a VM applies depends upon the community a user belongs to. As an example, discretionary access control policies may protect files shared within a community, whereas mandatory policies may rule access to files shared among communities. After describing the overall architecture of Vinci, we present the VM templates and the performance results of a first prototype.

1   Introduction

Among the benefits of virtualization, the most well known one is the cost saving achieved by consolidating several servers on a single physical machine [1]. We believe that a further noticeable advantage is an increase of system robustness because we can include in a virtual architecture components that check and control the other ones in a transparent way. As an example, a virtual network can include nodes, i.e. virtual machines (VMs), which run the applications and other nodes that monitor the previous ones in a completely unobtrusive way [2]. Furthermore, the ability of accessing any component of a virtual node enables the definition of more rigorous and complete checks to detect anomalies or intrusions, as when special purpose hardware units are available. Finally, an architecture composed of a large number of virtual nodes can increase the robustness of each node, and of the overall system, by minimizing the software each node runs.

D. Hausheer and J. Schonwalder (Eds.): AIMS 2008, LNCS 5127, pp. 65–78, 2008.

These considerations have led to the definition of *Virtual Interacting Network Com-munIty* (Vinci), a software architecture that aims to exploit at best virtualization tech-nologies to share in a secure way an information and communication technology (ICT) infrastructure. To this purpose, Vinci adopts a two-tier approach where several virtual networks, or overlays, are introduced and each overlay is highly parallel because it composes a large number of VMs. To increase the robustness of each overlay, Vinci minimizes the functionalities of each VM by defining several *VM templates*. As an ex-ample, Vinci instantiates *Application VMs* to run user applications, according to the applications trust level and to the user privileges, i.e. user security levels, so that each Application VM only runs the smallest number of software packages and libraries to support the considered applications. Other VM templates are introduced to control re-sources shared among Application VMs of the same overlay or of distinct ones, or in-formation flowing among VMs. In Vinci, each physical node of the infrastructure runs a virtual machine monitor (VMM) [3] on top of the hardware-firmware level to multiplex the node physical resources among VMs and strongly confine them.

The number of overlays that share the infrastructure depends upon user *communi-ties*, because a distinct overlay, or *virtual community network* (VCN), is introduced for each community. A community consists of a set of users that execute applications and of services that these applications exploit. The users and applications in a community can be handled in a uniform way because they have homogeneous security and relia-bility requirements. Communities can also cooperate and exchange information. Proper consistency and security checks are applied within a community, while more severe checks are enforced to cross the community border. When defining a community, an administrator pairs it with a *global level*, which defines the set of users that can join the community, the applications they can run and the resources they can access. In this way, the global level is the same for all the VMs in a community and they can be ho-mogeneously managed because they have similar requirements. Hence, the notion of community simplifies the management of the VMs, because VMs of the same com-munity require the same reliability level and the data they exchange can be protected through the same mechanisms.

The rest of the paper is organized as follows. Section 2 presents the overall archi-tecture of Vinci and discusses the various VM templates introduced to run user appli-cations, to build the overlays and to support the correct sharing of the infrastructure among VMs and among communities. Section 3 presents a first set of performance results. Section 4 reviews some related works. Finally, Sect. 5 draws some conclusions.

2   Vinci Overall Architecture

An example of an infrastructure where Vinci can be applied is the one of a hospital that is shared, at least, among the doctor community, the nurse community and the administrative community. Since each community manages its private information but also shares some information with the other ones, a community should be able to de-fine its own security policy, its reliability requirements and to control information to be shared with the other ones. As an example, users in a doctor community can update the information about prescriptions whereas those in the nurse community can read but not update the same information. The nurse community and the doctor one share some other information with the administrative community, which has to bill the patient insurances. In the most general case, each user belongs to several communities according to the applications she needs to run and the data she wants to access. Consider a doctor that is the head of the hospital: as a doctor she belongs to the doctor community but, because of her administrative duties, she belongs to the administrative community as well. Furthermore, the community the doctor joins to access critical health information differs from that she joins when surfing the Internet.

In the general case, we assume that the infrastructure architecture is a private network that spans several locations, it includes a rather large number of physical nodes, and it is centrally managed by a set of administrators. We also assume that most of the nodes of the infrastructure are personal computers that are only accessed by one person at time and that the infrastructure includes a set of server nodes, which store shared data and execute server applications. Vinci requires that each node runs a virtual machine monitor (VMM), a thin software layer on top of the bare machine that creates and manages several concurrent emulation environments, the VMs. The VMM is responsible of the confinement among the VMs and guarantees a fair access to the node resources.

One of the main advantages of virtualization is the ability of choosing the appropriate combination of OS and applications for each VM to minimize the overall complexity. To exploit at best this feature, Vinci defines a set of highly specialized and simple VM templates that are dynamically instantiated and connected into overlays, i.e. virtual community networks (VCNs). A Vinci VCN includes both VMs that run applications and VMs that support and monitor the previous ones. A VCN strongly resembles a virtual private network (VPN) but an important difference lies in the granularity of the computation because we are interested in minimizing the complexity of the services each VM implements. As an example, some VMs are introduced in a VCN just to apply consistency and security checks to the overall computation.

In Vinci, each VCN is built by composing VMs that are instances of the following templates:

1. *Application VM*: it runs a set of applications on behalf of a single user;
2. *Community VM*: it manages the private resources of a community by enforcing mandatory and/or discretionary access control (MAC/DAC) policies;
3. *File System VM*: it belongs to several VCNs to protect files shared among the corresponding communities. It can implement MAC and Multi-Level Security policies and a tainting mechanism to prevent illegal information flows across communities;
4. *Communication and Control VM*: it implements and monitors information flows among communities, i.e. flows among Communication and Control VMs of distinct communities, or private flows among VMs of the same community;
5. *Assurance VM*: it checks that Application VMs only run authorized software and attests the software of a VM.

Moreover, Vinci introduces *Infrastructure VMs* that do not belong to any VCN and extend the VMMs with new functionalities to manage the overall infrastructure. As shown in Fig. 1, since VMs that are instances of the same template have homogeneous requirements and system configurations, they are easy-to-deploy virtual appliances created on

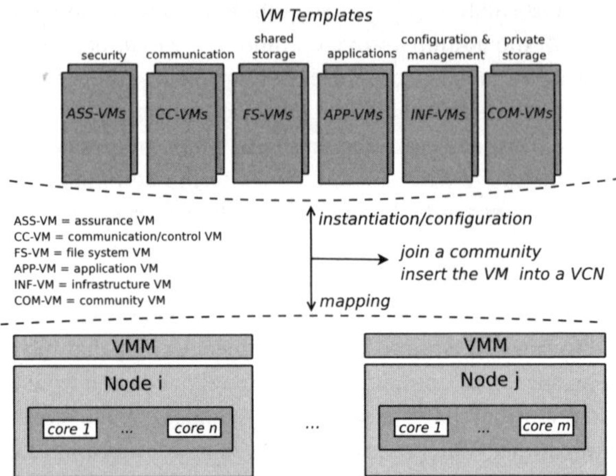

Fig. 1. VM Templates

demand from a generic baseline image. Moreover, when a VM is instantiated, its run-time environment is highly customized [4] according to the user and the community of interest through parameters such as the amount of memory, the running kernel modules, and the OS and applications versions. This results in the ability of strengthening each VM by tailoring its configuration to minimize the software it runs and avoid useless functionalities.

In the following, we describe the current implementation of Vinci that exploits Xen [5] to create the VMs and connect them into VCNs. NFSv3 [6] and Security-Enhanced Linux (SELinux) [7] [8] have been modified to apply security policies based upon the security levels of users or the global levels of communities. Finally, interconnections among VMs are handled through iptables [9] and OpenVPN [10].

2.1 Community and VCN

The key concepts of Vinci are those of community and of virtual community network (VCN). A community is composed by users and applications having the same security and reliability requirements. Users run their applications in Application VMs and, therefore, a community can also be seen as built around a set of Application VMs that share the same *global level*, i.e. the community level. This level constrains the security and reliability requirements of users that can join a community and the applications they can run. The number of communities reflects the distinct classes of users that share the private infrastructure. As an example, an administrator of a corporate enterprise can configure Vinci to support the following communities: sales, marketing, management, finance, R&D, engineering, customer support, Internet, etc. The adopted definition stresses the notion of a community as a collaborative environment where sharing of information among applications does not result in a loss of security or reliability. A VCN includes both the set of Application VMs of a community and further VMs that manage the resources of a community and interaction among communities.

2.2 Application VMs

Each Application VM runs applications of a single user and is paired with the global level inherited from the corresponding community. In general, the resources and services an Application VM can access depend upon the user security level and the global level of the community the VM belongs to. Since a user can join distinct communities through distinct Application VMs, she can access distinct resources/services according to the global level of each community. In some cases, there may exist some resources a user can access regardless of the community she currently belongs to. As an example, each user can always access its private files. While the global level of a community constrains the users that can join the community and the applications they can run, an administrator can also dictate which resources a community can access and/or share with other communities. Thus, when a user wishes to join a community, and she has the rights to do so, the community statically defines the set of applications that the Application VM can run and the resources it can access.

In Vinci, during the login phase, a user chooses the community she wants to join. Then, the Infrastructure VM of the local node configures and starts up a corresponding Application VM to run those applications that the community policy allows and it inserts the Application VM into the proper VCN. A user can run several Application VMs on the same node concurrently, each belonging to the same community or to distinct ones.

In the current prototype, each Application VM is associated with a minimal partition on one of the disks in the physical node, which stores the OS kernel loaded during the boot-up of the Application VM. Other files may be stored either locally, in a Community VM in the same VCN, or in a File System VM shared with other VCNs. To simplify the implementation of security policies, at boot time an IP address is statically assigned to an Application VM and both the VM global level and the user security level are paired with this address. Since the IP address uniquely determines the resources the VM and the user can access, Communication and Control VMs implement proper checks to detect any spoofed traffic in a VCN.

2.3 Community VMs

A Vinci VCN always includes at least one Community VM to manage and control the resources shared within the corresponding community, i.e. among its Application VMs only. This VM stores the community private files, which includes configuration files, system binaries, shared libraries and user home directories.

In the current prototype, files shared through Community VMs are protected by MAC and DAC security policies where the subject of the policy is the user security level, which is deduced from the IP address of the requesting Application VM. To this purpose, we have extended SELinux and NFS so that the NFS server enforces a policy where the subject is the user paired with the IP address of the requesting Application VM. In more detail, SELinux labeling and access rules have been extended to introduce a new subject that corresponds to an Application VM, and to define the operations it can invoke. We have also extended the object class of SELinux network object (*node*) to insert the operations that the NFS server executes on behalf of the requesting Application VM such as read, write or create files or directories. A node object is used to control the network traffic, for example to grant or deny a process the permissions to exchange data with a specific IP address and it is associated with the IP address of an Application VM. In this way, the administrator can define a distinct protection domain for each Application VM by dynamically pairing the NFS server process with the security context of the Application VM currently requesting the operation on a file.

SELinux stores most runtime security information about the running processes in the `task_security_struct` structure. We have extended this structure to include the security identifier bound to the node type and, therefore, to the corresponding subject. Moreover, we have introduced a function, `map_ip`, which maps the Application VM IP address into a security identifier (SID) according to the current policy in the SELinux security policy database. In this way, the security context can be deduced from the IP address of the Application VM that is trying to access a shared file. Every time the NFS server processes a request, if the policy pairs the requesting IP address with a node type, `map_ip` returns the SID of the requesting Application VM. Otherwise, `map_ip` returns a default unprivileged SID. Before invoking the file system operation, the Application VM SID is copied into the `task_security_struct` paired with the NFS daemon process serving the request. In this way, anytime the NFS server invokes an operation on a shared file system on behalf of Application VMs, the Community VM kernel triggers a Linux Security Module (LSM) hook to delegate the security controls to SELinux. Accordingly, we have modified the LSM hooks paired with file system operations so that the subject of the security policy is the SID paired with the IP address of the Application VM that has invoked the operation rather than the NFS server.

2.4 File System VMs

A community can share some files with other communities through a file system implemented by a File System VM that belongs to several VCNs. The security policies that this VM enforces extend those of a Community VM by considering both the user security level and the community each user belongs to. Furthermore, File System VMs exploit the capabilities of a *Tainting module* to prevent the flowing of information among predefined communities. This module has been introduced to: (i) confine information flows among communities; (ii) increase the robustness with respect to contamination attacks; (iii) log the actual flow of information among communities. To this end, the Tainting module pairs each community with a bit mask, i.e. the community mask, with exactly one bit set to 1 that represents the community. Furthermore, it pairs each file with a mask that represents the communities that either have interacted with the file or have exchanged some information through the file. Anytime a user tries to apply an operation on a file, the module computes an OR of the masks of the file and of the user community. If the result shows an illegal information flow among communities, then the operation is forbidden, otherwise the result becomes the new mask of the file, in the case of a write operation, or of the community, in the case of a read operation. In any case, the Tainting module logs into a file the operation type, the name of the community and of the file and the original and the new masks.

Periodically, the Tainting module parses the log file and updates in an incremental way the dependency graph [11] that represents the information flows among communities and files. Each node in the graph represents either a file or a community and it is

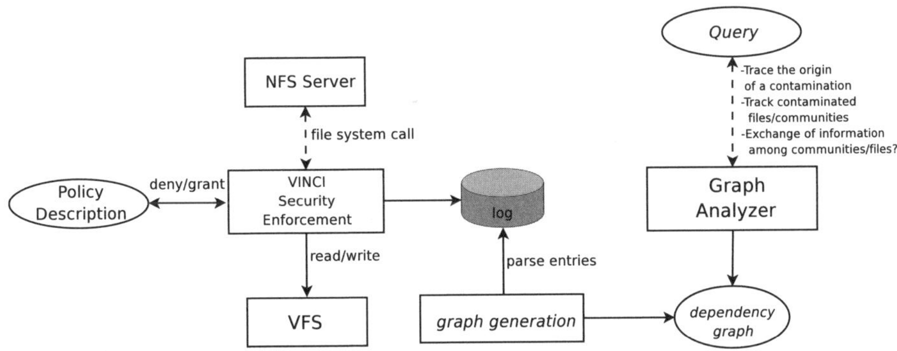

Fig. 2. File System VM Policy Enforcement and Query Generation

paired with a unique identifier of the community or of the file as well as with the corresponding mask. A node that represents a file is created the first time the file is involved in an operation. An arc represents an operation and is associated with the information about the requested operation. To identify how information flows, a read operation is represented by an arc from a node that represents a file to one that represents a community, while a write operation by an arc from a community to a file. As shown in Fig. 2, an administrator can query the module to analyze the dependency graph to discover those communities that have exchanged some information, to trace the source of a contamination and track all the files/communities that may have been contaminated by a community/file.

Since the implementation of a File System VM generalizes that of a Community VM, the same extensions of Community VMs have been applied to File System VMs as well. Moreover, we have extended the File System VM Linux kernel to insert the Tainting module in-between the NFS server and the Virtual File System (see Fig. 2). To this purpose, we have modified the `nfsd_permission` function, which verifies file requests, and `nfsd_vfs_read` and `nfsd_vfs_write` to check, respectively, read and write requests.

2.5   Communication and Control VMs

A Communication and Control VM protects and monitors information flows by implementing and managing a local virtual switch that supports communications among VMs. Communication and Control VMs can be further specialized in: (i) *Virtual Private Network (VPN) VMs*, which create an authenticated and protected communication channel among VMs of the same community on distinct physical nodes of the infrastructure; (ii) *Firewall VMs*, which filter information flows so that only authorized Application VMs can access the infrastructure and interact with other communities; (iii) *IDS VMs*, which monitor information flowing among VMs in the same community or in distinct ones. The introduction of a Firewall VM enables the administrators to define which communities can interact and, hence, to define the legal interconnections among distinct VCNs. As an example, a community can be isolated or communities with a lower global level may not be allowed to communicate with those with higher global levels. Firewall VMs can decide whether to forward a packet, based on the source and destination communities. Furthermore, Firewall VMs support the authentication of shared resource requests through the IP address of the originating VM because they control that Application VMs do not spoof traffic on the virtual switches interconnecting the VMs. Finally, IDS VMs monitor information flows among VMs in the same or in distinct communities to discover attacks. An IDS VM can also retrieve and correlate partial information from other IDS VMs in the same VCN or in distinct ones to minimize the time to detect a distributed attack [12].

2.6 Assurance VMs

Assurance VMs exemplify the advantages of virtualization to build a robust system. In fact, these VMs have been introduced just to monitor critical Application VMs and the VMs of a VCN that manage critical components, to attest their integrity and to authenticate their configuration as well. Furthermore, to define severe tests, Assurance VMs use virtual machine introspection [13] to retrieve critical data structures in the VM memory and evaluate assertions on these structures. Each assertion is an invariant for the original application and it is false only if the application has been attacked.

The software attestation implemented by Assurance VMs enables a VM to verify the integrity of critical code in another VM. As an example, an Assurance VM can compare a hash of the software of a VM against a value computed offline to discover anomalous updates of the configuration of the VM. Consider a critical server in an Application VM that is remotely accessed by other Application VMs. In this case, the server Application VM may require not only the client authentication but also have some assurance that the software stack of the client VM is not compromised and that the client version is correct.

2.7 Infrastructure VMs

Infrastructure VMs extend the VMMs to configure and manage the VCNs. In particular, distinct Infrastructure VMs cooperate to monitor the overall infrastructure and update the topology of the virtual overlays and their mapping. The adoption of these VMs simplifies the implementation of some functionality too complex to be applied at the VMM level, thus minimizing the VMM size. An Infrastructure VM runs a minimal kernel, it does not run any Internet service and the functionalities it implements cannot be directly accessed by any user but the administrators.

As shown in Fig. 3, all the Infrastructure VMs, one per node, belong to a *Management Community* that does not interact with any other community. During the creation of the Management Community, one Infrastructure VM is designated as the *Master Infrastructure VM* that contacts the other Infrastructure VMs to set up proper communication channels to support cooperation in the Management Community. To properly configure the Vinci runtime environment, Infrastructure VMs can: (i) create/kill, freeze/resume any VM in their node or request this operation to another Infrastructure VM; (ii) configure a VM through specific parameters such as network configuration, amount of memory, the number of VCPUs; (iii) retrieve information about the current mapping of VMs and the resulting resource usage; (iv) update the mapping by migrating VMs, which requires an interaction with some Communication and Control VMs

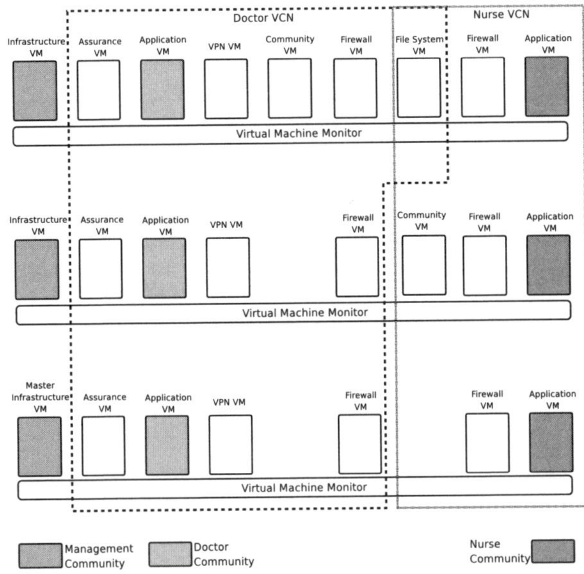

Fig. 3. Example of Communities and VCNs

to manage the resulting communications; (v) setup, compile and deliver to each File System and Community VM the general security policy it has to enforce.

Among the challenges that the Management Community has to face, one is concerned with data management issues, to enable a fast access of a community to its data [14], or with VMs mapping. Alternative mapping strategies may evenly distribute Application VMs running server applications on the available nodes, or map Community VMs onto physical nodes directly connected to those that run the Application VMs of the corresponding community. The Management Community may migrate VMs among physical nodes to handle errors and faults, to reduce the communication latency or to balance the computational load.

Infrastructure VMs also authenticate users through a centralized authentication protocol, so that users can log on Application VMs with the same combination of username and password anywhere in the infrastructure. In this way, the association among users and privileges is managed in a centralized way. The set of users of all the communities that share the infrastructure is globally known so that Vinci can uniquely identify users through their user-name or their associated user identifier (UID). The UID is paired with the privileges of the user, i.e. with its security level. Whenever a user has been authenticated and has chosen the community she wants to join, the Infrastructure VM starts up an Application VM, which includes only those applications that the community policy allows and with the proper global level. After the login and boot-up phases, the local Infrastructure VM contacts the proper Communication and Control VMs to update the topology of the VCN to insert this Application VM into a VCN and to add communication rules to handle the corresponding information flows. Finally, the security policies of Community VMs and File System VMs may be updated. Figure 4

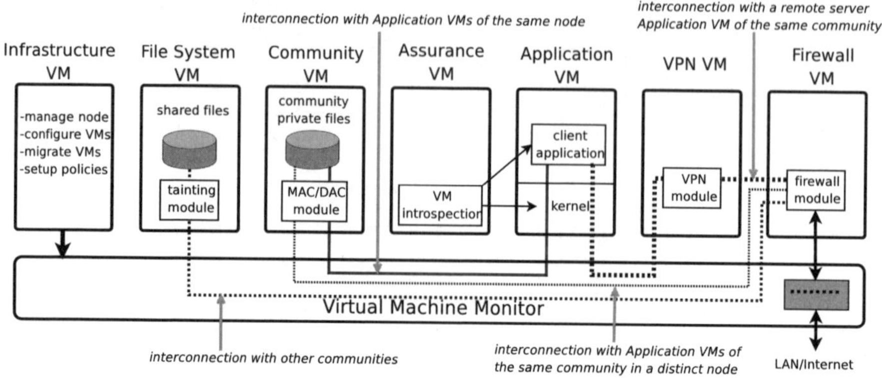

Fig. 4. Interactions among Communities

shows the various interactions among the VMs running on a physical node. Currently, Infrastructure VMs are assigned to Xen Domain 0 VMs, i.e. they are privileged VMs that can access the control interface to manage a physical node and the VMs that the node runs.

If a high degree of assurance is required, Vinci may require that some nodes of the infrastructure are equipped with a Trusted Platform Module (TPM) subsystem [15], which can also be virtualized on the VMs the node runs [16]. The TPM acts as a *root of trust* to build and setup the software environment and its mechanisms may be exploited to ensure that a platform has loaded its software properly and that the VMM and the Infrastructure VM of the local node are started in a safe state. Moreover, the TPM can protect secrets such as the asymmetric and symmetric keys to establish secure communications among VMs, to authenticate the VMs or to remotely attest the software that a VM runs. If a high degree of assurance is required but a TPM is not available, administrator should guarantee that each node cannot be physically tampered with so that the VMM and the Infrastructure VM can be safely initialized. In this case, the Infrastructure VM may emulate the features of the TPM and export it to other VMs through the virtual TPM.

3   Performance Results

This section shows a preliminary performance evaluation of the current Vinci prototype. The tests were performed on several machines equipped with Intel Core 2 Duo E6550 2.33GHz CPUs. A first experiment evaluated in an integrated way the performance of file sharing through File System VMs and Communication and Control VMs. An Application VM on a node ran the IOzone [17] NFS test while a File System VM, on a distinct physical node, stored the requested files. Requests were transmitted along a communication channel implemented by two Firewall VMs and the physical nodes were connected through a 100MB Ethernet. Fig. 5 compares the throughput of the `write` test against the one of the insecure version that does not apply the security checks. The overhead due to the enforcement of the security policies, in the average case, is lower

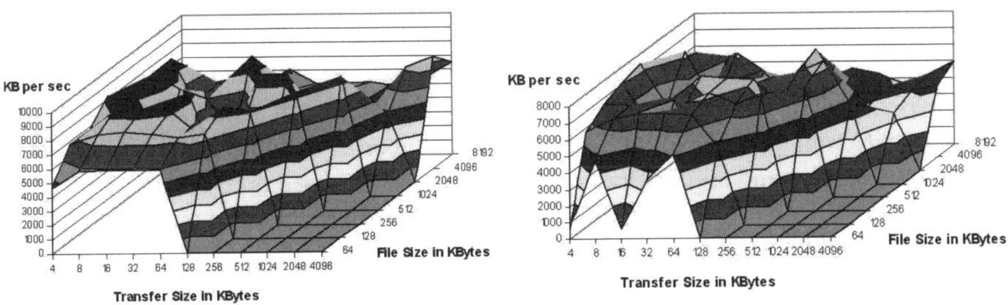

Fig. 5. IOzone NFS Read Performance without (left) and with (right) Policy Enforcement

than 9%. Instead, the tests on the enforcement of security policies by a Community VM resulted in a reduction of the final throughput lower than 5%. The same tests executed on an Application VM connected to a remote File System VM through two VPN VMs resulted in an overhead that, in the worst case, is lower than 13%.

We also evaluated the overhead due to the security checks enforced by an Assurance VM on the kernel code of an Application VM. To this purpose, an Application VM executed the command `tar -xjf linux-2.6.20.tar.bz2` while an Assurance VM, which runs on the same node, checked an increasing number of Application VM kernel pages by computing their hashes and comparing them against their original values. The period of time between two consecutive executions of the consistency checks was set to 2 seconds. The relative overhead was lower than 8% in the worst case. The coverage of these checks is rather satisfactory, because they quickly detect, for instance, any attempt to install a rootkit.

4   Related Works

[18] proposes an architecture where computing services can be offloaded into *Trusted Virtual Domains*, i.e. execution environments that meet a set of security requirements. *Trusted Grid Architecture* [19] is a framework to build a trustworthy grid architecture by using a combination of Trusted Computing and virtualization technologies. The proposed approach allows a user to check that a selected provider is in a trusted state before accessing a submitted grid job. Both the previous architectures consist of a grid of nodes where clients require services, using some form of negotiation to locate a trustworthy provider. Vinci, on the other hand, is more resemblant of a traditional client/server approach, where services and applications are mostly statically bound to physical nodes. Moreover, in Vinci users are managed by a central authority that also administers the whole architecture. [20] proposes an access control architecture that enables corporations to verify client integrity properties using a TPM, and to establish trust upon the capability of the client to enforce the policy before allowing the client to access the corporate Intranet. This framework could be easily integrated into Vinci, for example when a remote user tries to access the corporate infrastructure. *SVGrid* [21] introduces distinct execution environments for the applications and the storage areas, to protect file systems and network services from untrusted grid applications. In addition to these features,

Vinci aims also to provide assurance on the running software on critical VMs. Moreover, Vinci introduces a large number of VMs templates, so that each VM only runs a small amount of software. $Poly^2$ [22] is a framework aimed at segregating applications and networks and at minimizing OSes. The proposed approach separates network services onto different systems and it isolates specific types of network traffic. To this purpose, administrative and application-specific traffic are mapped onto distinct networks. Moreover, minimized OSes should only provide the services required by a specific network application. Vinci shares with this framework the minimization of OSes and applications but it introduces distinct overlay networks for each community and dynamically manages the configuration of these overlays. Moreover, Vinci applies introspection to provide assurance on the running software. [23] considers VMs as sandboxes that simplify the deployment of collaborative environments over wide-area networks. Each VM sandbox can be seen as a virtual appliance made available to several users by the administrator, so that new nodes can easily join and be integrated into the virtual network. A feature that characterizes Vinci with respect to the previous framework is the concept of community, which simplifies the management of users with similar security and reliability requirements. PlanetLab [24] is a global overlay network that runs concurrently multiple services in *slices*, i.e. networks of VMs that include some amount of processing, memory, storage and network resources. A slice is conceptually similar to a Vinci VCN, but in Vinci resources are those of a private infrastructure and their allocation is mostly static, whereas PlanetLab exploits the concept of an open grid of machines where resources can be dynamically allocated and discovered. Furthermore, Vinci introduces the concept of community, which allows administrators to define flexible security policies. Another important difference is that PlanetLab exploits OS-level virtualization, while Vinci exploits hardware-level virtualization and, therefore, it introduces a VMM that results in a better confinement among the VMs of the same node.

5   Conclusion

The focus of Vinci is on the definition of highly parallel overlays, i.e. VCNs, which simplify management and sharing of a private ICT infrastructure. Moreover, VCNs increase the overall robustness due to the introduction of specialized VMs that enforce security checks within and across VCNs. Each VCN supports a user community, i.e. a set of users with similar security and reliability requirements. This approach requires that each physical node runs a virtual machine monitor that manages and protects the physical resources and it results in the definition of several VM templates. Distinct templates are used to support the execution of user applications, to enforce consistency checks or to apply security policies that protect resources shared within or across distinct communities. We have shown that proper components can be introduced to protect the communities from contamination as well as to trace any contamination that can arise. Moreover, a specialized community includes a set of VMs that manage the configuration of the other VMs to achieve the required level of reliability and security. Preliminary results of our prototype show that Vinci can be adopted in a real-world scenario, such as the one of a hospital, a bank, or a corporate enterprise, which need to guarantee high security requirements and confine critical resources.

Concerning the shortcomings of state-of-the-art virtualization, we note that managing and configuring a node to support virtualization and to run a set of VMs, each with a customized OS, requires more effort than managing a node that only runs a standard OS, especially in the case of a para-virtualization approach that requires the OSes to be modified to run inside the virtual environment. However, since virtualization is becoming increasing popular, there is a large amount of tools that help the administrator to set-up and manage virtual nodes. Another counterpart of the advantages of virtual, highly parallel and secure overlays is the overhead due to the context switching that the VMM applies to multiplex the physical resources. A multi-core architecture [25] can strongly reduce this overhead because of the native support for multiplexing. Moreover, it can run several VMs in consolidation and assign a dedicated core to some VMs. This guarantees that VMs that implement critical tasks, such as management and protection of other VMs, are never delayed. Moreover, the virtualization overhead can be strongly reduced because of the extension of hardware instruction sets to efficiently support virtualization technology [26].

Acknowledgments

We would like to thank the anonymous reviewers for their valuable comments and suggestions.

References

1. Uhlig, R., Neiger, G., Rodgers, D., Santoni, A., Marting, F., Anderson, A., Bennett, S., Kagi, A., Leung, F., Smith, L.: Intel Virtualization Technology. Computer 38(5), 48–56 (2005)
2. Dunlap, G.W., King, S.T., Cinar, S., Basrai, M.A., Chen, P.M.: Revirt: enabling intrusion analysis through virtual-machine logging and replay. SIGOPS Oper. Syst. Rev. 36(SI), 211–224 (2002)
3. Goldberg, R.P.: Survey of virtual machine research. IEEE Computer 7(6), 34–45 (1974)
4. Huang, W., Abali, B., Panda, D.: A case for high performance computing with virtual machines. In: Proc. of the 20th annual international conference on Supercomputing, pp. 125–134 (2006)
5. Dragovic, B., Fraser, K., Hand, S., Harris, T., Ho, A., Pratt, I., Warfield, A., Barham, P., Neugebauer, R.: Xen and the art of virtualization. In: Proceedings of the ACM Symposium on Operating Systems Principles (October 2003)
6. Callaghan, B., Pawlowski, B., Staubach, P.: NFS V3 Protocol Specification. RFC 1813
7. Loscocco, P., Smalley, S.: Integrating flexible support for security policies into the linux operating system. In: Proceedings of the FREENIX Track: 2001 USENIX Annual Technical Conference, Berkeley, CA, USA, pp. 29–42. USENIX Association (2001)
8. Loscocco, P.A., Smalley, S.D.: Meeting critical security objectives with security enhanced linux. In: Proceedings of the 2001 Ottawa Linux Symposium. (2001)
9. Netfilter.org: Netfilter/Iptables project, www.netfilter.org/
10. OpenVPN: OpenVPN - An Open Source SSL VPN Solution, http://openvpn.net/
11. King, S.T., Chen, P.M.: Backtracking intrusions. ACM Trans. Comput. Syst. 23(1), 51–76 (2005)
12. Cheetancheri, S.G., et al.: A distributed host-based worm detection system. In: LSAD 2006: Proc. of the 2006 SIGCOMM workshop on Large-scale attack defense, pp. 107–113. ACM Press, New York (2006)

13. Garfinkel, T., Rosenblum, M.: A virtual machine introspection based architecture for intrusion detection. In: NDSS (2003)
14. Figueiredo, R.J., Dinda, P.A., Fortes, J.A.B.: A case for grid computing on virtual machines. In: ICDCS 2003: Proceedings of the 23rd International Conference on Distributed Computing Systems, Washington, DC, USA, p. 550. IEEE Computer Society, Los Alamitos (2003)
15. Pearson, S.: Trusted Computing Platforms, the Next Security Solution. Trusted Computing Group Administration, Beaverton (2002)
16. Berger, S., Cáceres, R., Goldman, K.A., Perez, R., Sailer, R., van Doorn, L.: vTPM: virtualizing the trusted platform module. In: USENIX-SS 2006: Proceedings of the 15th conference on USENIX Security Symposium, Berkeley, CA, USA, pp. 21. USENIX Association (2006)
17. IOzone: IOzone Filesystem Benchmark, http://www.iozone.org/
18. Griffin, J.L., Jaeger, T., Perez, R., Sailer, R., van Doorn, L., Caceres, R.: Trusted Virtual Domains: Toward secure distributed services. In: Proc. of 1st IEEE Workshop on Hot Topics in System Dependability (HotDep) (2005)
19. Löhr, H., Ramasamy, H.V., Sadeghi, A.R., Schulz, S., Schunter, M., Stüble, C.: Enhancing Grid Security Using Trusted Virtualization. In: Xiao, B., Yang, L.T., Ma, J., Muller-Schloer, C., Hua, Y. (eds.) ATC 2007. LNCS, vol. 4610, pp. 372–384. Springer, Heidelberg (2007)
20. Sailer, R., Jaeger, T., Zhang, X., van Doorn, L.: Attestation-based policy enforcement for remote access. In: CCS 2004: Proceedings of the 11th ACM conference on Computer and communications security, pp. 308–317. ACM Press, New York (2004)
21. Zhao, X., Borders, K., Prakash, A.: SVGrid: a secure virtual environment for untrusted grid applications. In: MGC 2005: Proceedings of the 3rd international workshop on Middleware for grid computing, pp. 1–6. ACM Press, New York (2005)
22. Bryant, E., Early, J., Gopalakrishna, R., Roth, G., Spafford, E., Watson, K., William, P., Yost, S.: Poly^2 Paradigm: A Secure Network Service Architecture. In: Proceedings 19th Annual Computer Security Applications Conference, 2003, pp. 342–351 (2003)
23. Wolinsky, D.I., Agrawal, A., Boykin, P.O., Davis, J., Ganguly, A., Paramygin, V., Sheng, P., Figueiredo, R.J.: On the Design of Virtual Machine Sandboxes for Distributed Computing in Wide Area Overlays of Virtual Workstations. In: First Workshop on Virtualization Technologies in Distributed Computing (VTDC) (November 2006)
24. Chun, B., Culler, D., Roscoe, T., Bavier, A., Peterson, L., Wawrzoniak, M., Bowman, M.: Planetlab: an overlay testbed for broad-coverage services. SIGCOMM Comput. Commun. Rev. 33(3), 3–12 (2003)
25. Gepner, P., Kowalik, M.F.: Multi-core processors: New way to achieve high system performance. In: PARELEC 2006: International symposium on Parallel Computing in Electrical Engineering, pp. 9–13. IEEE Computer Society Press, Washington (2006)
26. Leung, F., Neiger, G., Rodgers, D., Santoni, A., Uhlig, R.: Intel Virtualization Technology: Hardware support for efficient processor virtualization. Intel Technology Journal 10(3), 167–178 (2006)

Statistical Behaviors of Distributed Transition Planning

Ning Wu and Alva L. Couch

Tufts University, Medford, 02155, USA
{ningwu,couch}@cs.tufts.edu

Abstract. The transition planning problem is to move a system from an existing starting configuration to a desired final configuration at the lowest possible cost. Prior work shows that the transition planning problem can be reduced to a bipartite matching problem and the stable marriage algorithm can be used to approximate a minimum cost transition in a distributed environment. In this paper, we study the efficiency of this mapping, including its best-case, worst-case, and statistical behavior. We discuss the relationship between algorithm performance and the distribution of the input data. We show that while there are cases in which this algorithm performs poorly, works well when the costs of transitioning between distributed resources follow a normal distribution. We discuss the applicability of this algorithm to real-world situations in which resources are thus distributed.

1 Introduction

The transition planning problem for a system (such as a network) is to design a plan of operations that – when executed – will move the system from its existing configuration to a new configuration having desirable properties. In a previous paper [8], we discussed the distributed transition planning mechanism. Transition planning is reduced to a matching problem whose solution is approximated by solving the stable marriage problem. We apply distributed algorithms to compute the transition plan. We show that although these algorithms do not always achieve optimal solutions, they return acceptable results in most cases. Thus they can be used for system management.

For example, suppose that there are three physical servers X, Y, and Z that act as web servers and serve three types of content that we call A, B, and C. Each server initially serves one form of content: server X serves content A, Y serves content B, and Z serves content C. We think of each kind of content as a *role* for the server. Initially, each server is matched to a unique role and the cost of changing roles is more than the cost of remaining at the same role. This is depicted as a bipartite graph, with X, Y, Z on one side and A, B, C on the other(Figure 1(a)). Edges represent cost of transition, which can be estimated by a variety of methods. In this bipartite graph, the cost of keeping the current server-role mapping is zero so we say that the system is at a *fixed point* [1, 2].

D. Hausheer and J. Schönwälder (Eds.): AIMS 2008, LNCS 5127, pp. 79–91, 2008.
© IFIP International Federation for Information Processing 2008

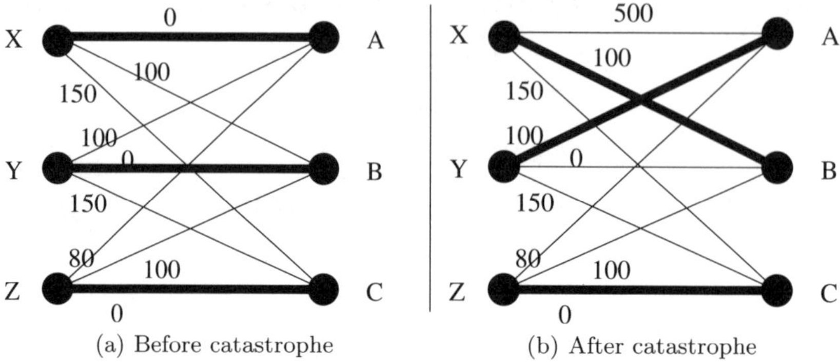

Fig. 1. The bipartite graph before and after the catastrophe

When the environment changes (e.g., the users of content A increase), the processing power of servers serving content A may not be enough. We call such a change a transition catastrophe [8], to distinguish it from policy changes that do not incur configuration change and incur no cost. To provide the same level of service, some servers serving other content need to be transitioned to serve content A. The goal is to find a plan to meet the new requirements so that the transition happens at minimum cost. The difference between this and the prior state is that remaining at the current roles now has a nonzero cost, e.g., including the cost of violating a service-level agreement(Figure 1(b)). The minimum cost matching for this graph will not be the status quo. The Hungarian method [4] can be used to compute the minimum cost matching, which represents the minimum cost solution. The new minimum-cost matching is shown with bold lines. The roles have been rearranged so that SLAs are again met. The resulting reconfiguration achieves a fixed point again, because the cost of remaining in this state is again zero.

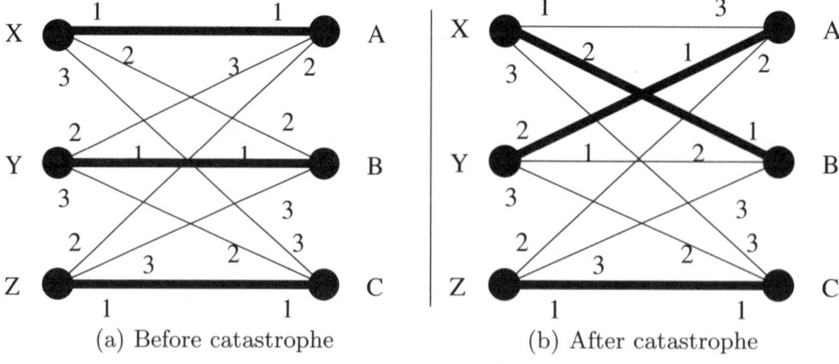

Fig. 2. The bipartite graph using rankings before and after the catastrophe

However, in a distributed environment, the bipartite matching method for transition planning may not work properly for several reasons. Agents might not agree on how the costs are computed, or their units for cost may differ. We proposed in [8] to use a stable marriage algorithm, the Gale-Shapley algorithm [3], to solve the distributed transition planning problem. The first step in using this method is to convert costs to rankings. Each node ranks the edges connected to it in order of preference, from lowest cost to highest cost. For example, for Figure 1(a), the rankings are shown in Figure 2(a). If costs are at a fixed point, so are rankings. When a catastrophe arises, instead of considering costs (as in Figure 1(b)), agents will consider rankings, as illustrated in Figure 2(b). Thinking of agents as representing both sides, agents will attempt to form a set of *stable marriages*, so that there is no advantage to any server switching roles. Such a matching is shown again in bold.

2   Hospitals/Residents Problem

The stable marriage problem results in a one-to-one mapping. Another related problem is the Hospitals/Residents problem (a.k.a college admission problem) [3], which computes a one-to-many mapping. The hospitals/residents problem describes the matching process that is used to match medical students and hospitals having openings for residents; because a hospital only has limited positions, only the top candidates ranked by that hospital will be admitted. This problem is also called the college admission problem. The hospital/residents problem can again be solved by the Gale-Shapley algorithm [3]. In each round, each unmatched applicant proposes to the most preferred hospital that has not rejected his proposal.

We can investigate the resource allocation and transition problem by reducing it to the hospitals/residents problem. Let us use the virtual machine assignment problem as an example. In virtual machine (VM) management, a common task is determining how to assign a VM to an appropriate physical machine. Figure 3 shows an example of assigning virtual machines to physical machines.

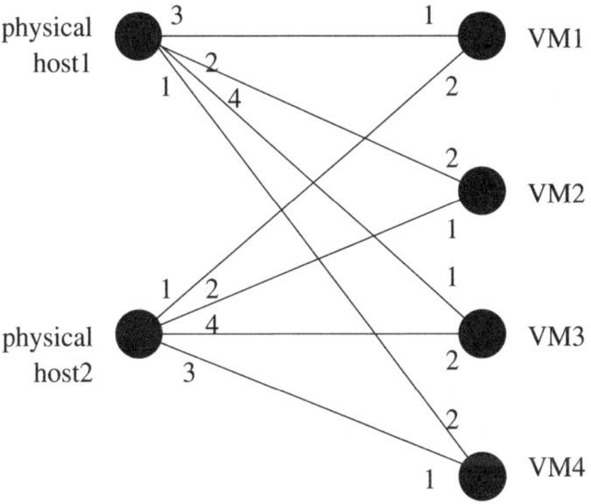

Fig. 3. Assign virtual machines to physical hosts

One challenge of applying the Gale-Shapley algorithm to VM assignment is how to determine the ranking of the VMs. An agent representing a physical host can rank VMs by many standards, such as the importance of the VM, the resource-utilization profile (e.g., CPU-bound, disk-bound) of the VM, or user preferences. We start from the simplest cases and build to a discussion of how to handle various kinds of constraints.

For example, suppose that there are four virtual machines VM_1, VM_2, VM_3, and VM_4, and two physical hosts PHY_1 and PHY_2 (Figure 3). The attributes of physical hosts are memory size, storage size, and network bandwidth. There are also several constraints that limit matching between the VMs and PHYs.

Suppose that our task is to deploy new applications to VMs that are hosted by physical hosts. First, the resources needed for applications are estimated, though these estimates can be adjusted later. The goal is to find steps (ideally in a distributed way) to provide resources for the new application and ensure minimum cost.

In the bipartite graph, the virtual machines are listed on the right side; the physical hosts are listed on the left side. Each node has a ranking of all the nodes on the other side, based on its own standard. The right side proposes to the agents representing the physical hosts and current VMs. As in the one-to-one case, once stabilized, the left side ranks current bindings the highest. The ranks among current bindings are decided by the physical host based on its own standard. The same three-step process applies here: first use the Gale-Shapley algorithm to get a stable matching; then change the bindings according to the matching; finally change the rankings on the left side to reflect the new bindings. This transition process is a deterministic fixed-point operator.

When a catastrophe arises, some VMs will be chosen to be served by other physical servers; this is called "swinging the physical servers to serve new VMs". Once transitioned, these VMs may be adjusted to meet the new requirements. For example, one problem might be to find enough bandwidth for a new application (by moving some existing applications around in the physical hosts).

Failover can be characterized as a transition catastrophe: when a physical server fails, the VMs running on it will try to locate new physical servers for their host environment. Agents monitoring these VMs will notice the outage and reflect it in their stable marriage rankings. Then these agents will propose to the rest of the physical hosts and determine whether the matching is feasible, because the capacity of each physical server is limited.

3   Quality of Stable Marriage and Hospital/Resident Solutions

The Gale-Shapley algorithm always produces a stable marriage, but there is some question as to how well that marriage substitutes for the more ideal transition plan based upon costs rather than ranks. We first develop a measure of how well stable marriage works compared to the theoretical best solution.

Definition 1. *The approximation ratio of a stable marriage solution is the ratio of the cost of the stable marriage solution to the cost of the ideal solution obtained through minimum bipartite matching.*

The ratio is always $>= 1.0$. Values near 1.0 indicate that the stable marriage algorithm is working well, while high values indicate that it is working poorly. A value of 1.0 means that the stable marriage algorithm did as well as a bipartite matching solution in which all weights (costs) are collected in a central location. The approximation ratio may be thought of as the "cost of distributing" the algorithm onto an agent network.

The approximation ratio is highly distribution dependent; it differs with the statistical distribution of the input weights.

Theorem 1. *When all the weights in the bipartite graph are identical, the ratio of the total cost computed through stable marriage to the optimal solution is 1.0.*

Proof. Suppose that d edges need to be selected. When all the weights are the same, the total cost in any mapping is always $d \cdot weight$. Thus the approximation ratio is always one. $\qquad\square$

Theorem 2. *Suppose the maximum ratio of two weights in the bipartite graph is k. In the worst case, the ratio of the total cost computed through stable marriage to the optimal solution (i.e. the approximation ratio) is less than or equal to k.*

Proof. Let $max(weight)$ and $min(weight)$ represent the maximum and minimum weights in the graph. Let $k = max(weight)/min(weight)$. In the worst case, the stable marriage or the hospital/resident algorithm selects the worst solution possible. Suppose that d edges need to be selected in the solution. The optimal solution has a total weight greater than or equal to $d \cdot min(weight)$, and the stable marriage or hospital/resident solution has a total weight less than or equal to $d \cdot max(weight)$. Thus the maximum ratio is less than or equal to k. $\quad\square$

The worst scenario is illustrated in the following example (Figure 4).

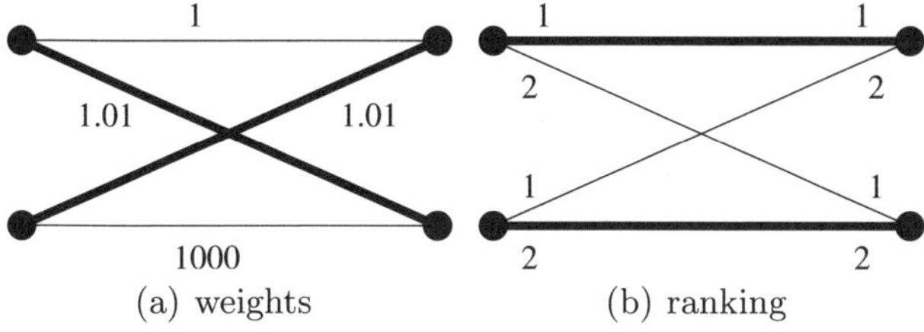

Fig. 4. The solution of the stable marriage problem vs. the solution of the assignment problem. Bold lines represent the matchings derived in each case.

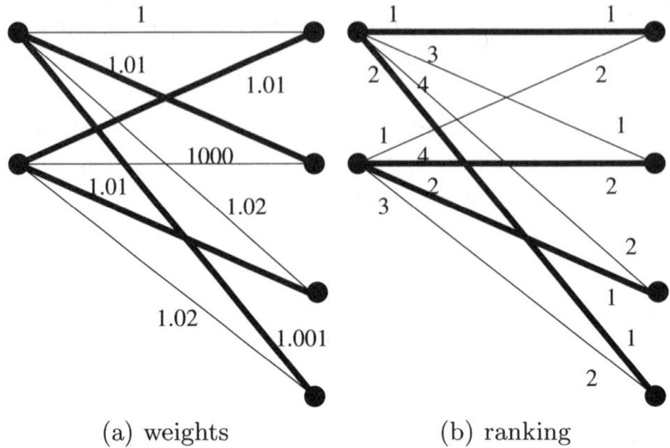

(a) weights   (b) ranking

Fig. 5. The solution of the hospitals/residents problem vs. the solution of the matching problem. Bold lines represent the matchings derived in each case.

Theorem 3. *Suppose that for one side of the bipartite graph, we select the maximum and minimum labels max_i and min_i for each node i on that side. Suppose that max and min are the sums of max_i and min_i over all i, respectively. Then the approximation ratio cannot be greater than max/min.*

Proof. The best possible outcome of a bipartite matching includes the minimum edge taken from every node, yielding a minimal score. The worst outcome of stable marriage includes the maximum edge taken from every node, yielding a maximum score.   □

In this example, the optimal solution has a total cost of $1.01 + 1.01 = 2.02$, whereas the stable marriage algorithm yields a total of $1000 + 1 = 1001$. The ratio is almost 500, which is less than $1000/1 = 1000$.

In the worst case, the approximation ratio can also be arbitrarily large in the hospitals/residents problem (Figure 5). In the figure, on the left side, each physical host has two slots and there are four VMs. The approximation ratio is almost 250.

In practice, the upper bound is tighter because there is no case in which the optimal solution chooses all minimum weights and the stable marriage solution chooses all maximum weights, because the stable marriage algorithm chooses at least one edge that has minimum weight.

4   Simulations

In the following we study the approximation ratio of the Gale Shapley algorithm and that of a variant utilizing a heuristic strategy.

4.1 The Gale-Shapley Algorithm

In the previous section, we showed several examples where the approximation ratio for stable marriage depends upon the choice of weights. In this section, we consider how the approximation ratio for stable marriage changes as we change the statistical distribution of the weights in the original bipartite matching problem. For some distributions, stable marriage yields low approximation ratios that are nearly optimal. For others, high approximation ratios are observed. We tested the stable marriage transition planning scheme in simulation and compared the resulting matching to that obtained from bipartite matching. We used different probability distributions to determine the weights of the transition edges. The results for the uniform, normal, and Pareto distributions are shown in Figure 6. We tried two uniform distributions. The first setting (uniform distribution 1) has a mean of 1000 in range (0,2000], and the second setting (uniform distribution 2) has a mean of 10000 in range (0,20000]. These yield almost identical results.

Next we simulated approximately normally distributed weights with mean 10000 and 3 different standard deviation parameters. The first setting (normal distribution 1) has a standard deviation of 2000; the second setting (normal distribution 2) has a standard deviation of 5000; the third setting (normal distribution 3) has a standard deviation of 10000. In the experiments, when a negative

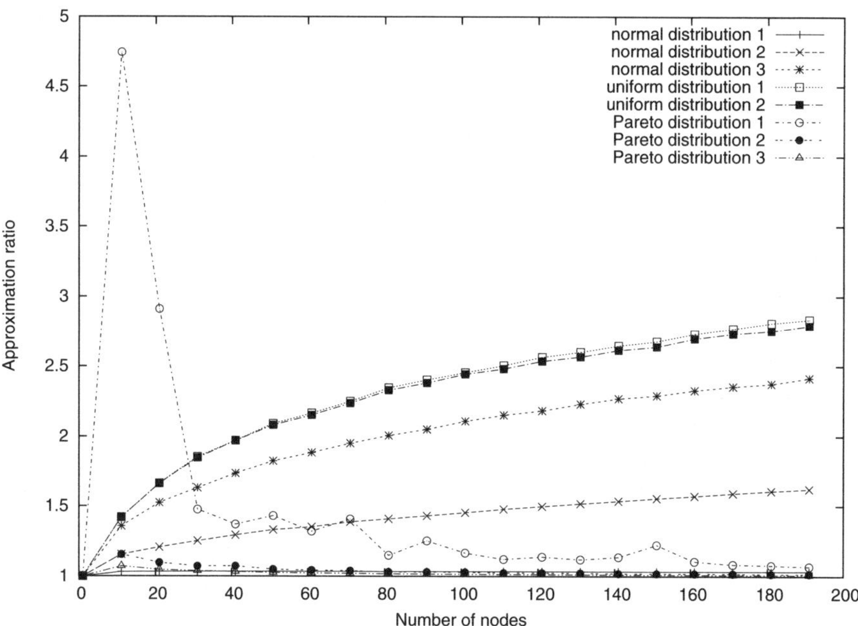

Fig. 6. The approximation ratio for weights following the uniform, normal, and Pareto distributions

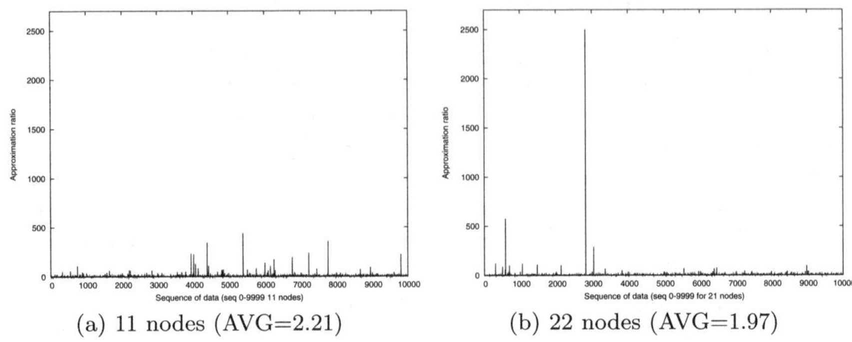

(a) 11 nodes (AVG=2.21)   (b) 22 nodes (AVG=1.97)

Fig. 7. 10000 data points collected from simulation for approximation ratio

random number is generated following these settings, we discard it and choose
another with the same distribution function. So the actual distribution function
slightly tilts toward positive numbers. The coefficient of variation (the ratio of
the standard deviation to the mean) is an important factor. When the coefficient
of variation is small (for example, 0.2 in normal distribution 1), the weights are
relatively clustered and the performance is near-optimal. When the coefficient of
variation increases, the approximation ratio moves towards that of the uniform
distribution.

We also tried the Pareto distribution. The Pareto distribution function is
$P(x) = ab^a/x^{a+1}$ [7]. We use several cases: distributions with $a = 1$ $b = 0.6$
(Pareto distribution 1), $a = 2$ $b = 0.6$ (Pareto distribution 2), and $a = 3$ $b = 0.6$
(Pareto distribution 3). The larger the value of a, the shorter the tail is in the
PDF function. In the case of Pareto distributions 2 and 3, the efficiency is near
optimal, but in the first case (Pareto distribution 1), the approximation ratio is
undesirable when the number of nodes is small.

For the above scenarios, the approximation ratio is good in most case, but
some cases have a high approximation ratio. Because of the long tail of the Pareto
distribution (especially with $a = 1$, where the probability distribution function
curve is relatively flat), a weight can be far away from other weights, and as we
have shown, this may results in a large ratio. In our experiment, because there is
no upper limit for the weights in the Pareto distribution, one case can generate
a large approximation ratio. Figure 7 shows the raw simulation data. While
most of the points in Figure 7(a) have low approximation ratios, there are many
with ratios that reach into the hundreds. By contrast, Figure 7(b) shows much
fewer ratios in the hundreds, but also uncovers a ratio high in the thousands.
For 21 nodes, there are less points with approximation ratios in the hundreds
but there is one data point whose approximation ratio is in the thousands. The
figure demonstrates that the long-tail distribution leads to poor approximation
ratios.

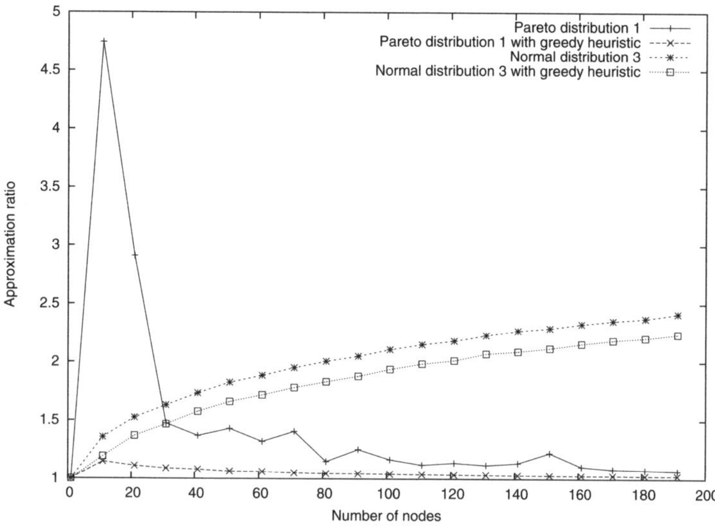

Fig. 8. The approximation ratio with and without using the greedy heuristic

4.2   The Gale-Shapley Algorithm Plus a Greedy Heuristic

To address the issue that occurs in the worst-case scenario, we propose a simple heuristic that could improve the efficiency of the stable marriage approximation. After running the Gale-Shapley algorithm once, the most expensive edge in the result is marked "infeasible", and the right side of that edge is forced to take its first preference as its match. Then the rest of the nodes use the Gale-Shapley algorithm to determine a stable marriage of the remaining bipartite graph. This process continues until the total cost can no longer be decreased. In practice, each agent will determine its own criteria for marking edges as expensive. The exclusion of edges will not be as close to optimal as that obtained in our simulation, which utilizes global knowledge. The simulation results can be viewed as the best-case result for this heuristic.

We selected two weight distributions to verify the effectiveness of this heuristic. First we use the long-tail Pareto distribution (Pareto distribution 1). Then we use the normal distribution with a large coefficient of variation (normal distribution 3). The greedy heuristic works very well for the Pareto distribution, but only slightly improves the result in the case of normal distribution. The result is shown in Figure 8.

4.3   Simulating Real Cases

In the first experimental simulations, the left and right sides of the graph share the same weight. In the next simulations, we try to evaluate the stable-marriage-based scheme under a more realistic environment. We now estimate their cost based on different formulas and use a cost function to derive the cost incurred by the bipartite matching.

We estimate the cost of a transition in two parts: file transfer cost and usage time lost due to downtime during the transition. The first part can be estimated based on the size of files transferred, and the second part can be estimated based on CPU cycles. It is known that in practice, file sizes follow the Pareto distribution. CPU speed follows a Moore's law [5] growth pattern. We estimate the speed of computer servers through a 3-year cycle. One third of the CPUs are the latest fastest, one-third are middling, and the last third are the slowest. The total cost formula is as follows:

$$totalCost = fileSize * coefficient1 + CPUSpeed * coefficient2 \qquad (1)$$

We collect the RPM package size on a typical Linux server and show the raw sizes and their counts in Figure 9. The X axis shows the package size and the Y axis shows the number of packages of that size. The distribution is Pareto; we use another distribution function $0.6/x^2$ to fit the curve. The Pareto distribution function is $P(x) = ab^a/x^{a+1}$, where $a = 1$, $b = 0.6$. Figure 10 shows these two PDFs.

For CPU, we select three products: AMD Athlon 64 3800+ X2 (Dual Core) (14,564 MIPS), Intel Core 2 X6800 (27,079 MIPS), and Intel Core 2 Extreme QX6700(57,063 MIPS) [6]. To normalize file sizes and CPU speeds, we multiply file size by 10 and average with CPU MIPS. For example, a 3MB file and a Intel

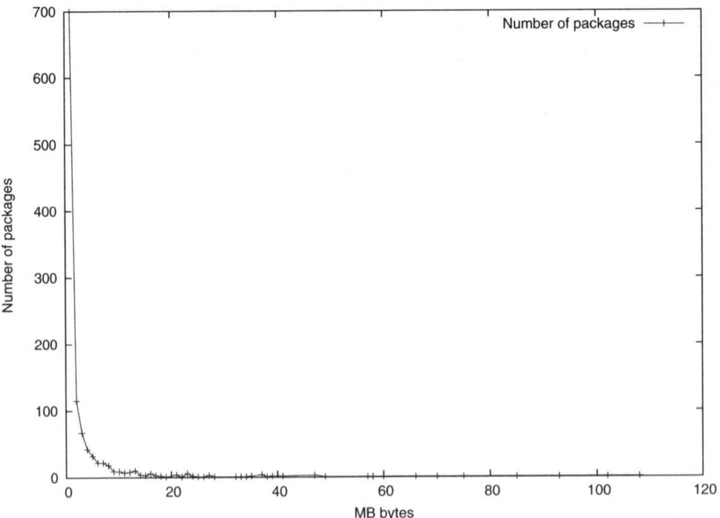

Fig. 9. The package size distribution on a typical Linux server

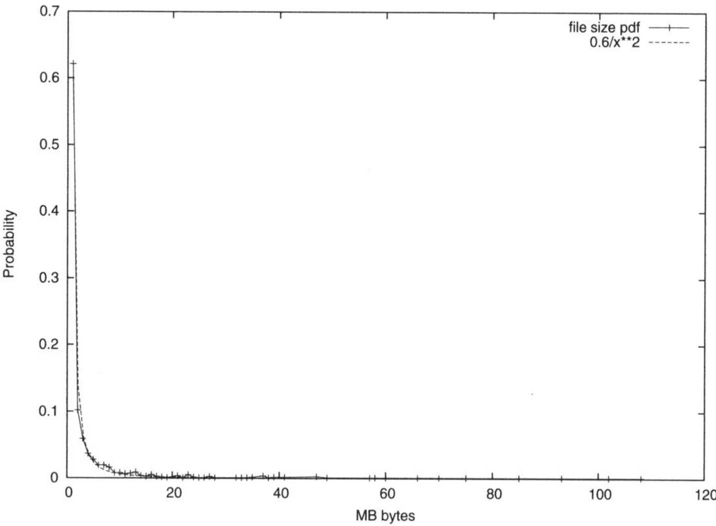

Fig. 10. The probability distribution function and the fitted curve of the package size distribution

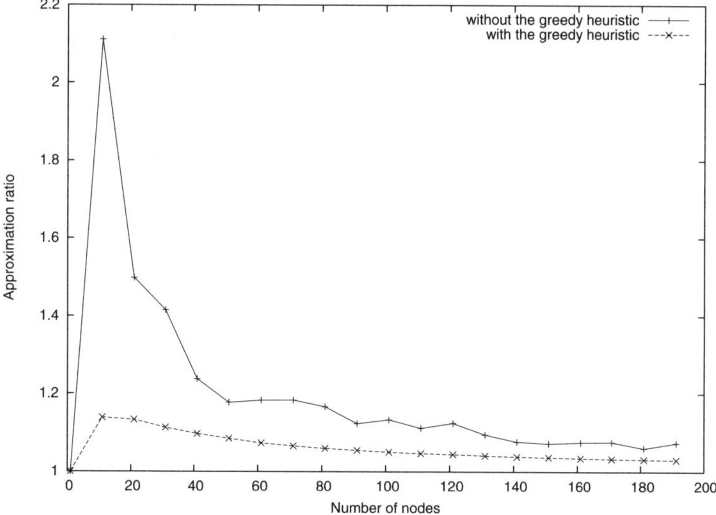

Fig. 11. Simulated approximation-ratio results when each side ranks according to a different cost standard, comparing that result to the minimum-cost transition based on a combined cost function

Core 2 CPU will give us $(3000*10 + 27079)/2 = 28539.5$. We use this model to explore the relationship between a cost function and individually decided rankings until we can find a more accurate cost model.

In this experiment, each side of the bipartite graph ranks the other side differently; the left side ranks using the file size, and the right side ranks using the CPU speed. The minimum cost transition uses weights computed from the cost function. The result is shown in Figure 11.

5   Conclusion and Future Work

In this paper, we investigate the statistical behaviors of transition planning mechanisms in a decentralized environment. The Gale-Shapley algorithm can be used to find transition plans. Theoretically, we can create an arbitrarily large approximation ratio by using the Gale-Shapley algorithm to simulate the optimal solution. But in practice, the worst case rarely arises and can be prevented via heuristics. We use simulation to study the impact of different probabilistic distributions. The result shows that the normal distribution has a very good performance when the coefficient of variation is low. When the coefficient of variation is high (for example, 1) the performance is similar to that of the uniform distribution. The uniform distribution has an average performance. But in a probability distribution that is flat and has a long tail, such as the Pareto, some settings (for example, $a = 1$) will produce a poor approximation ratio when the number of nodes is small. The performance improves dramatically when the number of nodes is increased. Thus, a minimum node size above 50 is recommended or the greedy heuristic should be used.

Although better stable marriage algorithms exist, which might address these issues, these algorithms take more time to settle than the Gale-Shapley algorithm. We propose a simple heuristic that greedily removes the most expensive edge from the mapping, and thus improves the stable marriage performance. In the future, heuristics can be investigated, that leave out some options in order to avoid obviously bad marriages.

Acknowledgement

We wish to thank Marc Chiarini for reading several versions of the paper and making timely comments.

References

1. Burgess, M.: An approach to understanding policy based on autonomy and voluntary cooperation. In: Schönwälder, J., Serrat, J. (eds.) DSOM 2005. LNCS, vol. 3775, pp. 97–108. Springer, Heidelberg (2005)
2. Burgess, M., Couch, A.: Autonomic computing approximated by fixed-point promises. In: 1st IEEE International Workshop on Modelling Autonomic Communications Environments (MACE 2006) (2006)
3. Gale, D., Shapley, L.S.: College admissions and the stability of marriage. American Mathematical Monthly (1962)

4. Kuhn, H.W.: The hungarian method for the assignment problem. Naval Research Logistic Quarterly (1955)
5. Moore, G.: Cramming more components onto integrated circuits. Electronics Magazine 38(8) (1965)
6. Voelkel, F.: Intel's core 2 quadro kentsfield: Four cores on a rampage (2006), http://www.tomshardware.com/reviews/cores-rampage,1316-13.html
7. Weisstein, E.W.: Pareto distribution. from mathworld–a wolfram web resource
8. Wu, N., Couch, A.: Transition planning via matchings and marriages. In: The 2nd IEEE International Workshop on Modelling Autonomic Communications Environments (MACE 2007) (2007)

Service Load Balancing with Autonomic Servers: Reversing the Decision Making Process

Remi Badonnel[1,2] and Mark Burgess[1]

[1] Oslo University College
St Olavs plass, 0130 Oslo, Norway
badonnel@loria.fr
[2] LORIA - INRIA Grand Est, Nancy University
Campus Scientifique, 54500 Vandoeuvre, France
burgess@iu.hio.no

Abstract. Load balancing faces new challenges in the framework of autonomic servers deployed in data centers. With traditional push-based strategies, the authoritative decision is made by the load balancer, which decides to which server the requests are forwarded. However, the autonomy of servers is often incompatible with these strategies, as they may accept or refuse to process a request on a voluntary basis. We present in this paper the benefits and limits of a pull-based load balancing strategy for transferring the authority from the load balancer to the autonomic servers. We describe the underlying functional architecture with two different schemes and quantify the performances through an extensive set of experiments.

1 Introduction

Autonomic computing has become a major paradigm for dealing with the growing complexity of systems and networks and simplifying their maintenance [1]. In particular, we can consider autonomic servers that are capable of managing themselves based on closed control loops in order to: configure their components, detect and correct their failures, monitor and control their own resources in an optimal manner, and diagnose and protect themselves against attacks. These servers can typically be deployed in data centers. They may provide support for multi-tier applications and services, and share the load of client requests.

A variety of algorithms [2] has been proposed in order to balance the workload among servers in an optimal manner. However, autonomic computing favors autonomous components that are weakly coupled rather than traditional hierarchical systems with strong couplings (based on an obligation model). Autonomic servers seem therefore to pose new challenges with regard to this load balancing.

In traditional approaches, the load balancing strategy is performed in a push-based (obligation) manner (see Sub-figure 1(a)), which means the decision of whether a server should receive a request or not made exclusively by the load balancer. Autonomics skeptics often imagine that this kind of approach is fundamental to the idea of "control" and the idea of component autonomy stands

D. Hausheer and J. Schönwälder (Eds.): AIMS 2008, LNCS 5127, pp. 92–104, 2008.

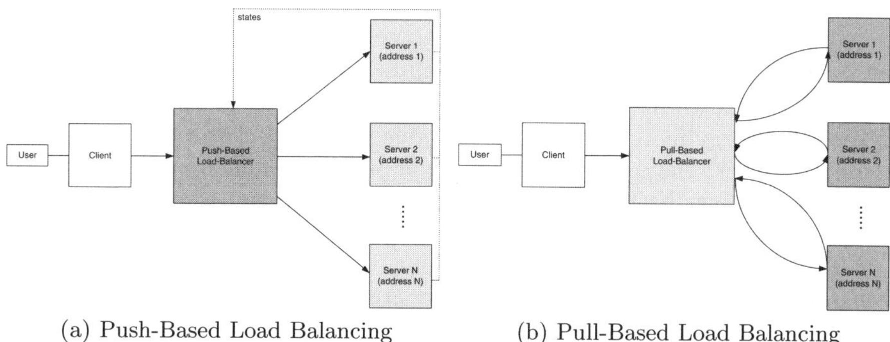

(a) Push-Based Load Balancing   (b) Pull-Based Load Balancing

Fig. 1. Push-Based vs Pull-Based Load Balancing with Autonomic Servers

in the way of proper resource sharing if servers will not do as they are told by an authoritative controller. We have already argued against this viewpoint [3] and show this belief to be erroneous below.

One might argue that a push-based load balancer can easily estimate server resources by observing network parameters such as on-going connections. Monitoring agents can also be deployed on the servers to evaluate their performance. While server-state information can improve the load balancing mechanism with traditional servers, this adds an unnecessary overhead with autonomic servers. The authoritative decision is kept by the load balancer, which decides to which server the request is forwarded. Moreover, this authority is in conflict with an autonomic server's preference to make decisions by itself and to interacting on a purely voluntary basis. So there are two reasons why push based sharing is undesirable in autonomic networks.

Why then should we preserve a push-based strategy for balancing load among autonomic servers? In this paper we explore the arguments in favor of *pull-based* load balancing strategy (see Sub-figure 1(b)) where autonomic servers can manage load at their own convenience. Each server knows its own capabilities and state more quickly and accurately than any external monitor, so it seems reasonable to explore the idea that it is the best judge of its own performance.

By pulling service requests from a load balancer servers can decide to take on work depending not only on their available resources but also on many other internal parameters including their willingness to interact, their internal scheduled management operations, protection procedures when attacks are detected, and any policy. The authoritative decision is therefore transferred from the load balancer to the autonomic servers.

The paper is structured as follows: we present in Section 2 our pull-based load balancing strategy for autonomic servers. We describe the underlying architecture and show how this scheme can be instantiated with two different return path strategies. We evaluate the performance and scalability of the solution through an extensive set of experimentations in Section 3. A survey of related work is given in Section 4. Finally, Section 5 concludes the paper and presents future research efforts.

2 Pull-Based Load Balancer

In this work, we explore the benefits of a pull-based load balancer for distributing workload among autonomic servers. The key motivation is to make the load balancing strategy more flexible and adaptive with respect to the servers. This is compatible with the goals of autonomic computing. Autonomic servers interact only on a voluntary basis. Their autonomy contradicts the basic tenets of push-based load balancing.

With the push-based strategy, the decision of whether a host should receive a request or not, is taken by the load balancer. Some solutions permit to a load balancer to exploit state information transmitted (voluntarily and hopefully on time) by the servers, but the push-based load balancer takes the final decision. In [4] with traditional servers, it was shown in actual hardware that this decision making could be a limitation on the dispatch rate. For instance, the least-connections algorithm [5] keeps track of the number of active connections each server currently has. The dispatcher then forwards requests (i.e., new connections) to the server with the fewest active connections. Another example consists of sending server-state information to the balancer using a dedicated protocol such as the Dynamic Feedback Protocol [6]. The balancer then determines based on that information which server will handle the request. This adds overhead to the process. By considering a pull-based strategy, the authoritative decision is transferred from the balancer to the servers themselves since this is where the important information is located. Indeed, we can view the interaction between balancer and server as a competitive game. If the balancer acts first, it has imperfect information about its opponent's condition and the coalition of dispatcher and servers can lose productivity through poor forwarding decisions, but if the server acts first it does not need information about the dispatcher's state to make the most economically motivated decision since there is no penalty if there is "no work to be done". Hence, the servers have effectively perfect information as far as the overall productivity is concerned. The load balancer role can typically be played by the client itself, by a DNS server or by a dedicated dispatcher (interacting as a proxy).

We consider the pull-based load balancer to be a dispatcher with a central queue. All of the requests from clients are kept by the dispatcher so that the autonomic servers can pull requests from this queue at their own convenience i.e., whenever the server makes a voluntary decision to process a request. This includes whenever the server has free resources, but is not limited to that particular condition. A server may refuse to process requests for other reasons: when failures have been detected, when new components have to be installed and configured, when attacks have been detected and protection procedures have to be executed, or when the server simply does not want to (unable or unwilling to comply). In any event, the other servers adapt automatically to the best of their own ability and policy.

2.1 Underlying Architecture

We will detail in this section how this pull-based strategy can be instantiated using two different return path strategies. A first possible architecture consists in using a dispatcher with NAT (Network Address Translation). Let consider the application example of web servers. The dispatcher receives multiple HTTP requests from clients via its public address. When a client sends such a request to the load balancer, the request is first stored into the central queue of the load balancer. The requests are usually processed according to a FCFS (First Come First Serve) queue scheduling discipline [7]. The key difference with the push-based scheme is that the requests have to stay at the load balancer stage until autonomic web servers start to pull requests.

Each of the servers can pull requests from the dispatcher at any time. If client requests have been issued and are waiting in the balancer central queue, the web server is dynamically served by the dispatcher. We can observe that the load balancing process has been reversed and that server pulls have to be managed by the dispatcher. The dispatcher uses the NAT mechanism to transfer a client request to a given web server. The dispatcher translates the target IP address to the one of the client using Reverse NAT and sends the reply to the client.

The NAT mechanism requires that the load balancer keeps state of each ongoing connection. This may contribute to a bottleneck effect [8] at the load balancer when the traffic rate is high.

With the NAT mechanism, the web server has to send the resulting reply back to the pull-based load balancer. An alternative solution consists in modifying the return path. Three different strategies [9] can usually be considered to send the reply to the client: (1) the bridge path strategy when the dispatcher is implemented at level 2 and interacts as bridge, (2) the route path strategy when the dispatcher is implemented at level 3 and interacts as an intermediate router, and (3) the direct server routing strategy when the reply is directly sent back by the server to the client. The pull-based load balancer with NAT corresponds to the second strategy. We propose to deploy the pull-based scheme using a direct server return, in order to decrease the bottleneck effect i.e., so that the reply is not forwarded by the load balancer.

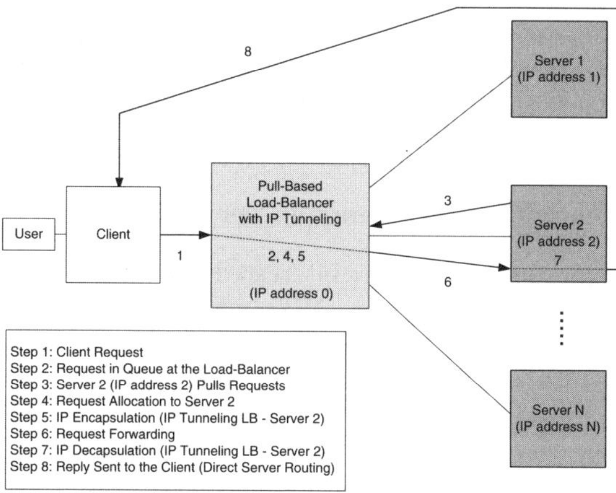

Fig. 2. Pull-Based Load Balancer with Direct Server Return

This second architecture is depicted in Figure 2. It requires to establish IP tunneling between the pull-based load balancer and the web servers. The load balancing process essentially differs from the previous one by the manner how requests are forwarded among components. The pull-based load balancer is also implemented as a dispatcher, but uses IP tunneling instead of NAT. When receiving client requests (Step 1), the dispatcher first stores them into the central queue (Step 2) according to a FCFS scheduling. A server can then pull requests from the dispatcher (Step 3). It may be served by the dispatcher if client requests are queuing (Step 4). In that case, the dispatcher establishes IP tunneling with the web server: the request is encapsulated into another IP packet (Step 5) and is forwarded to the web server (Step 6). The server then decapsulates the request (Step 7). When it has successfully processed the request, the server can directly send the reply back to the client using a direct server return. This return path increases the load balancer performance as it does not require to keep state of the connections at the load balancer.

3   Experimental Results

We evaluated the performance of our pull-based load balancing scheme through an extensive set of experiments, which can be compared directly with earlier physical experiments performed in [4] (these previous experiments were however limited to push-based load balancing with regular servers). The simulations were performed with the JMT open source suite for queuing network modeling and workload analysis [10] developed by the Performance Evaluation Lab at the Polytechnic University of Milan. We extended it so that we can model the behavior of a pull-based load balancer with direct server return. We considered during the experiments a system composed of a load balancer L at the front office and a set of n servers $S = \{S_1, S_2, ..., S_n\}$ at the back office. The load balancer L implements either a push-based scheme or a pull-based scheme depending on the scenario. We assume that the arrival and completion process distributions follow a typical Poisson distribution in discrete time. Despite the controversy regarding the inter-arrival times, we use Poisson distributed arrivals, this allows a direct comparison with [4] and we would not expect the choice to affect the broad conclusions of our results.

3.1   Performance with Homogeneous Servers

In a first series of experiments, we were interested in analyzing the performance of our solution with homogeneous servers. We modeled a system with three servers $\{S_1, S_2, S_3\}$ of same capabilities. Each server is capable of processing an average of 100 requests per second. We measured the average response time obtained with the pull-based load balancer while varying the request rate from 5 to 300 requests per second. We assume here the natural notion of response time perceived by users, that is, the time interval between the instant of the submission

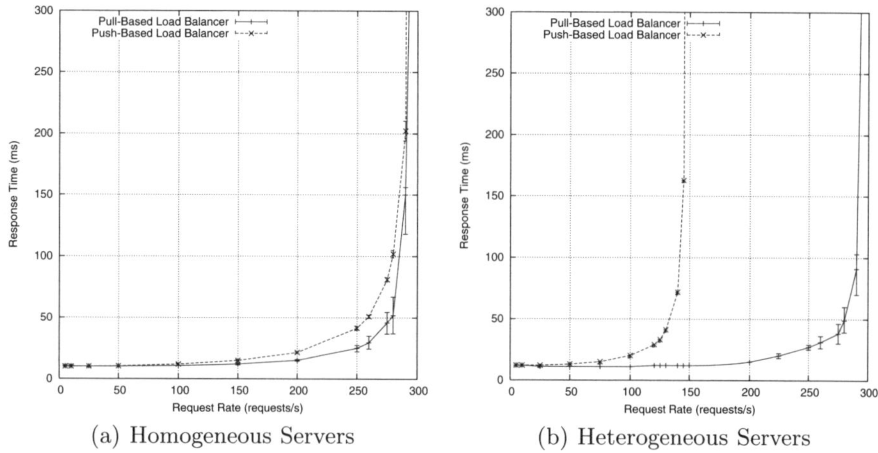

(a) Homogeneous Servers   (b) Heterogeneous Servers

Fig. 3. Response Time with Autonomic Servers

of a request and the instant the corresponding reply arrives completely at the user. We compared these values with the response time provided by a load balancer implementing a classic push-based scheme where servers are taken without consideration of their current queue length or latency. Indeed, autonomic servers may refuse to provide any server-state information, and we consider that they interact in a voluntary basis making least-connection algorithms inefficient. The experimental results are summarized in Figure 3(a). The horizontal axis corresponds to the different request rate values. We plotted for each of them the average response time obtained with the pull-based load balancer (plain line) compared to the one obtained with the push-based load balancer (dotted line). The two graphs show the same tendency when we increase the request rate: the response time first stays relative low and stable (on the left of the figure), then grows exponentially when we tends to 300 requests per second (on the right of the figure). This value corresponds to the theoretical maximal processing rate of the system (the sum of three servers capable of processing 100 requests per second each). When comparing the two load balancing schemes, we can observe that the performance is quite similar at a low response rate (from 5 to 100 requests per second). The push-based load balancer is even better than the pull-based strategy at the lowest rates. However, at high response rates (from 100 requests per second), we clearly see that the pull-based load balancer produces faster response times than the push-based load balancer.

Additional parameters need to be taken into account to complete and refine this comparison. In particular, as load balancer and servers have finite queue sizes, we measured the request drop rate while varying the request rate values. The drop rate is the number requests per second never processed at all by an element of the system. We plotted these rates in Figure 4 for respectively the load balancer and each of the three servers. When looking at these results, we first can observe that the system starts to drop requests at around 300 requests per

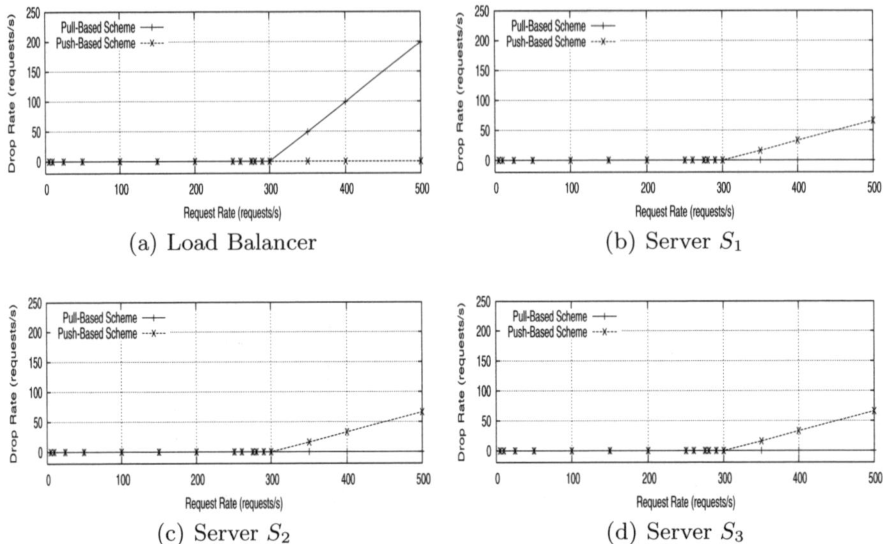

(a) Load Balancer   (b) Server S_1

(c) Server S_2 (d) Server S_3

Fig. 4. Drop Rates with Homogeneous Servers by using the Pull-Based Strategy (plain line) and the Push-Based Strategy (dotted line)

second (compare to [4]), when the request rate exceeds the maximal processing rate. However, the dropped requests are not distributed in the same manner in the system. In the push-based scenario (dotted line), the dropped requests are equally distributed among the three servers. The load balancer does not drop any requests during the experiments, even with high request rates. The reason for these results is that all the requests are dispatched by the load balancer to one of the servers whatever the server is overloaded or not (i.e., it simply pushes the problem downstream).

Intuitively, the pull based mechanisms needs a longer queue at the dispatcher since this is where waiting builds up at the system bottleneck, but this does not imply that greater resources are needed. The pull strategy is like an airport check-in queue: servers pull passengers from a single line that fills the same space as would multiple lines. The same resources are simply organized differently. Moreover, the reliance on a single dispatcher should not be a problem if redundancy is factored into the calculation [11].

As the servers have homogeneous capabilities and the load balancer takes servers each in turn, the dropped rate is almost identical for the three servers and corresponds to the third of the total drop rate in the system. In the pull-based scenario (plain line), requests are only dropped by the load balancer. The servers process requests on demand by pulling the load balancer. As a consequence, the servers are not overloaded and do not need to drop requests during the experiments. The requests are waiting at the load balancer and are directly dropped by it when the request rate is too high for the system.

3.2   Performance with Heterogeneous Servers

In a second series of experiments, we analyzed the same scenario with heterogeneous servers. The average service rate for servers S_1, S_2, S_3 is respectively of 50, 100 and 150 requests per second. The graphs in Figure 3(b) represent, as previously, the comparison of response times with the pull-based strategy and the push-based strategy. This scenario produces worst performances than the scenario with homogeneous servers. However, the impact has not the same scale on the two strategies: the difference is minor with the pull-based strategy while the difference is major with the push-based scheme. In the push-based scenario, the response time grows faster when the arrival rate tends to 150 requests per second. The server S_1 with the smallest capacity becomes overloaded earlier than the two other servers. The push-based load balancer is not capable of transferring the workload on servers S_2 and S_3. The workload is equally distributed on the three servers (a third per server). The response time therefore increases significantly at around 150 requests per second when server S_1 is overloaded (a third of 150 requests per second). In the pull-based scenario, server S_1 can reduce its workload by pulling less requests from the load balancer. In that manner, the load balancer can maintain the requests on its queue and dispatches them to the higher capacity servers. As the total processing capacity $(50 + 100 + 150)$ is the same than in the homogeneous scenario (3×100), the response time grows exponentially when the arrival rate tends to the same saturation value of 300 requests per second.

We observe the same phenomenon by measuring the drop rates of servers (see Figure 5). In the push-based strategy, the load balancer does not drop requests.

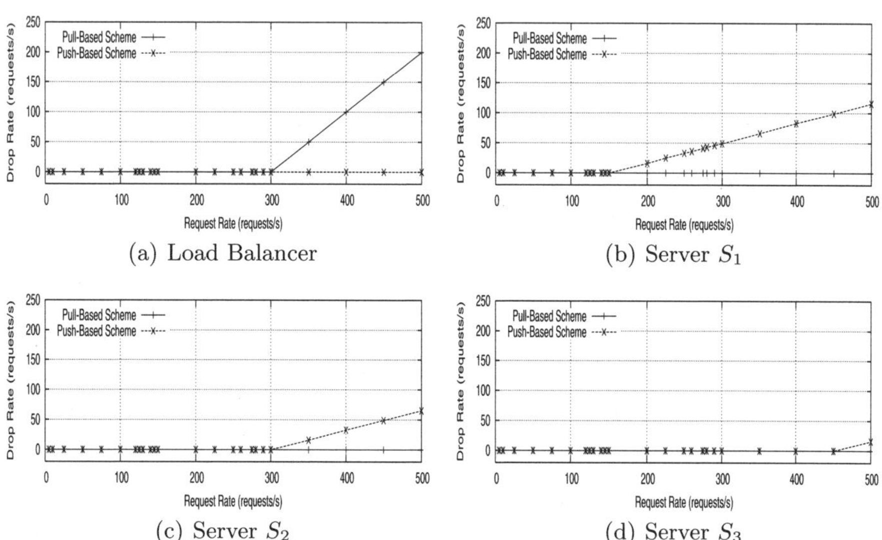

(a) Load Balancer   (b) Server S_1

(c) Server S_2 (d) Server S_3

Fig. 5. Drop Rates with Heterogeneous Servers by using the Pull-Based Strategy (plain line) and the Push-Based Strategy (dotted line)

The drop rate is unequally distributed among the three servers, as they start to drop requests when they becomes overloaded e.g., when the total workload is three times equal to their processing capacity. Server S_1 drops requests earlier (at 150 requests per second) than servers S_2 and S_3 (at around 300 and 450 requests per second). In the pull-based strategy, the load balancer is the only element which drops requests in the system (at 300 requests per second), as the servers can reduce the workload by their own in order not to be overloaded.

3.3   Scalability and Bottleneck Effect

The third series of experiments evaluates the scalability of our pull-based load balancer when adding extra servers. We measured the average response time while varying the number of servers from 2 to 6 in the system and calculated the profit in percentage of the pull-based strategy compared to the push-based one. We considered during the experiments that the servers are homogeneous with a same processing capacity of 100 requests par second on average. We plotted the experimental results for four different request rates $\{100, 200, 400, 600\}$ in Figure 6.

We can first observe that the profit generated by the pull-based load balancer for a given request rate decreases when we add extra servers. For instance, Sub-figure 6(a) shows that the profit at a rate of 100 requests per second goes from around 12 percents with 2 homogeneous servers to around 2 percents with 6 homogeneous servers. The pull-based strategy is therefore much more valuable if the server resources are scarce. Indeed, the push-based strategy with homogeneous servers stays relatively competitive as long as the resources are sufficiently dimensioned. Heterogeneous servers may produce a better profit with the same scenario, in particular when one of the servers has a significantly smaller capacity. In that case, the smaller server can regulate the request rate so that the load balancer forwards the requests to the other servers. Another natural question is to what extent the request rate impacts on the pull-based strategy. When comparing the four sub-figures, we can distinguish two major phases. In a first phase (Sub-figure 6(a) and Sub-figure 6(b)), increasing the request rates improves the profit generated by the pull-base strategy. For instance, with three homogeneous servers, the profit grows from around 7 percents with a rate of 100 requests per second to around 28 percents with a rate of 200 requests per second. However, in a second phase (Sub-figure 6(c) and Sub-figure 6(d)), the profit starts to decrease when we continue to increase the request rate. The profit with three servers decreases to 19 percents at 400 requests per second and to 16 percents at 600 requests per second. The pull-based load balancer becomes even less interesting than the push-based load balancer in the worst cases. We mean, by worst cases, scenarios when the request rate is high and the server resources are sufficiently scaled. Both the pull-based and push-based load balancers suffer from the bottleneck effect at a high load. However, this phenomenon is significantly more important with the pull-load strategy. These experimental results are confirmed by the drop rates presented in figures 4 and 5, where we observed the requests are maintained and then dropped by the load balancer.

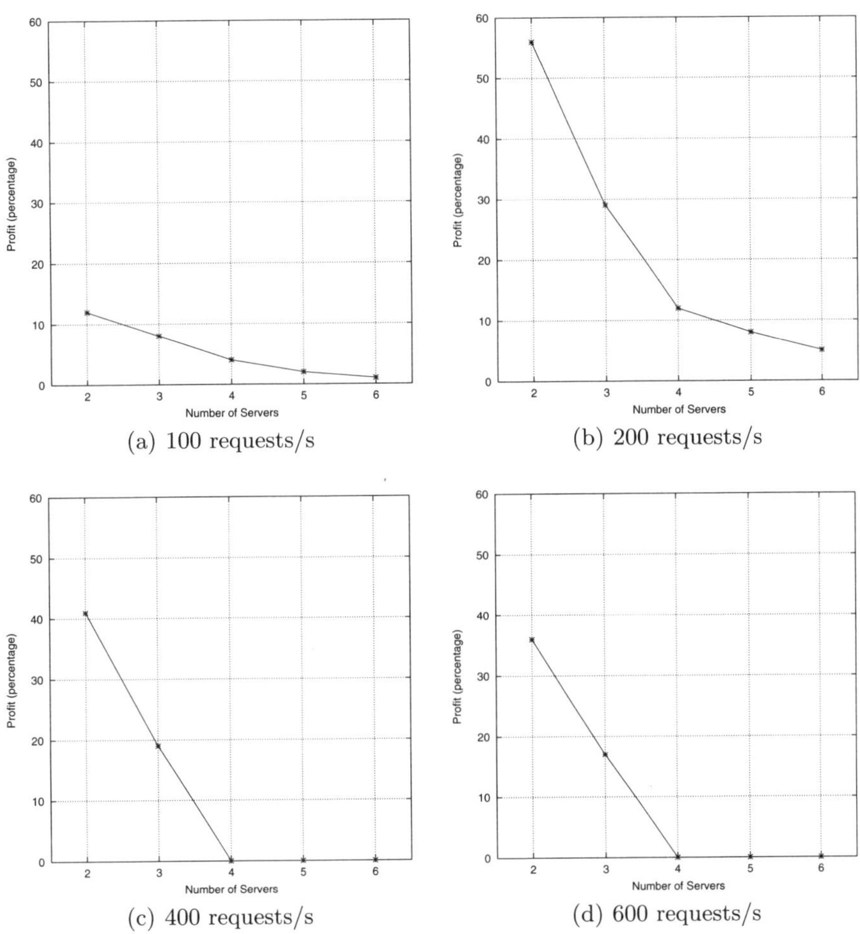

Fig. 6. Profit of the Pull-Based Strategy Compared to the Push-Based Strategy on Adding Extra Servers. Results can be compared to [4].

We also analyzed the behavior of our pull-based strategy, by comparing experimental results to queuing theoretical models [12]. In our experiments, the authoritative decision of servers is limited to a simple condition on a given resource (maximal processing rate). As a consequence, the system converges to a behavior very similar to a set of servers processing the same queue ($M/M/k$ queuing model). This convergence may be less evident if we consider the full autonomy of servers. Moreover, our research group attempted in [5] a direct implementation of a pull-based load balancer using a Java application in an attempt to demonstrate that pull-based methods would be superior to push methods. The prototype showed performance can often be hostage to implementation issues.

4 Related Approaches

A large variety of algorithms and techniques were proposed for balancing workload to traditional back end servers [5]. Dynamic algorithms can exploit client-state and server-state information. The server-state information can be obtained in an implicit manner: the load balancer estimates the load on the servers by passively monitoring network parameters such as ongoing connections or by activating probes. For instance, we previously mentioned that the least-connections scheme selects the server with the lowest number of ongoing connections. In all of these approaches, the load balancing is performed in a push-based manner. We have already described in [4] (but with traditional servers) a comparative study of these push-based load balancing algorithms used to distribute packets among a set of web servers. Server-state information can also be obtained in an explicit manner. For instance, the Dynamic Feedback Protocol (DFP) [6] permits a dispatcher to deploy agents directly on the back end servers. These agents periodically report relative weights to the load balancer in the form of load vectors. The load balancer then exploits the reported weights to select more efficient servers. This requires a substantial overhead and infrastructure. In distributed systems and grid computing, management platforms [13] and service middlewares [14,15] can dynamically align the allocation of resources to infrastructure and business requirements. A significant amount of effort has been expended to design resource management methods based on analytical queuing models [11], decision theory [16], and planning and scheduling techniques [17]. These optimizations are made possible thanks to server-state information collected by agents. In our approach, we show that there is no need for these feedback loops, completely autonomous behavior suffices to solve the problem effectively by voluntary cooperation [3].

5 Conclusions and Future Work

We have explored the motivation for the use of pull-based load balancing between autonomic servers and have quantified the benefits and limits of such a scheme, as one approaches the theoretical limit of a perfect implementation. Autonomic computing advocates greater decentralization of autonomy and only weak coupling of components through cooperative communication. It makes traditional server-state and least-connection inapplicable or inefficient. Our study shows that relaxing the desire for mandatory control of servers using a central controller, and instead allowing them to cooperate voluntarily through only weak coupling, is not the disadvantage that skeptics imagine; quite the opposite, it has the potential to exceed the performance of a push approach, while maintaining better security for each component.

Comparing experimental results to push-based results with autonomic servers we find, as expected, that the pull-based balancer is more sensitive to the bottleneck's resources than the push-based balancer. It surpasses the push-based balancer when the workload is high compared to the expected server acceptance rate (i.e., at high "voluntary utilization"), and when it is sufficiently low to avoid the bottleneck limitation. When we restrict the decision of autonomic servers to a simple condition on a given local resource, the pull-based load balancer converges as expected to an $M/M/k$ model. This convergence may be less evident with servers having a full autonomy. In future work, we are interested in measuring the performance of voluntary dispatch in a large scale virtualization environment [18] where these considerations are especially relevant. We are also planning to model the behavior of autonomic servers using high order internal chain architectures, and in evaluating how these new parameters impact on our pull-based load balancer.

Acknowledgment

This work was supported by the EC IST-EMANICS Network of Excellence.

References

1. Murch, R.: Autonomic Computing. IBM Press (2004)
2. Yu, P.S., Cardellini, V., Colajanni, M.: Dynamic Load Balancing on Web-Server Systems. IEEE Internet Computing 3(3) (June 1999)
3. Burgess, M.: An Approach to Understanding Policy Based on Autonomy and Voluntary Cooperation. In: Schönwälder, J., Serrat, J. (eds.) DSOM 2005. LNCS, vol. 3775, pp. 97–108. Springer, Heidelberg (2005)
4. Burgess, M., Undheim, G.: Predictable Scaling Behaviour in the Data Centre with Multiple Application Servers. In: State, R., van der Meer, S., O'Sullivan, D., Pfeifer, T. (eds.) DSOM 2006. LNCS, vol. 4269, pp. 49–60. Springer, Heidelberg (2006)
5. Berggren, A.: Presenting a Prototype for Pull Based Load Balancing of Web Servers. Oslo University College, Norway (May 2007)
6. Kersey, C.: Dynamic Feedback Protocol (DFP), IETF Internet Draft (August 2005), http://dfp.berlios.de/draft-eck-dfp-00.txt
7. Gross, D., Gross, D., Harris, C.M.: Fundamentals of Queueing Theory, 3rd edn. Wiley Interscience, New York (1998)
8. Jung, G., Swint, G.S., Parekh, J., Pu, C., Sahai, A.: Detecting Bottleneck in n-Tier IT Applications Through Analysis. In: State, R., van der Meer, S., O'Sullivan, D., Pfeifer, T. (eds.) DSOM 2006. LNCS, vol. 4269, pp. 149–160. Springer, Heidelberg (2006)
9. Bourke, T.: Server Load Balancing. O'Reilly and Associates (August 2001)
10. Bertoli, M., Casale, G., Serazzi, G.: An Overview of the JMT Queueing Network Simulator. Technical Report TR 2007.2, Politecnico di Milano - DEI (2007)
11. Cunha, I.S., Almeida, J.M., Almeida, V., Santos, M.: Self-Adaptive Capacity Management for Multi-Tier Virtualized Environments.. In: Proc. of the 10th IFIP/IEEE International Symposium on Integrated Network Management (IM 2007), Munich, Germany, May 2007, pp. 129–138 (2007)
12. Badonnel, R., Burgess, M.: Dynamic Pull-Based Load Balancing for Autonomic Servers. In: Proc. of the 11th IEEE/IFIP Network Operations and Management Symposium (NOMS 2008), Salvador, Brazil, Short Paper. IEEE Press, Los Alamitos (2008)

13. Singhal, S., Arlitt, M.F., Beyer, D., Graupner, S., Machiraju, V., Pruyne, J., Rolia, J., Sahai, A., Santos, C.A., Ward, J., Zhu, X.: Quartermaster - a Resource Utility System. In: Proc. of the 9th IFIP/IEEE International Symposium on Integrated Network Management (IM 2005), Nice, France, pp. 265–278 (2005)
14. Magaña, E., Lefèvre, L., Serrat, J.: Autonomic Management Architecture for Flexible Grid Services Deployment Based on Policies. In: Lukowicz, P., Thiele, L., Tröster, G. (eds.) ARCS 2007. LNCS, vol. 4415, pp. 157–170. Springer, Heidelberg (2007)
15. Adam, C., Stadler, R., Tang, C., Steinder, M., Spreitzer, M.: A Service Middleware that Scales in System Size and Applications.. In: Proc. of the 10th IFIP/IEEE International Symposium on Integrated Management (IM 2007) (May 2007)
16. Nassif, L.N., Nogueira, J.M.S., de Andrade, F.V.: Distributed Resource Selection in Grid Using Decision Theory. In: Proc. of the 7th IEEE Symposium on Cluster Computing and Grid (CCGrid 2007), Rio de Janeiro, Brazil, May 2007, pp. 327–334 (2007)
17. Diao, Y., Keller, A., Parekh, S.S., Marinov, V.V.: Predicting Labor Cost through IT Management Complexity Metrics. In: Proc. of the 10th IEEE International Symposium on Integrated Management (IM 2007), Germany, May 2007, pp. 274–283 (2007)
18. Begnum, K.M.: Xen Virtualization and Multi-Host Management using MLN. In: Bandara, A.K., Burgess, M. (eds.) AIMS 2007. LNCS, vol. 4543, p. 229. Springer, Heidelberg (2007)

An Architecture for Supporting Network Fault Recovery Management

Feng Liu, Antonis M. Hadjiantonis, Ha Manh Tran, and Mina Amin

MNM Team, Ludwig-Maximilians-University Munich, Germany
`liufeng@nm.ifi.lmu.de`
Centre for Communications Systems Research, University of Surrey, UK
`{a.hadjiantonis,m.amin}@surrey.ac.uk`
Computer Science, Jacobs University Bremen, Germany
`h.tran@jacobs-university.de`

Abstract. Highly available and resilient networks play a decisive role in today's networked world. As network faults are inevitable and networks are becoming constantly intricate, finding effective fault recovery solutions in a timely manner is becoming a challenging task for administrators. Therefore, an automated mechanism to support fault resolution is essential towards efficient fault handling process. In this paper we propose an architecture to support automated fault recovery in terms of traffic engineering, recovery knowledge discovery and automated recovery planning. We base our discussion on an application scenario for recovery from border router failure to maintain optimized configuration of outbound inter-domain traffic.

Keywords: Fault Management, Fault Recovery, Automated Planning, Policy-Based Management, Case-Based Reasoning, Peer-to-Peer, Inter-Domain, Traffic Engineering.

1 Introduction

Availability of networks is becoming more essential in today's networked world. Whereas network faults are inevitable facts, an efficient fault management process is decisive to decrease the fault resolution time and to increase the availability of the network. In case of failure, an efficient fault recovery process is expected to find fault resolutions quickly and recover the impacted network in a timely manner. Hence, recognizing the importance of minimum system downtime to maintain compliance with accepted Service Level Agreements (SLA), we propose a dual stage fault recovery process. The first stage is a short-term system reaction to minimize the immediate effects of a fault. In order to allow for quick system response, this first reaction is pre-planned in sets of recovery policies able to anticipate faults. The second stage is the long-term recovery plan and aims to discover the recovery knowledge and plans the recovery process.

The presented architecture involves traffic engineering, policy-based management and artificial intelligence approaches. Our research focuses on providing

D. Hausheer and J. Schönwalder (Eds.): AIMS 2008, LNCS 5127, pp. 105–119, 2008.

a comprehensive framework to facilitate an automated fault recovery process in large-scale networks. The motivations of the architecture are: (1) providing short-term recovery plans through fast recovery solutions, (2) providing long-term recovery plans through an efficient recovery knowledge discovery approach and (3) automating recovery planning for the long-term recovery process.

Application Scenario: To demonstrate the applicability of our approach, we choose a scenario related to inter-domain Traffic Engineering (TE) and examine a case study of automated recovery from an egress point (EP) failure. Since inter-domain links are the most common bottlenecks in the Internet [1], an efficient plan for fault recovery is necessary. We focus our interest on planning the recovery from border router faults to maintain optimized configuration of outbound inter-domain traffic. Once a border router (EP) fails, we follow a dual stage recovery process that will be detailed in section 4.

The first stage is to switch affected traffic flows to another EP, while at the same time optimize the EP selection (border router selection) for all outbound inter-domain traffic of a domain. To achieve a quick reaction that would minimize disruption, we execute in advance an outbound TE algorithm and store short-term recovery plans in a repository. The algorithm is designed with the goal of inter-domain link load-balancing and creates configuration sets for each case of the EP failures. In addition, the algorithm creates the initial configuration set for normal operation which is used until a failure is detected. Having responded to the border router failure and minimizing short-term disruption, the second recovery stage begins to discover a long-term solution and recover from the failure. Once notified about the failure, the recovery system relies on proposed policies and actions to decide an appropriate recovery plan. More specifically, the planning subsystem receives high-level directives and actions as input, then combines the input with received state information from the monitoring system in order to generate the appropriate sequence of actions for remedying the failed EP and recovering normal network operation.

This paper is organized as follows: in section 2 we present our proposed architecture and discuss the involved subsystems and their interactions. Section 3 summarizes the methodologies applied to our approaches and in section 4 we analyze our system based on the application scenario. Section 5 provides an overview on the related work and the paper concludes with section 6.

2   System Architecture

Our proposed system contains three subsystems: Automated Recovery Planning (ARP), Knowledge Discovery (KD) and Policy-based Management (PBM), see Fig.1. The planning subsystem obtains status reports from the monitoring component in order to carry out analyzing and executing recovery plans for the managed system with the support of the other subsystems that provide appropriate actions and policies respectively. The introduction of each subsystem is presented in the following subsections.

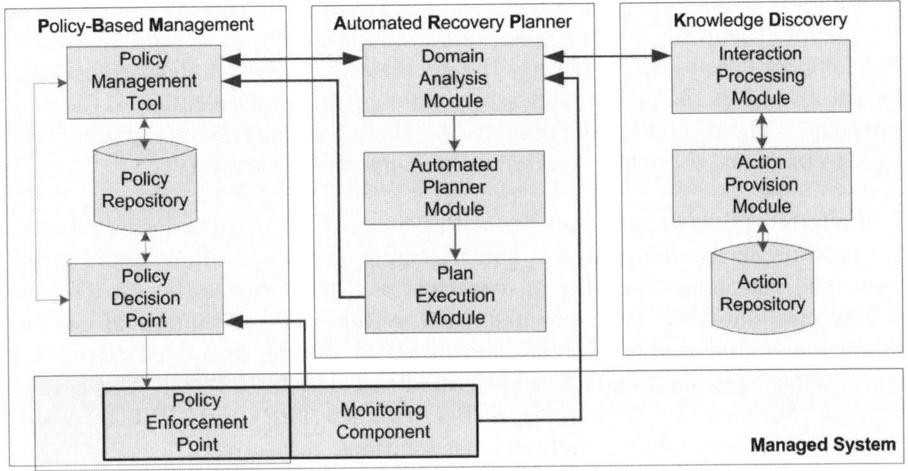

Fig. 1. Overview of System Architecture

Automated Recovery Planning: This central subsystem provides fault recovery plans for the managed system. Its tasks involve analyzing the status report from the monitoring component, collecting relevant information from the other subsystems for the recovery activities, producing relevant recovery plans and provisioning for plan executions on the managed system. In Fig. 1, the three modules responsible for these tasks include:

Domain Analysis (DA): This central module connects to KD, PBM subsystems and the monitoring component for aggregating the relevant information as plan knowledge to facilitate the operation of the automated planner module. Such plan knowledge includes the description on the current system state, e.g. which components are impacted by the failures and which components are still operational etc. Depending on the impacted components, it contacts KD for a set of relevant recovery measurements attached with meta-information. The meta-information describes under which situations a particular solution step could be applied and what consequences could be expected from it, i.e. how a particular solution step is going to affect the current system state. DA also contacts PBM to retrieve recovery policies.

Automated Planner (AP): This module derives recovery plans based on plan domain descriptions provided by DA. It contains an automated planning algorithm, which correlates relevant recovery knowledge and produces recovery plans by reasoning. Note that the selected planning algorithm is domain-independent and generic. The rationale to use domain knowledge as input is to accelerate the planning process and to increase the efficiency of the planning algorithm.

Plan Execution (PE): This module makes provision for the recovery plan executions. Plans generated by AP are described in a specific plan description language, therefore, to enable the plan executions, it is necessary to convert the format of the plan and map the recovery plan into executable actions. Since PE relies on PBM for plan execution, it converts the generated plan into a PBM-compatible format and sends the plan to PBM, where the mapping and execution of the plan take place. The results will be observed by the monitoring component and sent back to DA to see if further recovery measurements are necessary.

Knowledge Discovery: Case-Based Reasoning (CBR) [2] resolves a problem by searching for similar problems and reasoning on their solutions found in the past. The reasoning capability of a conventional CBR system is restricted by a local case database. A distributed CBR system takes advantage of computation power and problem-solving knowledge at various sites, thus improving performance and maintaining huge federated case databases better. This system exploits the integrated framework of Peer-to-Peer (P2P) and CBR [3], which involve retrieving problems and inferring solutions, respectively.

This subsystem acts as a distributed CBR system to provide actions for recovery plans. Its tasks involve communicating with various knowledge sources (e.g. the Internet, the operators), dealing with various requests from and responses to other modules, inferring proper actions corresponding to the failed status of the managed system and managing a case database (e.g. failure cases and actions). These tasks belong to three modules, shown in Fig. 1:

Action Repository (AR): This module involves storing cases and maintaining the case database. It regularly checks the usage of cases and the similarity of cases in order to deactivate obsolete cases or consolidate cases. Maintaining the case database is essential since the CBR system tends to be lumbering and inefficient with a large number of cases.

Action Provision: This module serves as an independent CBR engine which takes requests and the case database as input to provide actions. Its main tasks include (i) retrieving similar cases from AR, (ii) reasoning on these cases to figure out the most promising case, and (iii) updating the case database. To improve AR, the module regularly updates new cases from various sources including adapting instructions from operators to solutions, or updating cases by learning problems from monitoring systems, or extracting cases from the response of peers.

Interaction Processing: This module is responsible for establishing and maintaining a P2P network. Its main tasks are to interact with various sources including operators, surveillance systems or other peers for information exchange, resource search and lookup. Particularly, it deals with requests from peers forwarded to other peers, instructions and updates from the operators processed to update AR.

Policy-Based Management: PBM simplifies the complex management tasks of large scale systems, since high-level policies can be automatically enforced as appropriate network management [4]. In general, policies are defined as Event-Condition-Action (ECA) clauses, where on event(s) E, if condition(s) C is true, then action(s) A is executed. The components of PBM are shown in Fig. 1 along with their interactions with ARP and the managed system. The four functional elements, as defined by IETF, are described below:

Policy Management Tool (PMT): PMT is the interface between the operators and PBM. It allows the introduction and editing of policies and also provides notification about critical events requiring a manager's attention. Using this interface, the operators carry out the specification of operational policies by selecting the appropriate policies from the supported policy types and selecting the required parameters. We extend PMT's functionality by interfacing it with ARP. PMT provides relevant policies to ARP to assist the planning process.

Policy Repository (PR): PR encapsulates the management logic to be enforced on all networked entities, as expressed in policies. It is the central point where policies are stored by managers using PMT and can be subsequently retrieved either by the Policy Decision Point (PDP) or by PMT.

Policy Decision Point (PDP): PDP is responsible for evaluating policy conditions and deciding when and where policy actions need to be enforced. Once relevant policies have been retrieved from PR, they are interpreted and PDP in turn provisions any decisions or actions to the controlled Policy Enforcement Point (PEP). PDP receives input from the monitoring component of PEP to form a closed control loop.

Policy Enforcement Point (PEP): PEP enforces policy decisions, as instructed by PDP. Within our framework, PEP is enhanced by the *monitoring component* that reports local information to assist decision making.

The *monitoring component* is integrated to provide feedback to both PBM and ARP for decision making. It is not formally part of our architecture since fault detection and diagnosis are out of the scope of this paper. Critical events such as failures are reported to both subsystems in order to initiate the dual stage recovery process.

3   Methodology

In this section, we give detailed views on the methodologies the subsystems apply. The discussion focuses not only on individual subsystems, but also tries to provide an overview on the interactions between them.

3.1   PBM and ARP Collaboration

As networks become more and more complex, unavoidably faults occur more frequently. It is evident that frameworks with automated recovery capabilities can significantly expedite and simplify management tasks. Within our framework, policies work in two layers to express on one hand high-level business objectives and on the other hand, low-level configuration policies to anticipate faults. Policies can encapsulate the overall management logic at two functional layers: the business layer and the device layer. Using sophisticated algorithms, we translate high-level policies defined at the business layer to low-level configuration policies at the device layer. At the same time, the PBM interacts with ARP to provide policies and constraints to be used in the planning procedure.

By executing an outbound TE algorithm in advance, we create different policy sets that express those high-level goals in normal operation and in addition anticipate possible system failures. These low level policies, constitute short-term plans for the EP selection aiming for the recovery of outbound inter-domain traffic when an EP fails. The created recovery policy sets are stored in the Policy Repository and the policy set for normal operation is enforced. An outbound inter-Autonomous System (AS) TE algorithm that is able to optimize the EP selection (border router selection) for outbound inter-domain traffic of a domain has been developed in [5]. The algorithm is designed with the goal of inter-domain link load balancing. The output is $|L|+1$ ($|L|$ number of border routers) sets of EP selection configurations, one set for normal operation (i.e. no failure) that can be called PrimaryEgressPoint selection and one set for each case of EP failures that can be called BackupEgressPoint selections. In other words, PrimaryEgressPoint selection determines EP selection under no inter-domain link failure and BackupEgressPoint selection determines EP selection under Failure States. A common implementation of EP selection is by adjusting the local-preference value in the Border Gateway Protocol (BGP) route attribute [6]. According to the BGP route selection process, local-preference has the highest priority and its value indicates the preference of the route. The higher the local-preference, the more preferred is the route. The algorithm takes inter-domain connectivity, BGP routing information, inter-domain traffic matrix as inputs and then deterministically calculates the EP selection through local search heuristics. The reader is referred to [5] for more details.

High-level policies are used to express goals of inter-domain traffic management, e.g. *"optimize EP selection to achieve inter-domain load balancing"*, or *"optimize EP selection avoiding routing traffic to destination prefix p1 using domain D2"*. For security reasons we may wish to avoid routing the inter-domain traffic flows towards some particular destinations through some specific domains. The benefit of policy-based management is the ability to use different policies to achieve different goals, e.g. minimize peering cost. Furthermore, high-level or recovery policies could also be used by ARP in order to find the recovery plans which are in compliance with the management goals. It is possible that the fault recovery plan composition may result in several alternative plans to reach the same goal. In such cases, ARP should refer to policies in order to choose the right one which complies with the management objectives. A recovery policy can be interpreted as constraints for plan composition. Considering the previous example on EP optimisation, obviously a link failure recovery plan that involves the step which uses domain $D2$ to reach destination prefix $p1$ could not be considered as valid, because there is a management policy which forbids using this step. In this case, ARP has to search for other alternatives. Another example of using high-level policies to recover from router failure, assuming there are alternative steps involved to recover the router failure: one of them involves using router B as temporal fallback router, to which the traffic could be shifted to, while another step requires recalculating and applying the alternative links to route the current traffic. Obviously, both steps lead to same goal, namely, keeping the disruption on the current traffic to minimum. Nevertheless, the fallback solution maybe preferred in terms of shorter traffic disruption compared to link recalculation. If we assume that there is a policy that states *Router B can only be used as temporal failover for A between time 20:00 - 23:00* and the link failure on router A happens on $10:00$, apparently, the first alternative cannot be considered by the automated planner, because the constraint derived from the high-level policy restricts the usage of router B as failover router at the time of failure on A.

3.2 KD and ARP Collaboration

KD contains a P2P network for knowledge exchange and update. A peer shares resources (e.g. failure cases and actions) with other peers and provides search facilities for other peers. A peer also bears a CBR engine for choosing best solutions. The CBR engine, upon receiving requests from ARP, works on the case database to propose solutions for ARP. The design of KD below explains core issues related to building P2P network, case retrieval and reasoning in CBR regarding the focused problem domain. Some detail has been addressed in our related studies.

Communication: KD uses a Gnutella-style backbone network of super peers as an appropriate overlay [7]. The overlay sticks to the characteristics of Gnutella super-peer networks. Such networks organize peers into several clusters, any cluster contains peers connected to a super peer, and the connections among super peers form an unstructured overlay network. Any peer communicates with its super peer for sending queries, publishing resources or receiving answers. Any super peer, upon joining the overlay, has to perform several non-trivial tasks such as search and lookup, reasoning, or maintenance.

Case Retrieval: This issue involves case representation and similarity function. A case including failures and actions is represented by field-value vectors, where values are binary, numeric or symbolic. In particular, a case contains a vector v_f with symptoms sym_i for failure descriptions, a number of vectors v_a with an action act and conditions cnd_i for action descriptions, and a goal vector v_g with symptoms sym_i for verification descriptions. The following example explains how a case is represented:

- $v_f = <\ sym_1$: link_to_dest_failed, sym_2: no_traffic_flow, sym_3: primary_router_not_running, sym_4: second_brouter_exist, sym_5: second_brouter_ok, sym_6: bandwidth_reserv_required>
- $v_g = <\ sym_1$: link_to_dest_ok, sym_2: traffic_flow_ok, sym_3: bandwidth_ok>
- $v_a = <\ act$: use_alternative_link, cnd_1: link_to_dest_failed>
- $v_a = <\ act$: failover_to_secondary_router, cnd_1: second_brouter_exist, cnd_2: second_brouter_ok>

- $v_a = <$ *act*: establish_link$>$
- $v_a = <$ *act*: reserve_bandwidth, cnd_1: bandwidth_reserv_required$>$

Note that a request sent to the subsystem only contains v_f and v_g, the subsystem works on symptoms appeared in the request by communicating with other peers and looking into the local case database for similar symptoms and actions. Using this representation, evaluating case similarity is straightforward since it depends on comparing pairs of symptom and value; values avoid using textual fuzzy descriptions and the expert determines the weight values of symptoms. Similar cases are evaluated by the *global similarity* method $sim(r, c) = \sum_{i=1}^{n} w_i sim(r_i, c_i)$, where n is the number of matched symptoms; r_i and c_i are symptoms of request r and case c, respectively; $sim(r_i, c_i)$ is the distance between r_i and c_i, w_i is a weight value of the ith feature such that $\sum_{i=1}^{n} w_i = 1$ with $w_i \in [0, 1]$ $\forall i$.

Case Reasoning: This issue involves case adaptation (or reasoning, inference) and decision making. The conventional inference process carries out distinguishing a retrieved case from the problem to clarify main differences, modifying the retrieved case following the differences to obtain the final case. There are several alternative inference methods depending on problem domains, such as probabilistic inference using Bayesian network, classification using machine learning, optimization technique using genetic algorithms (GA). For the focused problem domain, the reasoning engine in KD employs optimization techniques to search for an optimal set of actions that satisfies symptoms from the request provided constraints from the goal vector and conditions from the action vectors.

To enable the planning process, ARP needs to aggregate the recovery knowledge from KD. After receiving the fault report from the monitoring component, the domain analysis module dispatches the knowledge search request regarding the impacted component to the interaction processing module of KD. The search results are returned by KD in the field-value vectors format. They include knowledge such as fault symptoms and solution steps. However, the results cannot be directly used by planner algorithm, the domain analysis module needs to convert the received data into some specific planning language, such as Plan Domain Description Language (PDDL) [8]. In the next section, we present examples on the representation of recovery domain knowledge.

As mentioned in section 2, the core of this subsystem is the automated planner module. This module utilizes the AI-based planning algorithm to generate plans accordingly to the domain description. A planning problem is based on the restricted state-transition system[9]. A state-transition system Σ could be represented as $\Sigma = (S, A, E, \gamma)$, where $S = \{s_0, s_1, s_2, \ldots\}$ is the finite set of states; $A = \{a_1, a_2, \ldots\}$ is set of actions; $E = \{e_1, e_2, \ldots\}$ is set of events and $\gamma : S \times A \times E \to 2^S$ denotes a state transition function.

A planning problem can be defined as a triple $P = (\Sigma, s_0, g)$, where $s_0 \in S$ is the initial state of a problem and $g \subset S$ is the set of states which satisfy the goal. Provided with problem domain descriptions, a planning algorithm operates on the provided information and finds one or more plans accordingly. Additionally, a planning algorithm observes different constraints if they are provided. The use of constraints serves two purposes: first, it reduces the plan searching space and second, it guides the plan searching in a correct way, e.g. some of the actions should be avoided according to constraints (policies).

4   System Analysis - Case Study

An outbound inter-domain TE scenario is chosen to investigate recovery from EP failure using the introduced architecture. Normally, upon an EP failure, traffic is shifted to another available EP in accordance to the BGP route selection policies. However, if a large amount of traffic is shifted, congestion is likely to occur on these new serving EPs. An intuitive approach to minimize this congestion is to redirect the traffic to another EP by adjusting BGP routing policies in an online manner until the best available EP has been found. Such online trial-and-error approach, however, may cause router misconfiguration, unpredicted traffic disruption and BGP route flooding, leading to route instability. It is desirable to have an efficient fault recovery plan and an optimization algorithm in order to proactively produce a configuration for optimal performance under normal and failure scenarios. Therefore, we focus our interest on outbound inter-domain TE and recovery planning in case of any EP failure. Once one of the EP fails, our recovery plan follows the proposed dual stage recovery process. First, PBM enforces appropriate policies (Table 2,P1-3) and a short-term solution is used to minimize disruption. Then ARP, through its interaction with KD, attempts to discover a long-term solution to recover from the fault. The topology for the described scenario is shown in Fig. 2.

4.1   Automated Recovery Using Outbound TE Algorithm

Based on the proposed architecture, the first step after a failure is detected is to react with a short-term solution to minimize disruption. This solution is preplanned by executing an EP selection algorithm in advance and storing its output as policies on the Policy Repository. The algorithm's output is based on a generated synthetic inter-domain traffic matrix. The traffic matrix consists

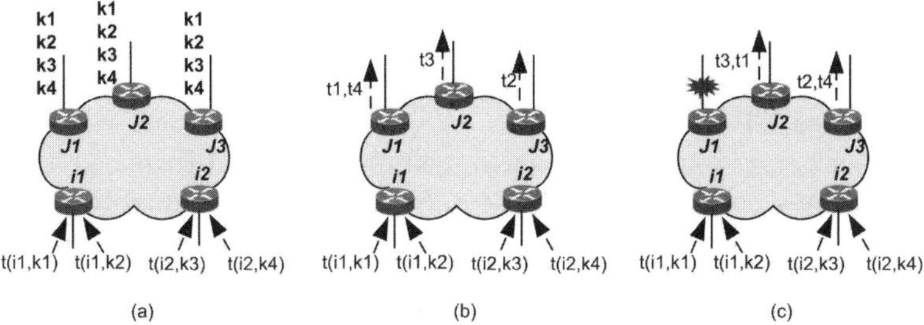

Fig. 2. Scenario Topology: (a) EP selection problem inputs, (b) PrimaryEgressPoint selection, (c) BackupEgressPoint selection if j1 fails

Table 1. Assignment of Primary and Backup Egress Point selection

Prefix	Primary	Backup		
		if J1 fails	if J2 fails	if J3 fails
k1	J1	J2	J1	J1
k2	J3	J3	J3	J2
k3	J2	J2	J3	J2
k4	J1	J3	J1	J1

of a set of inter-domain traffic flows that originates from each ingress point towards each of the considered destination prefixes. Each inter-domain traffic flow is associated with a randomly generated bandwidth demand according to uniform distribution. We use a sample topology and traffic flow to demonstrate the applicability of our recovery methodology. Details about the algorithm and evaluation results can be found in [5].

For a better understanding of our EP selection algorithm, we provide an example in Fig. 2. Figure2(a) illustrates the inputs for the EP selection problem, comprising ingress routers i1 and i2, EP j1, j2 and j3, inter-domain traffic demands $t1 = t(i1, k1)$, $t2 = t(i1, k2)$, $t3 = t(i2, k3)$ and $t4 = t(i2, k4)$. The destination prefixes k1, k2, k3 and k4 that can each be reached through all the three EP are also shown. Recall that the task of the EP selection problem is to determine, for each destination prefix, both a PrimaryEgressPoint to be used under no failure and a BackupEgressPoint to be used when its PrimaryEgressPoint has failed. Figure2(b) shows a potential solution of PrimaryEgressPoint selection, where t1 and t4 reach their destination prefix k1 and k4 respectively through EP j1, t2 reaches its destination prefix k2 through EP j3 and t3 reaches its destination prefix k3 through EP j2. This assignment corresponds to Table 1 column 2. In addition, Figure2(c) illustrates a potential solution of BackupEgressPoint selection when EP j1 has failed. As shown, t1 has been re-assigned to EP j2 to reach k1 and t4 has been re-assigned to EP j3 to reach k4 as their BackupEgressPoint. This assignment corresponds to Table 1 column 3 and according to the high-level goal, this solution achieves inter-domain link load balancing. To implement this solution, e.g. for prefix k1 the largest value of BGP local-preference, e.g. 100, should be assigned to its selected PrimaryEgressPoint (i.e. EP j1), the second largest value, e.g. 80, should be assigned to its selected BackupEgressPoint (i.e. EP j2) and any BGP local-preference value less than 80, e.g. 50, can be assigned to the remained EP (i.e. EP j3).Also for prefix k4 the largest value of BGP local-preference, e.g. 100, should be assigned to its selected PrimaryEgressPoint (i.e. EP j1), the second largest value, e.g. 80, should be assigned to its selected BackupEgressPoint (i.e. EP j3) and any BGP local-preference value less than 80, e.g. 50, can be assigned to the remained EP (i.e. EP j2).Moreover since the other two prefixes reachable through j1 (i.e. k2 and k3) are assigned to j1 for neither Primary nor Backup, their BGP local preference should be any value less than 80 e.g. 50. Table 2 shows the assignment of BGP local-preference setting

Table 2. Local-pref setting and policies for prefixes on Egress Points

Egress Point	Prefix	BGP local preference	Policies (Event==setupEP()
J1			*if* (EP==j1)
	k1	100	*then*[(set-local-pref(k1)=Prim-val)
	k2	50	(set-local-pref(k2)=Low-val)
	k3	50	(set-local-pref(k3)=Low-val)
	k4	100	(set-local-pref(k4)=Prim-val)][*P1*]
J2			*if* (EP==j2)
	k1	80	*then*[(set-local-pref(k1)=Back-val)
	k2	80	(set-local-pref(k2)=Back-val)
	k3	100	(set-local-pref(k3)=Prim-val)
	k4	50	(set-local-pref(k4)=Low-val)][*P2*]
J3			*if* (EP==j3)
	k1	50	*then*[(set-local-pref(k1)=Low-val)
	k2	100	(set-local-pref(k2)=Prim-val)
	k3	80	(set-local-pref(k3)=Back-val)
	k4	80	(set-local-pref(k4)=Back-val)][*P2*]
Initial configuration policy			
Event==BGP-conf			
if (-)			
then [(set-local-prefs([Prim-val,Back-val,Low-val],[100,80,50]))			
,gen-event-setupEP(j1,j2,j3)] [P0]			

for prefixes k1 to k4 on all EPs. These configuration settings are enforced on the EPs by their PEP based on policies (P1,P2,P3). An initial configuration policy (P0) is used by the network administrator, to configure the proper values for BGP local-preference. The benefit of combining a TE algorithm with a PBM approach is the creation of a flexible management environment able to quickly react to failures. In parallel, our framework automatically works to recover from the failure and recovery policies are used as input to the ARP subsystem. With the cooperation of KD, ARP outputs a new recovery plan that PBM can enforce to the network and reinstate normal operation.

4.2 Automated Recovery Using Planning Algorithm

To show how the planning and knowledge discovery subsystems collaborate, we present here an example based on the aforementioned border router (EP) failure scenario. The objective of collaboration between the two subsystems is to produce long-term fault recovery solutions.

After the router failure is recognized, the first stage recovery procedure is activated in order to sustain the current traffic and minimize the disruption of the failure. Whereas such a solution can be regarded as a short-term measure, a long-term recovery measure is still needed to completely recover from the failure and reinstate normal operation.

Algo. 1: Automated Planning	**Algo. 2:** Action Optimization
Input: O: set of actions	Input: C: set of retrieved cases c_i;
s_0, g: initial state, goal state	R, τ: request with symptoms r_j, threshold
Output: π sequence of actions	Output: σ optimal set of actions
1 $s \leftarrow s_0$	1 $\Sigma \leftarrow \emptyset$
2 $\pi \leftarrow \emptyset$	2 $\Sigma^* \leftarrow \emptyset$
3 **while** True **do**	3 **for each** $c_i \in C$ & $r_j \in R$ **do**
4 **if** s satisfies g **then**	4 $\sigma \leftarrow \{a | a \in c_i$ & a satisfies any $r_j \in R\}$
5 **return** π	5 $\Sigma \leftarrow \Sigma \cup \sigma$
6 $A \leftarrow \{a | a \in O$ & precond(a) true in $s\}$	6 **while** True **do**
7 applicable $\leftarrow A$	7 **for each** $\sigma \in \Sigma$ **do**
8 **if** applicable$= \emptyset$ **then**	8 evaluate $f(\sigma)$
9 **return** failure	9 **if** σ is optimal **then**
10 choose $a \in$ applicable	10 **return** σ
11 $s \leftarrow \gamma(s, a)$	11 $\Sigma^* \leftarrow \{\sigma | \sigma \in \Sigma$ & $f(\sigma) > \tau \}$
12 $\pi \leftarrow \pi.a$	12 $\Sigma \leftarrow \{\sigma | \sigma$ generalized by σ^* & $\sigma^* \in \Sigma^*\}$

The long-term recovery process is activated by the reports from then monitoring component. The domain analysis module analyzes the monitoring report and extract the current global state. The current global state includes the information on the impacted component and other relevant information. Note that the granularity of monitoring information will affect the later planning process. For example, a report states *The primary router is impacted by failure and it has OS version 2.3* will be more useful for planner to compose a better plan than just states *The primary router is impacted.* The global states are represented by the set of predicates.

After the failure source is known, the domain analysis module dispatches a search request to KD in order to find possible resolution steps to recover the component. KD collects solutions from various sources, then runs the reasoning engine on the retrieved solutions before returning the proposed actions to the analysis module. The reasoning engine uses the optimization technique based on the GA algorithm to provide an optimal set of actions, see Algo. 2. The discovered recovery actions have to be translated into a planning-specific language. For example, if a recovery action involves upgrading the router OS, this action could be described in PDDL [8] as:

```
(:action fetch_update
    :parameters(?r - router ?p - patch ?cv - currentversion
                ?nv - latest version )
    :precondition( and ( (failed ?r) (patch_at ?r ?p ?cv)
                  ( < (?cv ?nv) ) ) )
    :effect( and ( (updated ?r ?nv ?p) (= (?cv ?nv) ) ) ) )
```

The **parameter** field denotes which parameters are needed for this action. The field **precondition** describes the conditions, under which the **fetch_update** action could be applied. The **effect** field denotes the consequence of this action, i.e. how this action is going to effect the global state. The question mark denotes the variables. The initial state, goal state and recovery options formulate a planning domain. The automated planner operates on the planning domain for one or more feasible plans. The planning algorithm[9] is described by Algo. 1. Note that only those actions ($a \in O$) which cause state changes and the current state *s* are considered as parameters of γ function in this algorithm, events are left out for the sake of simplicity.

Recovery actions are selected based on their preconditions and current global state. Each action leads the current global state into a new state, this iteration finishes when the new state equals goal state. The generated plan is a sequence of actions which transit the initial state into the goal state.

5   Related Work

The study of Mark et al. [10] has proposed an automatic system for finding known software problems. The system matches the symptoms of the current problems with the symptom database to find the closest matches. The matching algorithm is designed to work with structured symptoms that contain program call stack, not arbitrary data. The recent study of Stefania et al. [11] has proposed a CBR system for self-healing in software systems. The description of the system lacks some details. Any case is represented in features which contain binary and symbolic values. Cases are retrieved by using the k-NN algorithm; where the similarity distance function evaluates case features with the corresponding weight values, but the weight function for features is not provided. The system mainly depends on the retrieval process to classify problems.

Policy-Based Management (PBM) simplifies the complex management tasks of large scale systems, since high-level policies monitor the network and automatically enforce appropriate actions [4,12,13]. Industry and PBM have been closely related in autonomic computing and self-management approaches [14]. The main advantage which makes a policy-based system attractive is the functionality to add controlled programmability in the management system without compromising its overall security and integrity. Policies can be viewed as the means to extend the functionality of a system dynamically and in real time in combination with its pre-existing hard-wired management logic [4,13]. Policies are introduced to the system and parameterized in real time, based on management goals and gathered information. Policy decisions generate appropriate actions on the fly to realize and enforce those goals.

Outbound inter-Autonomous System (AS) Traffic Engineering [5,6,1] is a set of techniques for controlling inter-AS traffic exiting an AS by assigning the traffic to the best egress points (i.e. routers or links from which the traffic is forwarded to adjacent ASes towards destinations. The general problem formulation of outbound TE is: given the network topology, BGP routing information and inter-domain Traffic Matrix (TM), determine the best Egress Point (EP) for each traffic demand so as to optimize the overall network performance,such as inter-AS link load balancing [1].

Srivastava et al. [15] discussed the feasibility and theoretical aspects on using planning methods in autonomic computing. They concluded that automated planning is an evolutionary next step for autonomic systems that possess the self-managing capabilities. Kephart [14] addresses in his paper the challenges of using AI-based planning methods to the autonomic computing. Arshad et al.

[16] presented a planning based recovery system for distributed system. However the proposed approach has several disadvantages; e.g. the recovery knowledge elicitation is not considered and lack of details in many aspects of applying automated planning methods in fault recovery.

6   Conclusion

Motivated by the need for an efficient fault recovery management, we have presented our initial efforts towards an integrated architecture. By combining the strengths of three paradigms: Automated Recovery Planning, Knowledge Discovery and Policy-based Management, we attempt to provide an automated framework. We have demonstrated a dual stage recovery process based on a case study of border router (EP) failure, aiming to maintain optimized configuration of outbound inter-domain traffic and quickly reinstate normal operation.

Beyond initial architecture design, we intent to investigate further interactions among subsystems and define generic and reusable interfaces. This will allow the extension of the architecture to a variety of case studies. We will aim to increase the automation of recovery and plan execution, thus minimizing human intervention and recovery times. Our future work will focus on intelligent planning algorithms that will combine system knowledge and business goals, aiming to gradually migrate to fully automated fault recovery management.

Acknowledgments. The work reported in this paper is supported by the EC IST-EMANICS Network of Excellence (#26854).

References

1. Bressoud, T., Rastogi, R., Smith, M.: Optimal configuration for bgp route selection. In: Proc. IEEE INFOCOM (2003)
2. Aamodt, A., Plaza, E.: Case-based reasoning: foundational issues, methodological variations, and system approaches. AI Communications 7(1), 39–59 (1994)
3. Tran, H.M., Schönwälder, J.: Distributed Case-Based Reasoning for Fault Management. In: Proc. 1st International Conference on Autonomous Infrastructure, Management and Security, pp. 200–203. Springer, Heidelberg (2007)
4. Verma, D.C.: Simplifying network administration using policy-based management. IEEE Network 16(2) (2002)
5. Amin, M., Ho, K., Howarth, M., Pavlou, G.: An integrated network management framework for inter-domain outbound traffic engineering. In: Helmy, A., Jennings, B., Murphy, L., Pfeifer, T. (eds.) MMNS 2006. LNCS, vol. 4267, pp. 208–222. Springer, Heidelberg (2006)
6. Feamster, N., Borkenhagen, J., Rexford, J.: Guidelines for interdomain traffic engineering. SIGCOMM Comput. Commun. Rev. 33(5), 19–30 (2003)
7. Tran, H.M., Schönwälder, J.: Heuristic Search using a Feedback Scheme in Unstructured Peer-to-Peer Networks. In: Proc. 5th International Workshop on Databases, Information Systems and P2P Computing. Springer, Heidelberg (2007)
8. McDermott, D., et al.: Pddl - the planning domain definition language (1998)

9. Nau, D., Traverso, P., Ghallab, M.: Automated Planning - Theory and Practic. Morgan Kaufmann, San Francisco (2004)
10. Brodie, M., Ma, S., Lohman, G., Syeda-Mahmood, T., Mignet, L., Modani, N., Champlin, J., Sohn, P.: Quickly finding known software problems via automated symptom matching. In: Proc. 2nd International Conference on Automatic Computing, Washington, DC, USA, pp. 101–110. IEEE Computer Society Press, Los Alamitos (2005)
11. Montani, S., Anglano, C.: Case-based reasoning for autonomous service failure diagnosis and remediation in software systems. In: Proc. 8th European Conference on Case-Based Reasoning, pp. 489–503. Springer, Heidelberg (2006)
12. Hadjiantonis, A.M., Charalambides, M., Pavlou, G.: A policy-based approach for managing ubiquitous networks in urban spaces. In: Proc. IEEE International Conference on Communications (ICC 2007) (2007)
13. Flegkas, P., Trimintzios, P., Pavlou, G.: A policy-based quality of service management system for ip diffserv networks. IEEE Network 16(2) (2002)
14. Kephart, J.O.: Research challenges of autonomic computing. In: Proc. 27th International Conference on Software Engineering (ICSE 2005). ACM, New York (2005)
15. Srivastava, B., Kambhampati, S.: The case for automated planning in autonomic computing. IEEE, Los Alamitos (2005)
16. Arshad, N., Heimbigner, D., Wolf, A.L.: A planning based approach to failure recovery in distributed systems. In: Proc. 1st ACM SIGSOFT workshop on Self-managed systems, pp. 8–12. ACM, New York (2004)

RLTE: Reinforcement Learning for Traffic-Engineering

Erik Einhorn and Andreas Mitschele-Thiel

Technical University Ilmenau,
Integrated Hardware and Software Systems Group,
98684 Ilmenau, Germany
{erik.einhorn,mitsch}@tu-ilmenau.de

Abstract. Quality of service (QoS) is gaining more and more importance in today's networks. We present a fully decentralized and self-organizing approach for QoS routing and Traffic Engineering in connection oriented networks, e.g. MPLS networks. Based on reinforcement learning the algorithm learns the optimal routing policy for incoming connection requests while minimizing the blocking probability. In contrast to other approaches our method does not rely on predefined paths or LSPs and is able to optimize the network utilization in the presence of multiple QoS restrictions like bandwidth and delay. Moreover, no additional signaling overhead is required. Using an adaptive neural vector quantization technique for clustering the state space a considerable speed-up of learning the routing policy can be achieved. In different experiments we are able to show that our approach performs better than classical approaches like Widest Shortest Path routing (WSP).

1 Introduction

NETWORK traffic has become very versatile within the last few years. Each network application makes different demands on the underlying network infrastructure. Streaming Video on Demand (VoD) for instance requires a high bandwidth while for Voice over IP (VoIP) a small delay is more important. The ability to guarantee certain network parameters like bandwidth, delay, jitter, loss or availability usually is referred to as Quality of Service (QoS). However, most networks are still IP-based. Since IP is a connectionless protocol, IP packets do not use specific paths between two communicating endpoints. This results in unpredictable QoS in a best-effort network. In contrast, the connection oriented Multiprotocol Label Switching (MPLS) standard [1] allows a better control for traffic routing and Traffic Engineering [2]. Traffic Engineering decides how to map the traffic requirements to the physical network in order to optimize the whole network resource utilization [3].

However, the problem of optimal routing in the presence of multiple independent QoS requirements is known to be NP-hard [4]. Therefore, heuristic or approximation algorithms are applied to solve this problem. The most often used algorithm for routing LSPs is the Min-Hop-Algorithm [5]. From all possible paths

D. Hausheer and J. Schönwälder (Eds.): AIMS 2008, LNCS 5127, pp. 120–133, 2008.

between a source and a destination of a connection that fulfill the desired QoS constraints, the one with the least number of links is chosen. This behavior often results in bottlenecks and consequently connection requests are rejected although other parts of the network still have enough resources available. The widest-shortest path routing (WSP) [6] tries to solve this problem by choosing the path with the largest residual bandwidth from all possible paths for a connection. Thus, it avoids the usage of heavily loaded links. One major drawback of this approach is the necessity for each node to have global knowledge about the current load situation of the network. It therefore imposes an additional signaling and information flooding overhead on the network. A more sophisticated technique is used for the Minimum Interference Routing Algorithms MIRA [4], LMIR [7] and DORA [8]. The main idea of these approaches is to route an incoming connection along a path that least interferes with other routes that may be crucial to satisfy possible future requests. For this purpose, MIRA manages a list of critical links and tries to preserve these links as long as alternative paths are available. As a consequence, some links will remain underutilized leading to a suboptimal usage of the network resources. Similar to WSP these approaches also require global knowledge about the network state and therefore increase the additional signaling overhead.

Apart from the aforementioned "classical" routing approaches a couple of alternative methods have been researched recently. Some of them use Ant Colony Optimization (ACO) for QoS routing in MPLS networks [9]. Other researchers have studied how reinforcement learning can be used to solve routing problems. In contrast to the classical routing protocols based on heuristics, where the routing decision is explicitly specified within the routing algorithm, routing approaches based on reinforcement learning are able to learn the routing on their own depending on a feedback given by the network. At first reinforcement learning was used for routing in IP networks. Boyan and Littman [10] use Q-Learning to learn an optimal routing policy that minimizes the delay for packet transmissions. In [11] the optimal policy is obtained using policy search via gradient ascent. In both publications the authors are able to show that their approach performs better than shortest path routing. In [3] a "Distributed Adaptive Path Selection Scheme" for MPLS networks (MAPS) is presented. This method uses reinforcement learning agents located at the networks edge routers. In comparison with Widest Shortest Path (WSP) MAPS significantly reduces the blocking probability without having global knowledge about the core network and hence without additional signaling traffic. However, the approach only focuses on the selection of predefined paths. Feasible paths must be established using a k-shortest path algorithm beforehand [3]. Therefore, the approach can not dynamically react to changes in the network topology or link failures. The same disadvantage applies for an approach that is described in [12] and that uses reinforcement learning to obtain a set of load-sharing factors for optimal load-sharing among different LSPs in MPLS networks.

In this paper we present a novel QoS routing algorithm based on reinforcement learning which can be used in MPLS networks or other connection oriented networks that support QoS. In contrast to the approaches mentioned above our algorithm does not rely on predefined paths. Instead it learns feasible paths depending on the connection requests while minimizing the blocking probability. Our approach is distributed and does neither need any global knowledge about the network topology nor the current load situation of the whole network, instead local information is sufficient. Moreover, it does not only consider the bandwidth as one QoS parameter as most of the above approaches do, instead it also takes delay restrictions into account. Furthermore, our approach should attain the following goals that we consider important:

1. Compared to heuristic routing approaches like WSP that rely on global knowledge about the network, the approach should at least achieve a similar performance although it uses local information only.
2. The learning time - a major drawback of reinforcement learning approaches - must be reduced to a minimum and should scale well if the network size increases.
3. The approach must be able to react dynamically on changes in the network topology such as link and node failures.

The organization of this paper is as follows. In the next sections the QoS routing problem is defined. Thereafter our algorithm is described in detail and we present techniques to achieve the goals mentioned above. In section 4 we present the results of different simulations and experiments before we conclude the paper with a summary.

2   Problem Definition

We consider a network described by the quadruple $G = (N, L, B, D)$ consisting of a set of n nodes (routers) $N = \{1, \ldots, n\}$ and a set of m links (arcs) $L = \{1, \ldots, m\}$. Furthermore, the functions $B : L \mapsto \mathbb{R}$ and $D : L \mapsto \mathbb{R}$ assign a certain bandwidth $B(l)$ and some delay $D(l)$ to each link $l \in L$. In contrast to other approaches, neither bandwidth nor delay need to be integers. Furthermore, it is not necessary to distinguish between ingress, egress and core routers. In our approach each node $n \in N$ actually can be sending or receiving node. However, if the algorithm is used in MPLS networks, the differentiation between core and edge routers will be induced by the MPLS network.

Let $R = (r_0, \ldots, r_i, \ldots)$ be the (generally infinite) sequence of connection requests that arrive at the network, where each connection request or call $c_i = (d, \beta, \delta)$ sent from some source node $s \in N$ specifies the address of the destination node $d \in N$ a bandwidth demand $\beta \in \mathbb{R}$ and a maximum delay restriction $\delta \in \mathbb{R}$ for the desired connection. Since we do not rely on predefined paths or LSPs, the QoS routing algorithm has to find an appropriate path $p = (l_1, l_2, \ldots, l_k)$ of adjacent links that connects the ingress-egress pair (s, d) and that fulfills the desired QoS requirements, namely:

1. the required bandwidth demand:

$$\min_{i=1}^{k} \check{B}(l_i) \geq \beta$$

2. the maximal delay constraint:

$$\sum_{i=1}^{k} D(l_i) \leq \delta$$

where $\check{B}(l_i)$ denotes the residual bandwidth that is available for link l_i. If the path does not satisfy these constraints, the connection request is blocked and rejected. Otherwise the connection can be established and the required bandwidth is reserved. The resources remain reserved until the connection is released.

The concern of an optimal QoS routing approach now is to find an optimal routing policy that maximizes the number of accepted requests or in other words minimizes the blocking probability of the connection requests.

3   Reinforcement Learning for Traffic Engineering

Our reinforcement learning approach for finding such a routing policy is based on the SARSA-Learning algorithm [13], a variant of Q-Learning. Since SARSA-Learning and Q-Learning are quite common techniques for reinforcement learning they will not be described in detail here. Further information can be found in [13,14] and [15].

Reinforcement learning (RL) is one type of Machine Learning, where a RL-agent learns how to map situations (states) to actions to maximize a numerical reward signal [15]. This mapping of states S to actions A is called *policy* π : $S \mapsto A$. In SARSA- and Q-Learning the policy can be determined by learning an *action-value function* $Q : S \times A \mapsto \mathbb{R}$. This function gives the expected reward $Q(s_t, a_t)$ for starting in state $s_t \in S$, taking action $a_t \in A$ and then following policy π thereafter. For choosing action a_t in state s_t the RL-agent receives a reward r_t and attains to state s_{t+1} where it again selects some action a_{t+1}. The SARSA-Learning rule will then update the Q-values as follows [15]:

$$Q(s_t, a_t) \leftarrow (1 - \beta)Q(s_t, a_t) + \beta\left[r_t + \gamma Q(s_{t+1}, a_{t+1})\right] \tag{1}$$

where the β notates the learning rate and γ the so-called discount rate.

For selecting an action the *softmax action selection* can be used. It is based on the Boltzmann distribution and chooses a certain action $a \in A$ in state s with the following probability:

$$P(a) = \frac{\exp\left(\frac{Q(s,a)}{T}\right)}{\sum_{b \in A} \exp\left(\frac{Q(s,b)}{T}\right)} \tag{2}$$

where the parameter T is called the *temperature*. High temperatures cause the actions to be all (nearly) equi-probable [15]. For low temperatures the softmax action selection converges to a greedy action selection that chooses the action with the highest Q-value. In our experiments a temperature between 0.1 and 0.25 gives the best results.

Overview

In our approach we use one RL-agent $\mathfrak{A}$ that is distributed over the network. Each node (router) $i \in N$ of the network contains one part $\mathfrak{A}_i$ of the RL-agent that is responsible for learning just one part $\pi_i : S_i \mapsto A_i$ of the whole policy π. Without loss of generality we assume that adjacent links for each node i are renumbered in ascending order from 1 to m_i. Moreover, we assume that the partial agent $\mathfrak{A}_i$ at each node is able to measure the residual bandwidth $\check{B}(j)$ and the delay $D(j)$ of each adjacent link $j \in (1, \ldots, m_i)$.

For signaling the connection requests and for establishing the paths we use a simple protocol similar to RSVP-TE [16]. The protocol uses a few messages only, that are described afterwards. For each incoming connection request a PATHRESV-message is sent hop-by-hop to the destination node. Analogous to [10] the partial RL-agent $\mathfrak{A}_i$ at each node $i \in N$ has to select one of its outgoing links for forwarding the PATHRESV-message to the next hop (see Fig. 1a). If the PATHRESV-message successfully arrives at its targeted node, a RESVACC-message is sent back to the sender of the connection request. This RESVACC-message takes the reverse path as the corresponding PATHRESV-message and reserves the required resources for the connection. Additionally, this RESVACC-message contains a positive reward, that reinforces the action each partial agent has selected (see Fig. 1b). If one of the demanded QoS parameters could not be satisfied at some chosen link, a RESVREJECT-message is sent back to the sender taking the reverse path of the PATHRESV-message. In contrast to the RESVACC-message the RESVREJECT-message contains a negative reward. By including the reward into the necessary signaling messages any additional signaling overhead is avoided.

In a real world implementation the reward can be easily included as additional object into the signaling messages of the RSVP-TE protocol.

Detailed Algorithm

As stated above, for each incoming PATHRESV-message containing a connection request $c_t = (d, \beta, \delta)$ the agent $\mathfrak{A}_i$ chooses one of its outgoing links as action $a_t \in A_i$ using the softmax action selection. Since the links are numbered in ascending order, the discrete action space can be described by $A_i = \{1, \ldots, m_i\}$. The action selection depends on the current state of the agent, which is determined by taking the destination address d, the bandwidth requirement β and the delay restriction δ of the connection request $c_t = (d, \beta, \delta)$ into account. Additionally, the residual bandwidths $\check{B}(1), \ldots, \check{B}(m_i)$ of all of adjacent links are measured. Using this information a state vector $\mathbf{s}_t \in S_i$ is formed:

$$\mathbf{s}_t = \left(d, \beta, \delta, \check{B}(1), \ldots, \check{B}(m_i) \right)^\top \tag{3}$$

Please note, that no global knowledge about the network state is required here at all.

Each partial RL-agent keeps track of its chosen action and the state which led to that action. This allows the agent to associate the correct state-action pairs to the delayed reward that arrives later with the corresponding RESVACC-message or RESVREJECT-message. However, although the RL-agent attains a new state with each arriving connection request, it does not need to maintain all of these states. In practice the state and the chosen action can be recovered when the RESVACC-message or RESVREJECT-message returns to the agent and do not need to be stored inside of each agent.

Corresponding to the selected action a_t the PATHRESV-message is forwarded along the chosen link j to the next node $k \in N$ and its partial agent $\mathfrak{A}_k$. Thereby, the delay restriction δ of the PATHRESV-message is decreased by the delay $D(j)$ of the chosen link. The connection request that arrives at node k can then be described by $c_{t+1} = (d, \beta, \delta - D(j))$. It will bring the distributed agent $\mathfrak{A}$ into a new state $\mathbf{s}_{t+1}$ that is observed by the partial agent $\mathfrak{A}_k$ according to equation 3 again using local information only. Once more an action a_{t+1} is chosen for forwarding the message (see Fig. 1a).

Using this forwarding mechanism the PATHRESV-message will finally arrive at its destination node d. As described earlier a RESVACC-message containing a positive reward r will be sent back to the sender taking the reverse path as the corresponding PATHRESV-message.

The PATHRESV-message is also used by each partial agent to propagate its Q-value $Q(\mathbf{s}, a)$ of the observed state s and the taken action a back to the previous node on the path. Therefore, each partial agent that was involved in forwarding the PATHRESV-message will receive a corresponding RESVACC-message containing a reward r_t and the Q-value $Q(\mathbf{s}_{t+1}, a_{t+1})$ of its subsequent node (see Fig. 1b). Together with its own state $\mathbf{s}_t$ and its chosen action a_t each agent is able to adapt its own Q-values $Q(\mathbf{s}_t, a_t)$ according to the SARSA-learning rule using equation 1. The same mechanism is used for RESVREJECT-messages, that are

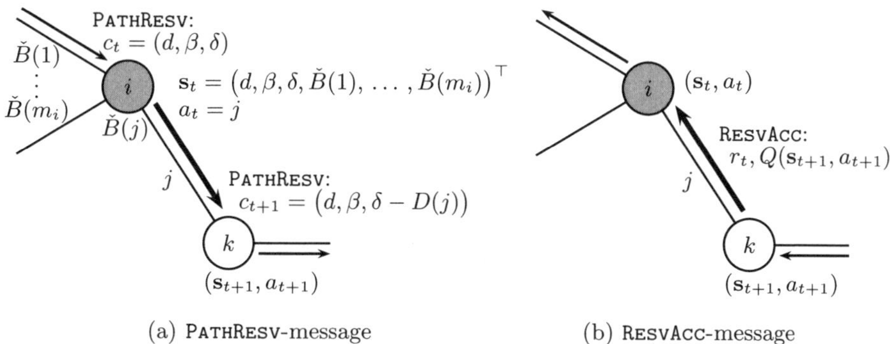

(a) PATHRESV-message   (b) RESVACC-message

Fig. 1. a: The PATHRESV-message containing the connection request c_t is sent hop-by-hop towards the destination node. Depending on the current state $\mathbf{s}_t$ each partial agent selects one link as action a_t for forwarding the message. This will bring the distributed agent into the state $\mathbf{s}_{t+1}$. Each state is observed by only taking local information of the concerning partial agent into account. **b:** The RESVACC-message takes the reverse path as the PATHRESV-message and carries the reinforcement r_t and the Q-value $Q(\mathbf{s}_{t+1}, a_{t+1})$ of each subsequent node.

sent if one of the QoS restriction is not satisfied during the path selection. The only difference is that RESVREJECT-messages contain a negative reward. If the RESVREJECT-message finally arrives at the sending node it depends on the upper layer protocols if the request is sent again or definitely rejected.

At the beginning all Q-values are initialized uniformly and each partial RL agent begins its learning *tabula rasa*. Hence, for the first arising connection requests the routing in the network will be random. After some time of exploration and learning the agents will develop a feasible routing policy and perform better with each new request. In section 4 we show that the required time for learning is acceptable in comparison to classical routing approaches.

State Space Clustering

Most related RL-based algorithms for routing [3][10] use a table where the Q-values of each state-action pair are stored. However, since our state space is continuous we cannot use such a table based Q-Learning approach here. Additionally, as seen in equation 3 each state consists of $3 + m$ elements, where m is the number of outgoing links. Hence, the dimension of the state space can become very high depending on the valency of the nodes. This would lead to a slow convergence while learning the optimal routing policy. Therefore, we have to apply some kind of state space clustering.

Similar to [17] we use a variant of Growing Neural Gas (GNG) [18] as adaptive neural vector quantization technique for optimal clustering of the continuous state space. The neurons of the GNG store the Q-values for the actions of the action space A and they are associated to reference vectors in the state space, which can be regarded as positions of the corresponding neurons. Depending on its position $\mathbf{w}_n \in S$ each neuron n is responsible for a certain (voronoi) region in the state space S.

To obtain the Q-value $Q(\mathbf{s}, a)$ for a given state-action pair $(\mathbf{s}, a)$ the best-matching neuron of the GNG is chosen, i.e. the neuron whose reference vector $\mathbf{w}_n$ has the smallest Euclidean distance to the state $\mathbf{s}$. Finally, the desired Q-value stored in the best-matching neuron can be obtained as seen in Fig. 2.

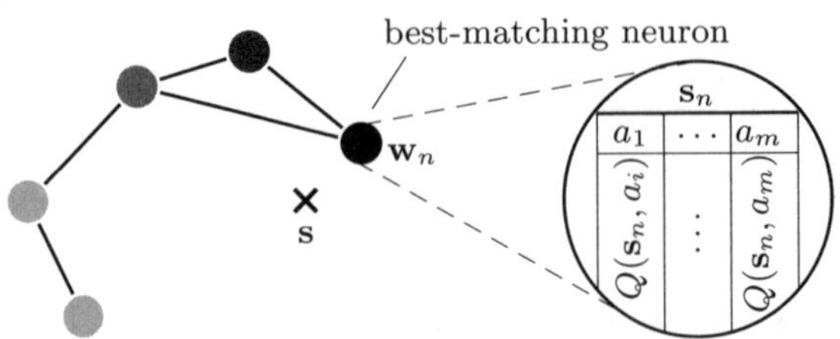

Fig. 2. The state space is clustered using a GNG *(left)*. For obtaining a certain Q-value $Q(\mathbf{s}, a)$ the best-matching neuron for the state $\mathbf{s}$ is chosen. It contains a table with the corresponding Q-values for each action *(right)*. The different colors indicate, that the Q-values of neurons close to the state $\mathbf{s}$ are adapted more than the values of neurons in larger distances during a learning step.

Similar to [19] we insert new neurons if the distance between the best-matching neuron and the state exceeds a certain threshold. While learning we do not only adapt the Q-values of the best-matching neuron according to the learning rule in equation 1 but also the Q-values of the topologically neighboring neurons, since they represent similar states. Neurons close to the best-matching neuron are adapted more (with a higher learning rate) than neurons in larger distances. This method is elaborately described in [17] and increases the speed of learning dramatically as shown in section 4.

In our approach each partial RL-agent at each node uses its own GNG to cluster its state space. However, the destination address of the connection request that is specified in each state is not yet included into the state space clustering. Hence, our next step will be to perform the clustering over the whole state space comprising the destination addresses. To do so a topological addressing scheme and an appropriate metric must be chosen. If two nodes in the network were separated by one or a few hops only, the metric should yield a small distance for the addresses of both nodes. If - on the other hand - both nodes were separated by many hops, the metric should yield a big distance for the addresses. Geographic addressing [20,21] and the Euclidean distance e.g. satisfy these requirements but do not support mobility. Therefore, we have to research other suitable addressing schemes first.

Convergence of the Approach

It has been shown that Q-Learning will converge to an optimal policy if certain conditions are met. One requirement is that the whole decision process must be Markovian and fully observable. However, we apply SARSA-Learning although we are dealing with a Markovian decision process that is only partial observable (POMDP). Additionally, our state space is not discrete. Therefore, the convergence to the optimal policy can not be guaranteed. Nevertheless, in section 4 we show that our approach at least converges to a routing policy that performs better than classical approaches.

Analysis of the Runtime and Learning Complexity

One advantage of our reinforcement learning routing approach is that it is computationally inexpensive and does not require extensive router hardware. The whole algorithm is distributed over all routers of the network. For a connection request each router merely has to look up some Q-values, select an action and adapt the Q-values afterwards. The adaption according to the learning rule is cheap. The look-up of the Q-values is more expensive since it includes finding the best-matching neuron in the GNG which usually is done by a *nearest neighbor search*. For a very high dimensional state space an *approximate nearest neighbor search* based on *locality sensitive hashing* is suitable. Using this method a query time of $O(dN^{O(1)})$ [22] can be achieved, where N is the number of neurons in the GNG and $d = 3 + m$ is the dimension of the state space of a router with m outgoing links as described earlier. Obviously, the runtime does neither depend on the number of routers nor the amount of links, therefore the runtime complexity of each routing decision is $O(1)$ in terms of the network size.

Unfortunately, the biggest problem of reinforcement learning based approaches is the required time for learning a feasible routing policy if they are applied to a completely new network without any prior knowledge. As stated earlier the routing will be random during the bootstrapping at the beginning and many requests will not reach their destination, which results in a high blocking rate. Depending on the network layout the number of possible paths between a source-destination pair that have to be learned by each RL-agent usually increases with the square of the distance between both nodes. Therefore, the learning complexity and time for bootstrapping increases according to $O(r^2)$ where r is the average number of hops between all source-destination pairs. However, in practice the size of networks increases incrementally by adding few new nodes or links only and hence the learning complexity will be smaller.

4   Results

We have implemented our QoS-routing approach and simulated the packet flow, the routing and the resource reservation using a discrete event network simulator. In our tests we have compared our RLTE approach to the often used Widest-Shortest-Path routing (WSP). As mentioned in section 1 WSP chooses the path with the largest residual bandwidth from all possible shortest paths between a source and a destination. Additionally, WSP needs information about the current load situation of the network. If a high refresh rate for updating this information is chosen, WSP will perform better but imposes a larger signaling overhead and vice versa. In the following results we have used different refresh intervals for WSP.

Since bandwidth and delay are inherently guaranteed by the routing approach, the blocking probability, i.e. the ratio of blocked and requested connections within a certain period of time, remains the most important measure of the routing performance. In the first test we have compared the blocking probability of our approach with WSP. We have used the topology shown in Fig.3a. It

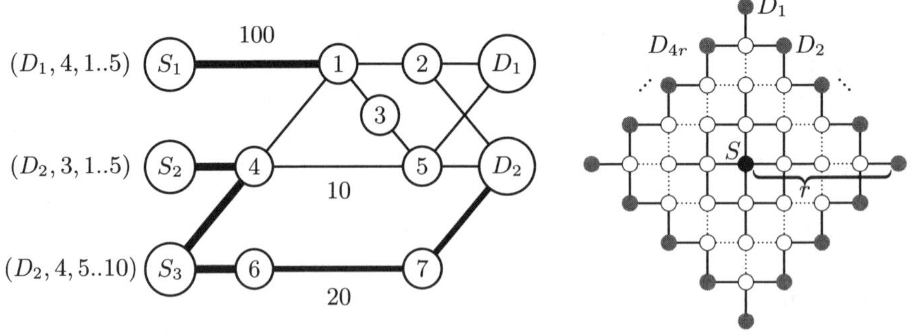

(a) topology for the first test   (b) regular meshed topology

Fig. 3. Different topologies that were used in our experiments. The radius r of the right topology can be changed to simulate different network sizes.

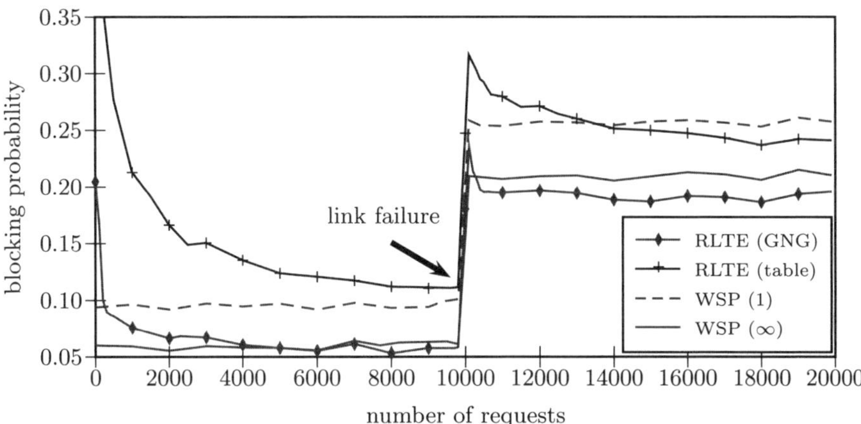

Fig. 4. Comparison of the blocking probability of our RLTE approach with WSP. State space clustering using GNGs speeds up the learning and our approach even performs better than WSP with an unlimited refresh rate. It is also able to handle link failures autonomously.

consists of three source nodes $S_1, \ldots, S_3$ and two destination nodes D_1, D_2. The bandwidth of the outgoing links of the source nodes is set to 100 in order to avoid bottlenecks here. The bandwidth for the two links between the nodes $6, 7$ and D_2 is set to 20, the bandwidth of the remaining links is set to 10. The delay of all links is 1. Each source node continuously sends connection requests to the destination nodes. The connection requests are shown left to each source node. S_1 for example requests connections to node D_1 with an allowed delay of 4 and a randomly chosen bandwidth between 1 and 5. The arrival and the holding time of new connections is exponentially distributed using an arrival rate of $\lambda = 1$ and an average holding time of $\mu = 1$, i.e. on average each source node requests one connection within one time unit and a duration of one time unit.

In Fig.4 our RLTE approach is compared to WSP. The blue graph marked with $+$'s shows the blocking probability for RLTE with table based SARSA-learning and the red graph marked with diamonds shows RLTE with state space clustering using GNGs. In both cases the RL-agents start without any knowledge about the network and cause high blocking rates at the beginning. It is obvious that the clustering dramatically speeds up the learning and reduces the blocking probability much faster. Hence, a smaller number of learning steps and therefore less connection requests are necessary to achieve a certain blocking probability.

After 100 requests and learning steps our proposed RLTE(GNG) approach performs better than WSP(1) with a refresh interval of 1 time unit (dashed green graph). Remember that the average inter arrival time of new requests also is 1 time unit, hence for WSP(1) the refreshs occur as often as connection requests and would impose a lot of signaling overhead in practice. After 4000 learning steps our approach even performs better than WSP(∞) with an infinite refresh rate, where each WSP router has access to the current global network state at any time (solid green graph). Of course an infinite refresh rate for WSP is not possible in practice. After 10000 requests we simulate a link failure between node 6 and 7. Hence the connections must be rerouted. Right after the link failure the blocking probability of our RLTE approach increases slightly more than WSP(∞) but stays below WSP(1). A few requests later our approach has adapted its routing policy and again performs better than WSP(∞). These tests reveal that our approach can achieve the goals mentioned in the introduction to this paper and performs better than WSP although it uses local information only. Moreover in comparison to WSP the learning time of RLTE is not a problem. 100 request for bootstrapping are negligible and right after the link failure RLTE still performs better than WSP(1).

To ascertain the impact of the network size on the required learning time during the bootstrapping phase we use the meshed network topology shown in Fig.3b. The radius r of the network graph can be varied in order to change the number of nodes and links in the network. Both increase with the square of the radius. At the center of the network we placed a source node S that continuously sends connection requests to a randomly chosen destination node D_i at the periphery of the network. The bandwidth of all links is 10.0. It is the advantage of the chosen network topology that all shortest paths between the source node and the destination nodes have the same length r. Therefore, at least r routing decisions have to be made in order to establish a connection between the source S and one destination D_i. For this network we use an arrival rate of $\lambda = 1$ and an average holding time of $\mu = 2$. As QoS parameters for each connection the allowed delay is set to $r + 2$ to allow slightly longer paths than the shortest ones and the required bandwidth is again chosen randomly between 1.0 and 5.0.

In Fig.5 the number of learning epochs and requests, that are needed to achieve a blocking probability below a certain value, is plotted against the radius of the network. As reference we use the blocking probability that WSP(1) and WSP(10) with a refresh time of 1 and 10 respectively produce in the network with the given size.   The solid red graph for example shows, that after 200 learning epochs RLTE(GNG) starts to perform better than WSP with a refresh time of 10 for a network with the radius $r = 4$. Again RLTE with state space clustering outperforms its table based variant. As expected at the end of the previous section the learning time increases with the square of the network size. To reduce the learning complexity we have tried a different way for initializing the Q-values. Instead of initializing the RL-agents tabula rasa, we provide them with rudimental information about the network topology. At the beginning of each simulation we apply the Dijkstra algorithm to compute the distance to each destination node and initialize the Q-values of each agent depending on these distances. The two green graphs marked with circles show that this significantly reduces the necessary time for learning.

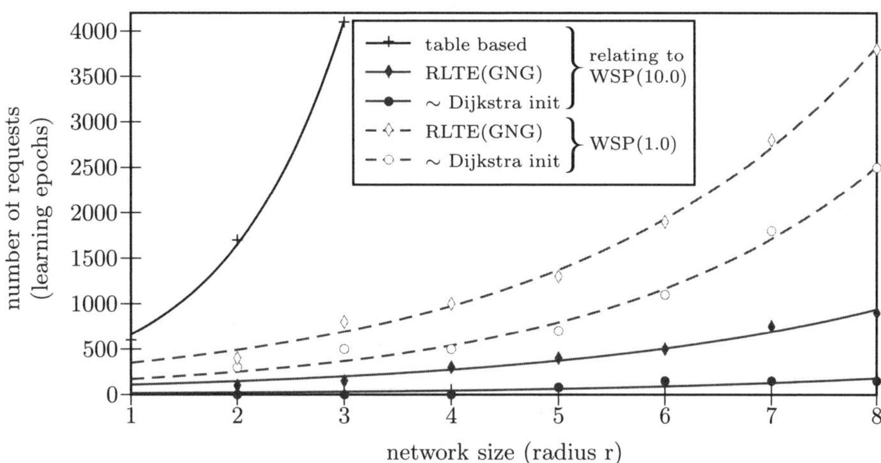

Fig. 5. Influence of the network size on the necessary time for learning. The graphs show the required learning epochs to achieve at least the same blocking probability as WSP with an refresh interval of 1 (dashed lines) and 10 (solid lines). Again state space clustering reduces the learning time (red graphs). Initialization of the Q-values using the Dijkstra algorithm leads to a further reduction (green graphs).

5   Conclusion and Future Work

In this paper we have presented a novel distributed and self-organized QoS routing approach that is based on reinforcement learning. In contrast to other reinforcement learning approaches our algorithm combines optimal path planing and path selection and does not depend on predefined paths.

We have shown that our approach performs better than WSP routing although it uses local information only and therefore does not impose any additional signaling overhead. Since we use a constant learning rate to achieve life long learning our algorithm is able to react to link failures. While learning an alternative optimal routing policy a differentiation between local and global repair is no longer necessary. For the first time we have applied state space clustering in a routing approach based on reinforcement learning. We have shown that the state space clustering dramatically reduces the necessary time for learning the routing policy to an acceptable level. This is essential if reinforcement learning approaches shall be used for routing in "real life" networks. Moreover, we have shown that the time for learning can be reduced if the RL agents are initialized using basic network knowledge obtained by applying the Dijkstra algorithm.

In the future the learning time can be further decreased if a topological addressing scheme is used and the destination addresses are included in the clustering as described in section 3. Then each agent will automatically cluster the destination addresses and build its own optimal subnets. In contrast to most other approaches our algorithm already takes two QoS constraints into account. However, it can easily be extended to handle much more parameters just by expanding the state vector. In addition to the continuous state space a continuous action space can be used. This will allow the agents to learn an optimal load sharing policy. Thus, routing approaches based on reinforcement learning have a high potential and provide many more possibilities that are worth to be investigated in future research.

References

1. Rosen, E., Viswanathan, A., Callon, R.: Multiprotocol Label Switching Architecture. IETF RFC 3031 (2001)
2. Evans, J., Filsfils, C.: Deploying IP and MPLS QoS for Multiservice Networks: Theory and Practice. Morgan Kaufmann, San Francisco (2007)
3. Liu, Y., Tham, C., Hui, T.: MAPS: A Localized and Distributed Adaptive Path Selection Scheme in MPLS Networks. In: Proc. of IEEE Workshop on High Performance Switching and Routing (HPSR) (2003)
4. Kodialam, M.S., Lakshman, T.V.: Minimum Interference Routing with Applications to MPLS Traffic Engineering. In: INFOCOM, vol. (2), pp. 884–893 (2000)
5. Awduche, D., Malcolm, J., Agogbua, J., O'Dell, M., McManus, J.: Requirements for Traffic Engineering Over MPLS. IETF RFC 2702 (1999)
6. Guerin, R., Williams, D., Orda, A.: QoS Routing Mechanisms and OSPF Extensions. In: Proc. of Globecom (1997)
7. Figueiredo, G., da Fonseca, N., Monteiro, J.A.S.: A minimum interference routing algorithm. In: Proc. of the IEEE Int. Conf. on Communications, vol. 4 (2004)
8. Boutaba, R., Szeto, W., Iraqi, Y.: DORA: Efficient Routing for MPLS Traffic Engineering. Journal of Network and Systems Management, Special Issue on Internet Traffic Engineering and Management 10, 309–325 (2002)
9. Carrillo, L., Marzo, J., Vilà, P., Fàbrega, L., Guadall, C.: A Quality of Service Routing Scheme for Packet Switched Networks based on Ant Colony Behavior. In: Proc. of the Int. Symposium on Performance Evaluation of Computer and Telecommunication Systems, pp. 637–641 (2004)
10. Boyan, J.A., Littman, M.L.: Packet Routing in Dynamically Changing Networks: A Reinforcement Learning Approach. In: Advances in Neural Information Processing Systems, vol. 6, pp. 671–678. Morgan Kaufmann Publishers, Inc., San Francisco (1994)
11. Peshkin, L., Savova, V.: Reinforcement learning for adaptive routing. In: Proc. of the International Joint Conference on Neural Networks (IJCNN) (2002)
12. Heidari, F., Mannor, S., Mason, L.: Reinforcement learning-based load shared sequential routing. In: Proc. of the IFIP Networking (2007)
13. Rummery, G.A., Niranjan, M.: On-line Q-learning using connectionist systems. Technical Report CUED/F-INFENG/TR 166, Cambridge University Engineering Department (1994)
14. Watkins, C.: Learning from Delayed Rewards. PhD thesis, King's College, Cambridge University, UK (1989)
15. Sutton, R., Barto, A.G.: Reinforcement Learning: An Introduction. MIT Press, Cambridge (1998)
16. Awduche, D., Berger, L., Gan, D., Li, T., Srinivasan, V., Swallow, G.: RSVP-TE: Extensions to RSVP for LSP Tunnels. IETF RFC 3209 (2001)
17. Gross, H.M., Stephan, V., Krabbes, M.: A Neural Field Approach to Topological Reinforcement Learning in Continuous Action Spaces. In: Proc. 1998 IEEE World Congress on Computational Intelligence WCCI 1998, pp. 1992–1997 (1998)

18. Fritzke, B.: A Growing Neural Gas Network Learns Topologies. In: Tesauro, G., Touretzky, D.S., Leen, T.K. (eds.) Advances in Neural Information Processing Systems 7, pp. 625–632. MIT Press, Cambridge (1995)
19. Marsland, S., Shapiro, J., Nehmzow, U.: A self-organising network that grows when required. Neural Networks 15, 1041–1058 (2002)
20. Watteyne, T., Auge-Blum, I., Dohler, M., Barthel, D.: Geographic Forwarding in Wireless Sensor Networks with Loose Position-Awareness. In: Personal, Indoor and Mobile Radio Communications, PIMRC, pp. 1–5 (2007)
21. Navas, J.C., Imielinski, T.: GeoCast – Geographic Addressing and Routing. In: Mobile Computing and Networking, pp. 66–76 (1997)
22. Andoni, A., Indyk, P.: Near-Optimal Hashing Algorithms for Approximate Nearest Neighbor in High Dimensions. In: 47th Annual IEEE Symposium on Foundations of Computer Science, FOCS 2006, pp. 459–468 (2006)

SNMP Trace Analysis Definitions

Gijs van den Broek[1], Jürgen Schönwälder[2], Aiko Pras[1], and Matúš Harvan[3]

[1] Computer Science, University of Twente, Netherlands
j.g.vandenbroek@student.utwente.nl,
a.pras@utwente.nl
[2] Computer Science, Jacobs University Bremen, Germany
j.schoenwaelder@jacobs-university.de
[3] Computer Science, ETH Zurich, Switzerland
mharvan@inf.ethz.ch

Abstract. The Network Management Research Group (NMRG) started an activity to collect traces of the Simple Network Management Protocol (SNMP) from operational networks. To analyze these traces, it is necessary to split potentially large traces into more manageable pieces that make it easier to deal with large data sets and simplify the analysis of the data. This document introduces some common definitions that have been found useful for implementing tools to support trace analysis.

Keywords: simple network management protocol, traffic modeling.

1 Introduction

The Simple Network Management Protocol (SMMP) was introduced in the late 1980s. Since then, several evolutionary protocol changes have taken place, resulting in the SNMP version 3 framework (SNMPv3), published as full standard in 2002 [1,2]. Extensive use of SNMP has led to significant practical experience by both network operators and researchers. However, up until now only little research has been done on characterizing and modeling SNMP traffic.

Since recently, network researchers are in the possession of network traces, including SNMP traces, captured on operational networks. The availability of SNMP traces enables research on characterizing and modeling real world SNMP traffic. Experience with SNMP traces has shown that traces must be large enough in order to make proper observations. A more detailed motivation for collecting SNMP traces and guidelines how to capture SNMP traces can be found in [3].

The analysis of large SNMP traces can take a large amount of processing time. Therefore, it is often desirable to focus the analysis on smaller, relevant sections of a trace. This in turn requires a proper way to identify these smaller sections of a trace. This document describes a number of identifiable sections within a trace which make specific research on these smaller sections more practical.

The rest of the paper is structured as follows. An overview of the definitions is given in the next section and subsequent sections define messages, traces, flows, slices, slice prefixes, and slice types. Related and future work is discussed before the paper concludes.

D. Hausheer and J. Schönwälder (Eds.): AIMS 2008, LNCS 5127, pp. 134–147, 2008.

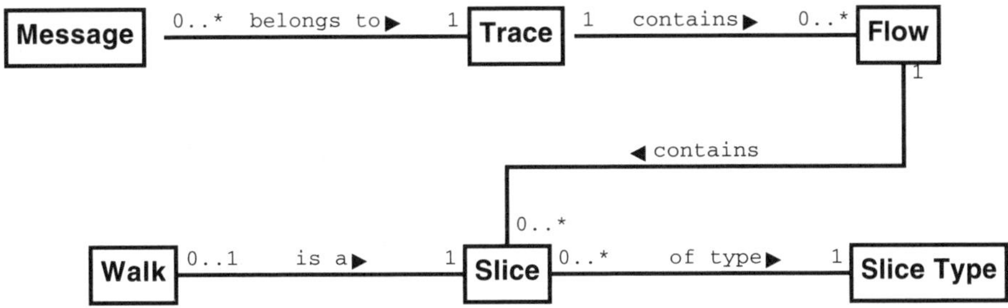

Fig. 1. Relationship between messages, traces, flows, slices and slice types

2   Overview

Fig. 1 shows the various entities associated with an SNMP trace and how they relate to each other.

The most central entity in Fig. 1 is an SNMP trace, consisting of a potentially large set of SNMP messages. An SNMP trace is the result of recording SNMP traffic on a specific network for a specific time duration. Such a trace may, depending on the number of hosts in the respective network, contain SNMP messages exchanged between possibly many different SNMP engines. The messages contained in a trace may be represented in different formats. For the purpose of this document, the simple comma separated values (CSV) format defined in [3] contains sufficient information to split a trace into smaller sections.

The SNMP messages belonging to an SNMP trace may have been exchanged between many different SNMP engines running on different hosts. Therefore, a first obvious way of separating a trace into smaller sets of SNMP messages is the separation of a trace into flows. Each flow contains only those SNMP messages of an SNMP trace that have been exchanged between two network layer endpoints. Such a separation may be necessary in case one wants to analyze specific SNMP traffic characteristics (e.g., number of agents managed by a management station) and wants to rule out network endpoint specific behaviour (e.g., different SNMP management stations may have different polling configurations).

Flows within traces can still be quite large in terms of the number of messages they contain. Therefore, it may be necessary to split a flow into even smaller sections called slices. A slice contains all SNMP messages of a given flow that are related to each other in time and referenced information. Splitting a flow into slices makes it possible to separate SNMP messages within traces that belong to each other.

For example, a slice may contain the SNMP messages exchanged between an agent and a manager, which polls that agent in a single polling instance. The manager may be configured to poll that agent every once in a while. If the requested information from the agent remains unchanged, then the respective slices of SNMP traffic occurring between this manager and agent will be highly comparable. In such a case the slices will be of the same slice type. Similar slices will thus be considered of the same slice type and incomparable slices will not be of the same slice type.

Besides the fact that each slice is of specific slice type, slices can also be of a specific form with respect to the messages encompassing a slice. For example, slices containing a sequence of linked GetNext or GetBulk requests are commonly called an SNMP walk. Note that only a subset of all slices will be walks.

3   Messages

SNMP messages carry protocol data units (PDUs) realizing a small set of well defined protocol operations [4]. The PDUs can be used to classify SNMP messages.

Notation 1. *The properties of an SNMP message M are denoted as follows:*

$$
\begin{aligned}
M.type &= \text{operation type of message } M \text{ (get, getnext, ...)} \\
M.class &= \text{class of message } M \text{ (according to RFC 3411)} \\
M.tsrc &= \text{transport layer source endpoint of message } M \\
M.tdst &= \text{transport layer destination endpoint of message } M \\
M.nsrc &= \text{network layer source endpoint of message } M \\
M.ndst &= \text{network layer destination endpoint of message } M \\
M.reqid &= \text{request identifier of message } M \\
M.time &= \text{capture timestamp of message } M \\
M.oids &= \text{OIDs listed in varbind list of message } M \\
M.values &= \text{values listed in varbind list of message } M
\end{aligned}
$$

These properties of an SNMP message can be easily extracted from the exchange formats defined in [3].

Definition 1. *This definition establishes the following message classes:*

1. *A **read request message** is a message M containing a PDU of type Get-Request, GetNextRequest, or GetBulkRequest.*
2. *A **write request message** is a message M containing a PDU of type Set-Request.*
3. *A **notification request message** is a message M containing a PDU of type InformRequest.*
4. *A **notification message** is a message M containing a PDU of type Trap or InformRequest.*
5. *A **request message** is a message M which is either a read request message, a write request message, or a notification request message.*
6. *A **response message** is a message M containing a PDU of type Response or of type Report.*
7. *A **non-response message** is a message M which is either a read request message, a write request message, or a notification message.*
8. *A **command message** is a message M which is either a read request message or a write request message.*

Report messages are treated like Response messages since the SNMPv3 specifications currently use Report messages only as an error reporting mechanism, always triggered by the processing of some request messages. In case future SNMP versions or extensions use Report messages without having a request triggering the generation of Report messages, we may have to revisit the definition above.

Definition 2. *A set of* **command group messages** *consists of all messages M satisfying either of the following two conditions:*

1. *M is a command message*
2. *M is a response message and there exists a command message C such that the following holds:*

$$M.reqid = C.reqid$$
$$M.tdst = C.tsrc$$
$$M.tsrc = C.tdst$$
$$(M.time - C.time) < t$$

The parameter t defines a maximum timeout for response messages.

This definition requires that the response message originates from the transport endpoint over which the request message has been received. This is not strictly required by SNMP transport mappings and in particular the UDP transport mapping allows to send responses from different transport endpoints. While sending response messages from a different transport endpoint is legal, it is also considered bad practice causing interoperability problems, since some management systems do not accept such messages.

It was decided to require matching transport endpoints since doing so significantly simplifies the procedures below and avoids accidentally confusing requests and responses. Implementations responding from different transport endpoints will lead to (a) a larger number of requests without related responses (and likely no retries) and (b) a similarly large number of responses without a matching request. If such behavior can be detected, the traces should be investigated and if needed the transport endpoints corrected. The requirement for matching transport endpoints only affects request / response pairs. It is perfectly fine for a manager to use different transport layer endpoints in different polling instances, or even different operations (i.e., slices) within the same polling instance.

Definition 3. *A set of* **notification group messages** *consists of all messages M satisfying either of the following two conditions:*

1. *M is a notification message*
2. *M is a response message and there exists a notification request message N such that the following holds:*

$$M.reqid = N.reqid$$
$$M.tdst = N.tsrc$$
$$M.tsrc = N.tdst$$
$$(M.time - N.time) < t$$

The parameter t defines a maximum timeout for response messages.

This definition again requires matching transport endpoints for notification group messages.

4   Traces and Flows

Traces are (large) sets of SNMP messages that are the result of recording SNMP traffic using a single traffic recording unit (e.g., using tcpdump) on a network segment carrying traffic of one or more managers and agents. Traces being used in the remainder of this document may be altered as a result of anonymization, which may result in some message information loss.

Traces may contain SNMP messages that have been exchanged between possibly many different network layer endpoints. One way of making an initial separation of such a trace into more manageable pieces is by splitting the messages into flows. Each flow contains only messages that have occurred between two network layer endpoints.

4.1   Trace and Flow Definition

Definition 4. *An SNMP **trace** (or short "trace") T is an ordered set of zero or more SNMP messages M. All messages M in T are chronologically ordered according to the capture timestamp M.time.*

Definition 5. *A **flow** F is the set of messages of an SNMP trace T with the following properties:*

1. *All response messages originate from a single network endpoint.*
2. *All non-response messages originate from a single network endpoint.*
3. *All messages are either command group messages with parameter t or notification group messages with parameter t.*

Parameter t defines the maximum timeout for response messages. The value of t should be chosen such that only response messages to the respective non-response messages are considered part of the same flow. Analysis of a large number of traces shows that 25 seconds is a proper default value for t.

It is possible that response messages of a trace cannot be classified to belong to any flow. This can happen if request messages triggering the response messages were not recorded (for example due to asymmetric routing), or because response messages were originating from transport endpoints different from the endpoint used to receive the associated request message.

This definition of a flow indicates that it can be either unidirectional (e.g., a manager sending non-response messages to a non-responding agent), or bidirectional (e.g., a manager reading a table from an agent). This is different from other flow definitions, like the NetFlow definition [5]. The flow definition is mostly consistent with the definition of an SNMP flow used in [6]. The difference is that the tool used to generate the data reported in [6] did only require that the network layer source endpoint of the response messages matches the destination network layer endpoint of the associated request messages.

Definition 6. *A **flow initiator** is the network layer endpoint of the two endpoints involved in a flow, which is responsible for sending the first non-response message.*

Notation 2. *The properties of a flow F are denoted as follows:*
$F.type$ $= type$ *of the flow F (command/notification)*
$F.nsrc$ $= network$ *layer source endpoint of F*
$F.ndst$ $= network$ *layer destination endpoint of F*
$F.start = timestamp$ *of the first message in F*
$F.end$ $= timestamp$ *of the last message in F*
$F.init$ $= initiator$ *of the flow F*
$F.t$ $= parameter\ t$ *of F (maximum timeout for response messages)*

Subsequently, flows containing only command group messages are called command flows. Similarly, flows containing only notification group messages are called notification flows.

4.2 Trace and Flow Example

Table 1 shows an example of a trace consisting of SNMP messages that were exchanged between different network layer endpoints. The network layer endpoints are represented by A, B, C and D.

The first flow F_1 consists of SNMP messages that have been exchanged between network layer endpoints A and B, where all response messages originate from B and all non-response messages originate from A. The minimum value of parameter t for this flow is 0.07 seconds, since that is the longest time between a request and its subsequent response message.

The second flow F_2 contains SNMP messages exchanged between network layer endpoints C and D, where all response messages originate from D and all non-response messages originate from C. The minimum value of parameter t for this flow is 0.04 seconds.

The third flow F_3 contains the remaining SNMP messages of the trace that occurred between network layer endpoints C and D. In this case the non-response message originates from D. There is no parameter t applicable to this flow, because there are no response messages.

Table 1. Example trace containing two flows

Message	Time [s]	Direction	Type	Reqid	Flow
0	0.00	$A \to B$	GetNext	1	F_1
1	0.04	$C \to D$	Get	10	F_2
2	0.05	$B \to A$	Response	1	F_1
3	0.08	$D \to C$	Response	10	F_2
4	0.11	$A \to B$	GetNext	2	F_1
5	0.15	$B \to A$	Response	2	F_1
6	0.18	$A \to B$	GetNext	3	F_1
7	0.22	$D \to C$	Trap	14	F_3
8	0.25	$B \to A$	Response	3	F_1

5   Slices

Flows can still contain a large amount of SNMP messages. A flow should therefore be split up into even smaller sets of messages. One way of identifying meaningful subsets of messages of a flow would be by considering the behavior of managers and agents. In the case of managers, they are usually configured to perform regular polling instances. In such a polling instance, the manager might poll a number of agents. Since a flow contains only the messages exchanged between two network layer endpoints, a flow therefore probably consists of only a subset of the messages that are part of a polling instance. So, one option of finding smaller, meaningful subsets of messages within flows, would be by looking for messages that belong to a particular polling instance. Such a smaller set of messages is called a slice.

5.1   Slice Definition

Definition 7. *A **slice** S with parameter e is a subset of messages in a flow F for which the following properties hold:*

1. *All messages are exchanged between the same two transport endpoints (a single transport endpoint pair).*
2. *All non-response messages must have a PDU of the same type.*
3. *All messages with a PDU of type Get, Set, Trap, or Inform must contain the same set of OIDs.*
4. *Each GetNext or GetBulk message must either contain the same set of OIDs as the preceding request or it must be linked to a response of the last previously answered request (i.e., the request must contain at least one OID that has been contained in the (repeater) varbind list of a preceding response message of the last answered request message).*
5. *All Response messages must follow a previous request message that is part of the same slice.*
6. *For any two subsequent non-response messages Q1 and Q2 with $Q1.time < Q2.time$, the following condition must hold:*

$$(Q2.time - Q1.time) < e$$

The first item in the slice definition requires that the messages of a single slice are exchanged between a single transport layer endpoint pair. This is different from the flow definition, which requires a single network layer endpoint pair. The choice of looking at the transport layer endpoints in the case of slices is based on the assumption that, for instance, multiple managers and agents might be operating from the same respective network layer endpoint. Another assumption is that a manager and an agent will only use a single transport layer endpoint respectively when they communicate for the duration of a slice (or even a polling instance). A previous section already mentioned some issues when a manager or agent uses different transport layer endpoints within a single polling instance.

The parameter e defines the maximum time between two non-response messages that belong to a slice. This parameter should be chosen such that unrelated non-response messages within a flow are not considered to be of the same slice. Unrelated non-response messages are those that, for instance, belong to different polling instances. The parameter e should therefore be larger than the retransmission interval in order to keep retransmissions within a slice and smaller than the polling interval used by the slice initiator.

The value of parameter e might be closely related to parameter t of the respective flow the slice is part of. For instance, if parameter e is very large, than t is also likely to be very large and vice versa. Also, if parameter e is very small, then t is probably also very small. However, it is not possible to strictly state that e and t are always closely related to each other, because parameter e is specific for a slice. This is in contrast with parameter t which is specific for a much larger set of messages, a flow.

Definition 8. *A **slice initiator** is one of the two transport layer endpoints involved in a slice, which is responsible for sending the chronologically first non-response message.*

Notation 3. *The properties of a slice S are denoted as follows:*

$S.type$ $= type\ of\ non\text{-}response\ messages\ in\ S$
$S.tsrc$ $= transport\ layer\ endpoint\ of\ initiator\ of\ S$
$S.tdst$ $= transport\ layer\ endpoint\ of\ non\text{-}initiator\ of\ S$
$S.start$ $= timestamp\ of\ the\ chronologically\ first\ message\ in\ S$
$S.end$ $= timestamp\ of\ the\ chronologically\ last\ message\ in\ S$
$S.init$ $= initiator\ of\ slice\ S$
$S.e$ $= parameter\ e\ of\ S\ (maximum\ time\ between\ two$
          $non\text{-}response\ messages)$

5.2   Slice Example

Table 2 shows an example of a flow containing messages exchanged between transport layer endpoints A, B, and C. Considering the timing of the messages, a proper value of e should be $0.14 \leq e \leq 299.82$ seconds. Such a value for parameter e will separate the flow into two apparent polling instances, which each contain the same set of messages.

The first slice S_1 consists of a Get request and its subsequent response. A similar request is recorded later in slice S_3 but since we assume e as discussed above, the slices S_1 and S_3 are distinct. The second slice S_2 also contains a Get request and its subsequent response. This slice is different from S_1 since a different OID is requested. The slice S_4 consists of a Set request that has not been answered. (A potential reason is that the SNMP engine listening on the transport layer endpoint C did not grant write access and dropped the message.)

The last slice S_5 contains a sequence of linked GetNext requests. The GetNext request message 10 is likely a retransmission of the GetNext request message 9. This example demonstrates that retransmissions are recorded in the slice that contains the original request.

Table 2. Example flow containing three slices

Message	Time [s]	Direction	Type	Reqid	OIDs	Slice
0	0.00	$A \rightarrow B$	Get	1	alpha.1	S_1
1	0.06	$B \rightarrow A$	Response	1	alpha.1	S_1
2	0.12	$A \rightarrow B$	Get	2	beta.1	S_2
3	0.17	$B \rightarrow A$	Response	2	beta.1	S_2
4	300.00	$A \rightarrow B$	Get	3	alpha.1	S_3
5	300.05	$B \rightarrow C$	Set	4	gamma.1	S_4
6	300.07	$B \rightarrow A$	Response	3	alpha.1	S_3
7	300.14	$A \rightarrow B$	GetNext	5	beta	S_5
8	300.19	$B \rightarrow A$	Response	5	beta.1	S_5
9	300.32	$A \rightarrow B$	GetNext	6	beta.1	S_5
10	300.52	$A \rightarrow B$	GetNext	7	beta.1	S_5
11	300.58	$B \rightarrow A$	Response	7	delta.1	S_5

6   Slice Signature and Prefix

As noted in the beginning of this document, it is desirable that slices can be tested for equality/comparability. This is where the slice prefix comes in. The slice prefix provides one of the means to compare slices. Using the slice prefix and a few other parameters of a number of slices, one can determine which slices should be considered "equal" and which of them are incomparable. This will assist in the process of finding potentially other relations.

The slice prefix is a set of OIDs. This set is constructed from the messages that make up a single slice. So, for example, a slice that is the result of a manager requesting the contents of a particular table (with OID alpha) on an agent using a simple single varbind GetNext walk, starting at the table OID alpha, shall yield a slice prefix which consists of the OID alpha.

Because the aim is to compare various slices using the slice prefix (along some other characteristics of a slice), this implicitly suggests the need to know whether a number of slices are the result of the same behaviour (i.e., specific configuration) of the initiating party of these slices. For example, one may want to know whether a number of slices that involve a single manager and a single agent were the result of just one specific configuration of that manager. Multiple slices, that may all be initiated by that same manager and each slice possibly occurred in different polling instances, may in fact be the result of the same specific configuration of that particular manager. So, since in this case the specific configuration of the manager is only relevant for determining the behaviour, the slice prefix should be constructed based on OIDs in messages originating from that manager only. More generally, only the messages within slices that are sent by the initiating party (the non-response messages) are considered for the determination of the respective slice prefix of a slice.

6.1   Slice Signature and Prefix Definition

Definition 9. *A **slice signature** S.sig of a slice S is a set of OIDs derived from the OIDs contained in the non-response messages of a slice. Let $r(S)$ denote the set of response messages of slice S and $n(S)$ the set of non-response messages of S. Then the set S.sig consists of the following OIDs:*

$$
S.sig = \begin{cases} \bigcup_{n \in n(S)} (n.oids) \setminus \bigcup_{r \in r(S)} (r.oid) & S.type \text{ is GetNext or GetBulk} \\[2ex] \bigcup_{n \in n(S)} (n.oids) & \text{otherwise} \end{cases}
$$

The slice signature summarizes which OIDs have been carried in a slice and is straightforward to compute. However, there are situations in some GetNext or GetBulk sequences where the signature might contain some unwanted OIDs as will be demonstrated by an example below.

To further condense signatures, it is necessary to introduce a prefix relationship between OIDs. This prefix relationship can then be used to reduce a slice signature to a slice prefix.

Definition 10. *An OID $a = a_1.a_2...a_n$ is a **prefix** of OID $b = b_1.b_2...b_m$ if and only if $n < m$ and $a_i = b_i$ for $1 \leq i \leq n$.*

Definition 11. *The **slice prefix** S.slice is the set of all OIDs o in S.sig for which there is no p in S.sig such that p is a prefix of o.*

6.2   Slice Signature and Prefix Example

The following example demonstrates how a slice prefix is determined. Consider the case that a single manager A is set to poll a specific agent B. Manager A is programmed to retrieve some values from B. A single slice may contain the messages shown in Table 3.

The slice shown in Table 3 has a number of interesting properties. First, not all columns in the retrieved table have an equal length. Second, the manager

Table 3. Example slice for calculating a slice prefix

Message	Direction	Type	OIDs
0	$A \to B$	GetNext	alpha, beta
1	$B \to A$	Response	alpha.1, beta.1
2	$A \to B$	GetNext	alpha.1, beta.1
3	$B \to A$	Response	alpha.2, beta.3
4	$A \to B$	GetNext	beta.2, alpha.2, sysUpTime
5	$B \to A$	Response	beta.3, alpha.3, sysUpTime.0
6	$A \to B$	GetNext	beta.3, alpha.3
7	$B \to A$	Response	gamma.1, alpha.4
8	$A \to B$	GetNext	alpha.4
9	$B \to A$	Response	delta.1

is set to request the sysUpTime on an irregular basis (i.e., every few requests). Third, the manager attempts to fill "holes" in the table and finally the order of referenced OIDs in GetNext messages changes.

All of these properties do not influence the process for determining the slice signature. The slice prefix is constructed as follows:

1. The union of all OIDs in non-response messages is the following set:

$$N = \{ \ alpha, beta, alpha.1, beta.1, beta.2, alpha.2,$$
$$sysUpTime, beta.3, alpha.3, alpha.4 \ \}$$

2. The union of the OIDs in response messages is the following set:

$$R = \{ \ alpha.1, beta.1, alpha.2, beta.3, alpha.3,$$
$$sysUpTime.0, gamma.1, alpha.4, delta.1 \ \}$$

3. Subtracting the two sets results in the slice signature $S.sig$:

$$S.sig = N - R = \{ \ alpha, beta, beta.2, sysUpTime \ \}$$

The element beta.2 exists, because the manager was trying to fill a "hole" in a table. Since these "holes" reside in the tables on the agent side and may change dynamically, they do not really help in describing the behavior of the initiating party.

4. Since beta is a prefix of beta.2, the slice prefix becomes the following set:

$$S.prefix = \{ \ alpha, beta, sysUpTime \ \}$$

The slice prefix does not include beta.2 anymore and thus a manager retrieving the same columns alpha and beta with and without "holes" will produce slices with the same slice prefix.

7   Slice Types

As described previously, the slice type allows for comparing slices. This means that any number of slices that are of the same slice type may be considered an equivalence class and may therefore be considered to be the result of the same behaviour of the slice initiator.

7.1   Slice Type Definition

Definition 12. *Two slices A and B satisfy the binary **slice equivalence** relation $A \sim B$ if the following properties hold:*

1. *All messages in A and B have been exchanged between the same network layer endpoints.*
2. *All read request messages, write request messages, and notification messages in A and B originate from the same network layer endpoint.*

3. All non-response messages in A and B are of the same type.
4. The slices A and B have the same prefix, that is $A.prefix = B.prefix$.

It can be easily seen that the relation $\sim$ is reflexive, symmetric, and transitive and thus forms an equivalence relation between slices.

Definition 13. *Let S be a set of slices, then all slices in the equivalence class*

$$[A] = \{s \in S | s \sim A\}$$

*with $A \in S$, are of the same **slice type**.*

7.2   Slice Type Example

The flow shown in Table 4 contains two slices. The first slice S_1 contains messages that have been exchanged between transport layer endpoints A and B while the second slice S_2 contains messages that have been exchanged between transport layer endpoints C and D. However, the network layer endpoints of this slice are the same as the first slice and all non-response messages in both slices originate from the same network layer endpoint.

Table 4. Example for slice equivalence and slice types

Message	Direction	Type	OIDs	Slice
0	$A \to B$	GetNext	alpha, beta	S_1
1	$B \to A$	Response	alpha.1, beta.1	S_1
2	$A \to B$	GetNext	alpha.1, beta.1	S_1
3	$B \to A$	Response	alpha.2, beta.2	S_1
4	$A \to B$	GetNext	alpha.2, beta.2	S_1
5	$B \to A$	Response	gamma.1, delta.1	S_1
6	$C \to D$	GetNext	alpha, beta	S_2
7	$D \to C$	Response	alpha.1, beta.1	S_2
8	$C \to D$	GetNext	alpha.1, beta.1	S_2
9	$D \to C$	Response	gamme.1, delta.1	S_2

As can be verified easily, the slices S_1 and S_2 satisfy the slice equivalence relationship, that is $S_1 \sim S_2$ and they form an equivalence class under $\sim$, which we call a slice type.

8   Related and Future Work

The performance of SNMP has been the subject of several studies. Some papers such as [7,8] compare the performance of centralized SNMP management to distributed management approaches while other papers compare the performance of the SNMP protocol with middleware systems such as CORBA or Web Services [9,10,11]. The impact of security protocols on SNMP performance has been studied in [12,13,14]. Some authors have formulated models for the SNMP protocol [15,16].

All these studies have in common that they make assumptions how SNMP is used in practice, due to a lack of commonly accepted models how SNMP is used in practice. To address this issue, some researchers active in the Network Management Research Group (NMRG) of the Internet Research Task Force (IRTF) started an effort to collect traces from operational networks and to build the necessary tools to analyze them [3]. First results were published in [6] and it became clear that precise definitions of basic concepts, such as those provided in this paper, are needed in order to produce meaningful and comparable results. The authors are currently using and extending these definitions in order to study the periodicity of SNMP traffic [17] and table retrieval algorithms.

9 Conclusions

The analysis of SNMP traces requires a collection of common and precise definitions in order to establish a basis for producing meaningful and comparable results. This paper provides such a collection of basic definitions that have been developed over time and are also being reviewed and discussed within the NMRG of the IRTF. This paper is a condensed summary of a more detailed document [18] submitted to the NMRG and written to provide an early stable reference while the work in the NMRG continues and to foster discussion within the broader network management research community.

Acknowledgement

The work reported in this paper is supported by the EC IST-EMANICS Network of Excellence (#26854).

References

1. Case, J., Mundy, R., Partain, D., Stewart, B.: Introduction and Applicability Statements for Internet Standard Management Framework. RFC 3410, SNMP Research, Network Associates Laboratories, Ericsson (December 2002)
2. Harrington, D., Presuhn, R., Wijnen, B.: An Architecture for Describing Simple Network Management Protocol (SNMP) Management Frameworks. RFC 3411, Enterasys Networks, BMC Software, Lucent Technologies (December 2002)
3. Schönwälder, J.: SNMP Traffic Measurements and Trace Exchange Formats. Internet Draft (work in progress) <draft-irtf-nmrg-snmp-measure-04.txt>, Jacobs University Bremen (March 2008)
4. Presuhn, R.: Version 2 of the Protocol Operations for the Simple Network Management Protocol (SNMP). RFC 3416, BMC Software (December 2002)
5. Claise, B.: Cisco Systems NetFlow Services Export Version 9. RFC 3954, Cisco Systems (October 2004)
6. Schönwälder, J., Pras, A., Harvan, M., Schippers, J., van de Meent, R.: SNMP Traffic Analysis: Approaches, Tools, and First Results. In: Proc. 10th IFIP/IEEE International Symposium on Integrated Network Management (May 2007)

7. Zapf, M., Herrmann, K., Geihs, K.: Decentralized SNMP Management with Mobile Agents. In: Proc. 6th IFIP/IEEE International Symposium on Integrated Network Management, Boston, May 1999, pp. 623–635 (1999)
8. Fuggetta, A., Picco, G., Vigna, G.: Understanding Code Mobility. IEEE Transactions on Software Engineering 24(5), 342–361 (1998)
9. Gu, Q., Marshall, A.: Network Management Performance Analysis and Scalability Tests: SNMP vs. CORBA. In: Proc. 2004 IEEE/IFIP Network Operations and Management Symposium, Seoul, April 2004, pp. 701–714 (2004)
10. Pras, A., Drevers, T., van de Meent, R., Quartel, D.: Comparing the Performance of SNMP and Web Services based Management. IEEE Transactions on Network and Service Management 1(2) (November 2004)
11. Pavlou, G., Flegkas, P., Gouveris, S., Liotta, A.: On Management Technologies and the Potential of Web Services. IEEE Communications Magazine 42(7), 58–66 (2004)
12. Du, X., Shayman, M., Rozenblit, M.: Implementation and Performance Analysis of SNMP on a TLS/TCP Base. In: Proc. 7th IFIP/IEEE International Symposium on Integrated Network Management, Seattle, May 2001, pp. 453–466 (2001)
13. Corrente, A., Tura, L.: Security Performance Analysis of SNMPv3 with Respect to SNMPv2c. In: Proc. 2004 IEEE/IFIP Network Operations and Management Symposium, Seoul, April 2004, pp. 729–742 (2004)
14. Marinov, V., Schönwälder, J.: Performance Analysis of SNMP over SSH. In: State, R., van der Meer, S., O'Sullivan, D., Pfeifer, T. (eds.) DSOM 2006. LNCS, vol. 4269, pp. 25–36. Springer, Heidelberg (2006)
15. Pattinson, C.: A study of the behaviour of the simple network management protocol. In: Proc. 12th IFIP/IEEE Workshop on Distributed Systems: Operations and Management, Nancy (October 2001)
16. Chen, T., Liu, S.: A Model and Evaluation of Distributed Network Management Approaches. IEEE Journal on Selected Areas in Communications 20(4), 850–857 (2002)
17. van den Broek, J.G.: Periodicity of SNMP Traffic. BSc Thesis (August 2007)
18. van den Broek, J.G., Schönwälder, J., Pras, A., Harvan, M.: SNMP Trace Analysis Definitions. Internet Draft (work in progress) <draft-schoenw-nmrg-snmp-trace-definitions-02.txt>, University of Twente, Jacobs University Bremen, ETH Zurich (April 2008)

Dynamic Consistency Analysis for Convergent Operators

Alva L. Couch and Marc Chiarini

Tufts University, Medford, Massachusetts, USA
`alva.couch@cs.tufts.edu`, `marc.chiarini@tufts.edu`

Abstract. It has been shown that sets of convergent operators with a shared fixed point can simulate autonomic control mechanisms, but many questions remain about this management technique. We discuss how an autonomous agent can reason about whether its convergent operators share a fixed point with the operators of other agents. Using a concept of time based upon operator repetition, we show that a failure to achieve convergence within specific time limits can be used as a probabilistic indicator of inconsistencies in local policy. We describe a statistical inference technique that determines if an agent's promise strategy is feasible. The strengths of this technique are that it is both scale-invariant and exterior to the operators whose consistency is being evaluated.

1 Introduction

How does a configuration agent in a highly complex and distributed network reason about the workability of its choices? What reasoning techniques work best in a situation in which agents have only local information? What strategies other than global information exchange can help agents reason? We attack these questions in a novel way.

This paper arose from a question asked at AIMS 2007 by Jan Bergstra: "How can you be sure that your [operators are] consistent?". By this, he meant "logical consistency", i.e., that the goals of the operators cannot embody a contradiction. We thought about this question for some time, and then decided upon a novel response: *logical* consistency of operators is useless in a ubiquitous computing environment, and *statistical* notions of consistency make more sense and are more useful.

To start to understand what consistency might mean in a ubiquitous computing environment, we combine and expand two threads of prior work: convergent operators and self-organizing precedences.

An *operator* is a management operation on a host or network. A *convergent operator P* is an operator with the specific behavior that – when repeatedly applied to a host or network – modifies the host or network so that it exhibits a state in some known set S_P of desirable states. A convergent operator P is *idempotent* on states in its result set S_P, i.e., it does not change any state that

D. Hausheer and J. Schönwälder (Eds.): AIMS 2008, LNCS 5127, pp. 148–161, 2008.

is already considered desirable. Thus every $s \in S_P$ is a fixed point of P, i.e. $P(s) = s$, and every convergent operator is also a *fixed-point operator*.

Convergent operators can take many forms, e.g., one operator might prune disk space for users who are over quota, while another might act on process space to prune runaway processes, and a third might modify the number of threads in a web server to optimize response time.

Prior work shows that autonomic computing can be "approximated" by a collection of convergent operators applied repeatedly at random, provided that these operators all share some common fixed-point state [1]. Each operator – in effect – embodies its own isolated control loop, and the set of operators behaves like a composition of multiple control loops.

2 Operator Consistency

To understand what consistency might mean for a set of operators $\mathcal{O}$, we point out that the set of fixed points S_P of an operator P is a representation of the *policy* of P. While we might be accustomed to expressing policies as a set of logical rules R_P, the set of states S_P that happen to obey those rules is a reasonable (though more sizable) substitute. Two sets of rules R_P and R_Q are consistent if their structure does not contain a logical contradiction. By analogy, we define:

Definition 1. *Two operators P and Q are* consistent *if the intersection of their fixed point sets is nonempty.*

Note that trivially, operator consistency is equivalent with rule consistency, in the sense that states matching contradictory rules have no intersection, and vice-versa [1]. Likewise,

Definition 2. *A set of operators $\mathcal{O}$ is* consistent *if the intersection of all fixed point sets of operators in $\mathcal{O}$ is non-empty.*

One must also ensure that consistency is practical as well as theoretically possible:

Definition 3. *A set of operators $\mathcal{O}$ is* reachably consistent *(with respect to a set of baseline states $\mathcal{S}$) if, through random applications of operators in $\mathcal{O}$, starting at a state in $\mathcal{S}$, the operators always achieve a common fixed point.*

If all operators are at a fixed point, then clearly their policies do not contradict one another, so reachable consistency is a sufficient condition for logical consistency. The converse, however, is not true. There may be a consistent state that, though it be fixed for all operators, can never be achieved. Suppose, e.g., that one operator's policy is that the web server serves subdirectories of students' home directories, but that no operator exists to actually set up a web server. Then the desired state is consistent with that of other operators, but not reachably consistent, because no operator exists that can achieve that state.

---

[1] Expanded definitions of consistency are explored in [5].

This notion of consistency is reasonable for a small, known set of operators, but in a ubiquitous computing environment, with no true centralized control, there is no clear notion of which operators are active at a given time. The contents of $\mathcal{O}$ is a moving target. From the point of view of any specific agent, the total set of operators and policies in effect *cannot* be known, because any snapshot of that state could potentially have changed since the snapshot.

Thus the concept of logical consistency – while well-defined – is simply not very useful. A new notion of consistency is needed; one that is useful to an agent with incomplete knowledge of the space of operators and/or policies being enforced.

3   Operator Precedence

Convergent operators only work properly if the precedences between operators are satisfied. For example, one operator might mount a filesystem, while another might start a service depending upon that filesystem. We refer to an active operator whose preconditions are fulfilled as being *operative*; an active operator with at least one unmet precondition is *inoperative*.

The effects of operators often depend upon precedences between them. For example, consider operator O_1 that mounts a filesystem on a host, and operator O_2 that sets up a web service on that filesystem. These operators have a precedence relationship: O_1 must precede O_2. Once O_1 completes its task, it has no further effect unless some *other* entity unmounts the filesystem, in which case O_1 mounts it *again*. Thus the mounted filesystem is a *fixed point* of operator O_1. Once this fixed point is achieved, operator O_2 can achieve its fixed point and we conclude that the set $\{O_1, O_2\}$ has a fixed point as well. The result of both operators is an *emergent* fixed point that is fixed for both operators, but fixed in *different ways* for each operator. Thus each operator can be thought of as acting on an *aspect* of the network, and the composition of operators into a set can be viewed as similar to *aspect composition* as defined in [6,7,8].

By contrast, consider an operator O_3 that removes any web service present. The *set* $\{O_1, O_2, O_3\}$ has no fixed point, because O_2 and O_3 *conflict*, and are thus *inconsistent*. This is analogous to a set of policy rules that are logically inconsistent. Anything O_2 does, O_3 undoes, and vice versa. Note that conflicts can be more subtle; it is just as damaging if O_3 simply breaks O_2's web server so that O_2 is forced to continually repair it. As another example, consider, e.g. operator O_4 that moves the service set up by O_2 to another filesystem. This can only happen after O_2 achieves a fixed point. Does O_4 conflict with O_2? This depends very much upon how O_2 is defined, and the difference between what it *assures* and the states it *accepts* as conforming to its needs. It is possible that a set of operators is consistent even though no consistent state is *reachable* via application of the operators.

As a first step in understanding precedences between operators, [2] shows that if operators are applied serially, and each operator is aware of its own needs, then it is possible to satisfy the precedences between operators *without* codifying the precedences separately or centrally. Instead, one applies n (distinct) operators in sequence n times. Since this sequence contains every permutation of the operators, it contains at least one permutation satisfying the actual precedences of the operators. If the operators are constructed to do no harm unless their preconditions are met, then all operators will become operative in the course of $O(n^2)$ trials, where n is the number of operators. We will call this result the *maelstrom theorem*, after the cyclic "whirlwind" motion of operators in the proof.

Reasons for this perhaps counter-intuitive result are twofold: facts about permutations and assumptions about operators. Operators are assumed to be *aware of their precedences* and *idempotent* unless precedences are fulfilled. An operator, applied to a network that is not ready for it because preconditions are lacking, will not affect network state or other operators. Likewise, an operator applied to a network to which it has already been successfully applied will do no harm. Changes will occur only in the case where an operator's preconditions have been fulfilled and the network does not already conform to the operator's expected outcomes.

This is the context in which prior results end and this paper begins.

4   Consistency as an Emergent Property

So far, we have translated the problem of rule consistency into the problem of determining whether fixed-point sets intersect. This change does not yet simplify matters. It remains difficult to analyze whether a given set of operators shares a fixed point, particularly when the operators act upon different parts of a distributed network. Static analysis of operator fixed-points is difficult enough when we have complete knowledge of the operators (the problem is equivalent to policy consistency[3]), and virtually impossible when we have incomplete knowledge of the operators[4]. Based upon prior work, *without further assumptions*, we conclude that the problem of statically determining whether a particular set of distributed operators share a fixed point is *intractable*, in the same way that it is computationally hard to determine consistency of an unconstrained set of rules.

But the maelstrom theorem described above provides a possible alternative to this quandary. If we know that a hidden order (e.g., a total ordering, or logical consistency) *must* emerge in a certain number of steps of a process (or in a known time interval), and it does *not* emerge, then *it must not be present*. If we can then determine *when* that order should emerge, then its emergence is a necessary and sufficient proof of its *existence*, while lack of emergence within time limits constitutes statistical (but not deterministic) proof of its *non-existence*. We call this last statement the *emergent ordering principle*.

The emergent ordering principle serves as a starting point for a very different notion of consistency than before. Prior attempts at determining consistency (of operators or – equivalently – of the policies that they enforce) relied upon describing the *intent* of operators (or, equivalently, the constraints of policy). The emergent ordering principle conveniently circumvents this requirement; we need not compute a total order of operators in order to know that such an order exists. Similarly, a proof of the existence of a set of consistent operators need not inform us as to exactly how or why they are consistent.

Perhaps most important, whether consistency and order emerge globally is relatively unimportant; what is important is whether consistency and order arise from one's own actions or not. From an agent's point of view, there is no meaning to global consistency; what the agent manages is either consistent or not. Thus we study how to test for consistency *without* describing intent, computing global information, or deriving causal information.

5 Kinds of Operators

In describing the properties of statistical consistency, there are many kinds of convergent operators and it will help us to consider each kind of operator separately.

Every result in this paper presumes the existence of a set of convergent operators, each of which has one or more fixed points, in the sense that once some fixed point is achieved (through some finite number of applications of the operator), the operator makes no further changes to the network unless some other force moves the network away from the operator's fixed point.

Many common operators are *single-step,* in the sense that they perform only one change if their precedences are fulfilled, and are idempotent on both sides of that step. Examples of a single-action operator include "mounting a filesystem" or "setting up a service". A single-step operator acts upon a non-conforming part of a network, checks that necessary preconditions have been fulfilled, and then effects a state change in that part to make it acceptable.

A "multiple-step" operator, by contrast, takes several steps to achieve a fixed point. Examples of a multiple-step operator include incrementing (or decrementing) the number of threads for a web server until response time is optimal. In this case, each operator invocation adds one thread, and the fixed point is achieved when a desired number of threads w (according to some externally defined criteria) have been invoked. This is one example of a *bounded multiple-step operator,* in which the number of invocations before achieving a fixed point is bounded by some constant L. In this case, L is the absolute bound on the number of threads the web server can support, which is always finite. Common "autonomic" operators, e.g., performance tuning, are all multi-step operators.

Note that neither of these definitions truly conforms to the definition of Burgess, who allows an operator to function in a continuous domain[1]. Burgess' definition of a fixed point operator is one whose result approaches a fixed point as the number of operator applications increases, possibly *without* bound. By contrast, we require an operator to approach a fixed point after a *finite and constant* number of iterations L. Thus, the results below cannot be extended to operators under Burgess' definition.

6 Fixed Points and Policies

Note in the above examples that the existence of a fixed point for a set of operators is in some sense *semantic rather than syntactic.* Whether O_2 and O_4

conflict depends upon what they *mean* or *intend*, rather than how they are *coded.* While the reader may suggest that they could be coded such that the fixed point of a set becomes a syntactic property, this would not simplify the problem of determining whether a fixed point exists. The reason for this is that the codings – and their semantics – are *distributed* in a network, and centrally collecting that information in a ubiquitous network is both intractable and unreasonable.

There is a strong relationship between "operator fixed points" in the semantic view of network management, and "policies" in the syntactic view. Presumably, the reason for constructing an operator is to enforce some (perhaps vaguely defined) policy. A policy, by contrast, is a very specific description of what should happen, independent of how it might be arranged to happen.

While it is quite obvious that one can construct an operator to implement a policy, the converse is not so obvious. By nature, an operator is imperative, while a policy is declarative. The difficulty arises in codifying what an operator does in declarative terms. For example, consider an operator that – through some complex and unknown process, perhaps enabled by machine learning – decides which user processes to kill. This is a perfectly usable operator, but might not be possible to codify in a policy by any more useful language than "do what this operator says to do." Thus we consider operators to be a more general mechanism than policies for managing network function.

We diverge from current work on policy consistency and take a new path. The problem of policy consistency is to determine – given a syntactic description of the desired fixed points of a policy – whether those fixed points conflict or not. Instead, we step *sideways* (figuratively speaking) and avoid syntactic coding of intent entirely. For us, consistency of a policy expressed as a set of operators means that they have a *semantic* fixed point that *emerges* over time, and is represented by a network's *state and behavior.* Operators are considered consistent if they together *achieve* a fixed point, regardless of whether we understand *how* they achieve it, and independent of whether we can even *codify* their intent.

The reason for this seemingly bizarre world-view comes from wanting to be able to analyze very large networks. In a ubiquitous network consisting of billions of nodes, determining "how" is intractable, while techniques for determining consistency may remain tractable.

7 The Quandary of Observability

When dealing with configuration management – and operators in particular – lack of observability is a common issue[9]. In the above, we are not assuming there is any concept of a globally observable action; in particular there is no way to *observe* global consistency. Agents reason *on their own* and *in isolation.* It is quite possible that each agent manages only one operator. The definition of an inconsistent set of operators is thus *relative to the observer.* Suppose, e.g., that each operator is applied by a different agent. It is plausible that one agent would discover an inconsistency that another could not observe, because the agent only sees that *its own operator* does not approach a fixed point.

As an example of this, consider a simple case in which one operator O_1 mounts an external filesystem and another operator O_2 establishes a web server on it. Suppose that the agents applying these operators cannot otherwise communicate. Suppose further that O_1 never achieves a fixed point, perhaps because the filesystem it desires to mount is improperly exported. Then from the point of view of O_2, the set of operators is inconsistent, while from the point of view of O_1, it is still consistent, because O_1 has never been able to observe any inconsistency. The fact that its poor view of the world results from its own lack of capability is not of consequence in the definition of consistency.

We handle this quandary as follows. The agents for which consistency is observed (by approaching a common fixed point) are the "haves", while the agents that never achieve a fixed point are "have nots". An agent who – from its own point of view – has achieved its aims, has no problems. It is the "have nots" that need to work on different strategies to achieve their aims. In any sufficiently complex system, there will always be *some* "have nots"; the goal is to minimize these and not allow them to dominate the network.

8   Synchronous Operator Activation

Our first exploration is to understand what happens in an environment in which operators can be applied in an ordered (synchronous) fashion. Results for synchronized clocks mimic the results in [2], except that non-emergence of order is now a distinct possibility.

Theorem 1. *Suppose that n single-step operators $O_1, \ldots, O_n$ are to be applied in sequential order. Suppose that the longest precedence chain in the n operators consists of k operators. Suppose that one repeats the sequence k times for a total of nk invocations. If there are no external effects, and a common fixed point has not been reached for all operators, then the operators are inconsistent.*

Proof. This is in essence the same result as stated in [2], except that this theorem is stated in converse form and adds the constraint that there are no more than k operators in any one chain of precedences.

The key to the theorem is that nk invocations contain all $k!$ permutations of the k operators in each precedence chain. Thus after nk invocations, all permutations have been tried, and if a fixed point has not been reached, then there is no permutation that produces consistency, and we can conclude that the operators are not consistent.

To demonstrate this claim, note that in each of k blocks comprising n steps, all n operators are tried. Thus one can construct an arbitrary permutation by choosing one operator from each block of n invocations. Thus nk iterations are sufficient to try all permutations.   □

It is important in the above proof that there are no functioning external operators about which one has no knowledge. If one is testing the consistency of $\{O_1, O_2, O_3\}$ and – unbeknown to us – an operator O_4 inconsistent with this set is sporadically being applied, then one may conclude erroneously that the set is inconsistent, even when it is consistent. However, the theorem's conclusion remains accurate if an unknown operator that is *consistent* with the set is being applied sporadically. This does not interfere with the theorem's inference in the same way as an inconsistent operator would.

We sidestep this issue in the following sections by changing the way operators are applied. If all operators are applied in the same fashion, and there are unknown operators being applied, then inconsistency is a property of the whole set of operators, not just those that are known. It is not necessary to know how many operators there are and what they are doing in order to know whether they are consistent or not. This is a fundamental strength of this form of analysis.

9   Heartbeats and Time

To apply the emergent ordering principle in the distributed case, we must define what time means in a distributed system. Our definition differs from that of Lamport[10] and researchers involved in distributed performance analysis; we have no need to synchronize the actions of agents.

To define our notion of time, we assume that there is a "heartbeat rate" λ at which, on average, all operators are applied to the network repeatedly. We assume that the time between applications of the same operator follows an exponential distribution with mean $1/\lambda$ and standard deviation $1/\lambda$. As a result, operator application is *memoryless*, in the sense that future frequency of operator invocations does not depend in any sense on past behavior. For now, we assume that the process of applying each operator is asynchronous from applying any other and that all operators share the same application rate λ.

The astute reader will realize that this model matches CFengine's[11,12,13] model of operator application; the operators are applied periodically to "immunize" the system against adverse effects[14,15]. As in Cfengine, it is not possible to assure that an operator occurs at a specific time, but one can assure the *statistical* behavior of an operator as it is applied over time. Our statistical model is chosen arbitrarily and is neither important nor essential, but it is convenient for the arguments that follow. Any other model of operator invocation can be substituted without changing the character of the following results.

10   Fixed Points and Time

The purpose of the "heartbeat" is to provide a coordination point for agents *without* requiring them to communicate. If an agent does not apply an operator at the "heartbeat" time, it is presumed to be down or out of compliance. It is not necessary for the heartbeat to be seen by an agent; one can observe its effect. The reason for this is the following:

Theorem 2. *Suppose we have a set of n single-action operators, repeatedly applied to a network at the same rate λ, where inter-arrival times are exponentially distributed. Suppose that in these operators there are chains of precedence* *of at most length k. Then the probability that the operators are consistent after time t, given that the network has not achieved a fixed point, is less than $1 - (1 - e^{-\lambda t/k})^{nk}$, which approaches 0 as $t \to \infty$.*

Proof. The proof utilizes Bayesian relationships between several hypotheses. Let t represent elapsed time since the reference time t_0 at which operators began to be applied. Let H be the hypothesis that the operators are consistent, let $R(t)$ be the hypothesis that all operators have been repeated in all permutations at time t, and let $F(t)$ be the hypothesis that a fixed point for all operators has been observed at time t.

At the outset, no operators have been applied, and we have no information about the likelihood of H except for its relationships with the other hypotheses $R(t)$ and $F(t)$, for which we also initially have no information.[2] Clearly, $F(t)$ implies H and – since $F(t)$ can only be observed over time – the probability $\text{Prob}(H)$ that the operators are consistent is a time-varying quantity.

If at a particular time t, $R(t)$ is true, and $F(t)$ is false, then H is false by Theorem 1. Thus $R(t) \wedge \neg F(t) \to \neg H$.

Now suppose at a particular time t that $F(t)$ is false. It follows that the only way that H can be true is if $R(t)$ is false; otherwise H is false by the above. Thus $\text{Prob}(H|\neg F(t)) \leq \text{Prob}(\neg R(t)) = 1 - \text{Prob}(R(t))$. The reason for the inequality is that $R(t)$ is sufficient but not necessary to disprove H. One might be able to infer that H was false long before $R(t)$ is true, e.g., by observing two operators conflicting over a short time.

$\text{Prob}(R(t))$ is difficult to compute, but we can bound it by approximation. Consider the hypothesis $S(t)$ which represents that all n operators have been applied each t/k seconds, so that each operator has been applied k times in t seconds. By Theorem 1, $S(t) \to R(t)$, so $\text{Prob}(S(t)) \leq \text{Prob}(R(t))$ and $1 - \text{Prob}(S(t)) \geq 1 - \text{Prob}(R(t))$.

To understand this relationship, consider the Venn diagram in Fig. 1. The circles in the diagram represent overlaps in probability space. If one hypothesis implies another, this is a containment relationship. In our case, we know that $S(t) \wedge \neg F(t) \to R(t) \wedge \neg F(t) \to \neg H$, which is depicted as a containment relationship between their probability masses.

The probability of S being true, unlike that of R, is easily computed. The probability of $S(t)$ with respect to elapsed time t is the result of k independent sets of events, each of which are composed of n independent events, where each event has probability $(1 - e^{-\lambda t/k})$. Thus the composite probability of these nk events is $\text{Prob}(S(t)) = (1 - e^{-\lambda t/k})^{nk}$, and we conclude that at time t,

$$\text{Prob}(H|\neg F(t)) \leq 1 - \text{Prob}(R(t)) \leq 1 - \text{Prob}(S(t)) = 1 - (1 - e^{-\lambda t/k})^{nk}$$

The exponential dominates the constant power, so this quantity approaches 0 as $t \to \infty$. $\qquad\square$

---

[2] One reviewer felt that the estimates would be greatly improved by use of a priori estimates of the likelihood of H. We agree, but at the outset of this process, we have no such information.

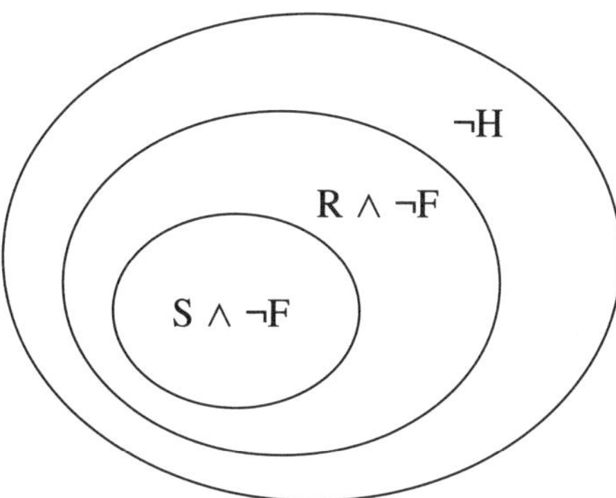

Fig. 1. If all permutations of operators have been tried and a fixed point was not observed ($R \wedge \neg F$), then the set of operators is inconsistent ($\neg H$), but this is not the only way to prove $\neg H$

In the theorem, n is the number of operators and k is the maximum dependency between them. In regular practice, the number of operators managing a network might be in the thousands, while the dependencies between them remain rather limited; an average service depends on at most 10 others.[3]

The practical uses of this theorem are easier to describe than the theorem. By assumption, all operators try to operate on average once each $1/\lambda$ seconds. There is a precedence chain of length k, where n is the number of operators. In this case,

1. After time $1/\lambda$, on average, one has operated.
2. After time $2/\lambda$, on average, a second has operated (depending upon the first).
3. ...
4. After time k/λ, on average, the last in the chain has operated.

On average, within time $k\lambda$, a set of operators is either proved consistent or there is enough evidence of inconsistency to safely assume that the set is inconsistent.

The key to the usefulness of this theorem in practice is that the agent discovering the inconsistency is exactly the agent whose operators should change to react to it. If an agent has been listening for time t, and can be 99% sure that the current set of operators is inconsistent, then it can act to preserve consistency. If we want $\mathrm{Prob}(\neg H) \geq .99$, we know that is true if $(1 - e^{-\lambda t/k})^{nk} \geq .99$. In turn, this is true when $t \geq -k \cdot \ln(1 - \sqrt[nk]{.99})/\lambda$. In general, .99 can be replaced with any confidence limit. A graph of time versus confidence for $\lambda = 1$, $k = 10$, and $n = 10, 20, 30$ is shown in Fig. 2. An alternate view is shown in Fig. 3.

---

[3] This estimate is based on the combined system and network administration experience of the authors, and is roughly the maximum depth of dependencies exhibited in software packages for Linux distributions.

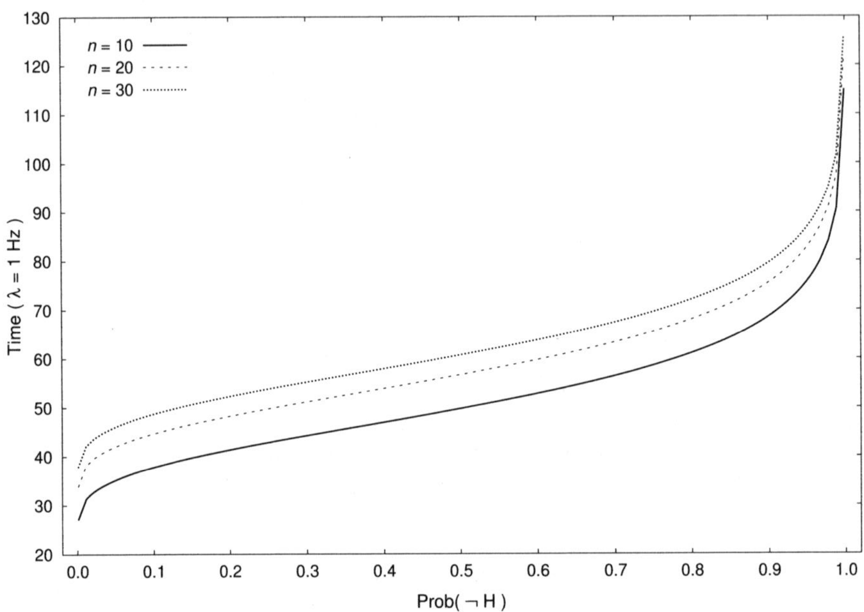

Fig. 2. The probability of inconsistency over time, given that a fixed point has not been observed, for sets of $n = 10$, $n = 20$, $n = 30$ operators containing no precedence chain over $k = 10$ operators long

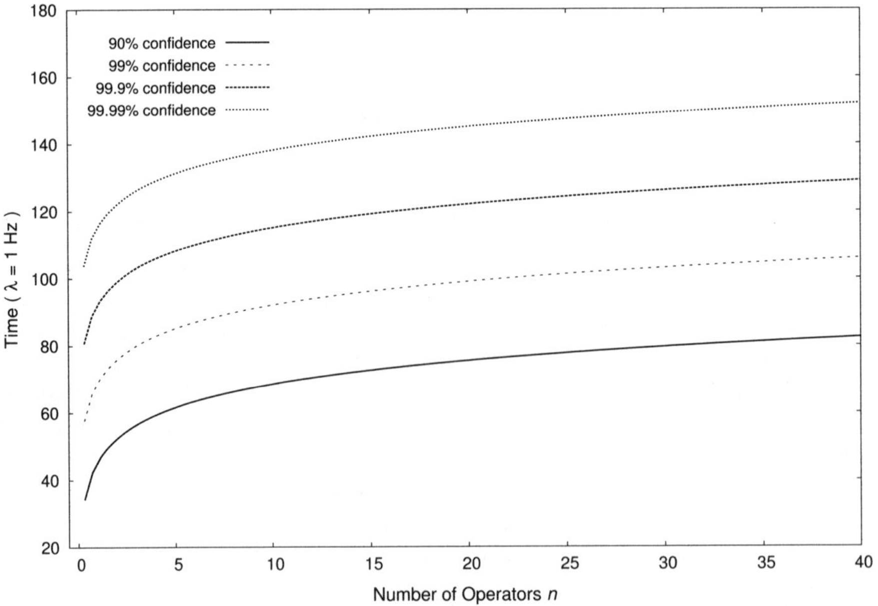

Fig. 3. Time taken to disprove H, given that a fixed point is not observed, for a precedence chain limit of $k = 10$ and increasing numbers of operators

Note also that the construction of the theorem is invariant of the particular distribution of operator invocations:

Corollary 1. *If invocations of operators in Theorem 2 are distributed according to a cumulative distribution function $c(t)$ (rather than the exponential distribution), and invocations are independent events, then the probability that the operators are not consistent at time t, given that consistency has not been observed, is less than $1 - c(t/k)^{nk}$.*

Proof. Substitute $c(t)$ for the exponential cumulative distribution function $1 - e^{-\lambda t}$ in the proof of Theorem 2. $\qquad\square$

Note that in our model, a security violation is modeled as an operator; it is just like any other operator, except that we do not have knowledge of its contents. It is typical for such an operator to introduce inconsistencies in policies, by trying to assert states that other operators attempt to prevent. Since our model does not require codification of the intent of each operator, it can be used to model effects of security violations without knowing the exact effect of a violation. Thus it is possible to model a security violation as the emergence of disorder in a previously ordered environment.

11   Multiple Time Bases

The assumptions in Theorem 2 are still too limiting for most practical cases. For example, we assume in Theorem 2 that all operators are applied at the same rate. The case in which different operators are applied at different rates is easy to handle:

Corollary 2. *Suppose operators $O_1, \ldots, O_n$ are applied at rates $\lambda_1, \ldots, \lambda_n$ and that $\lambda = min(\lambda_i)$. Then Theorem 2 applies to this system with rate λ and, given that a fixed point has not been observed after time t, the probability that the set of operators is consistent is less than $1 - \left(1 - e^{-\lambda t/k}\right)^{nk}$, which approaches 0 as $t \to \infty$.*

Proof. Exponential inter-arrival rates are additive; e.g., a process that is the sum of two rates λ_a and λ_b has a composite rate that is the sum $\lambda_a + \lambda_b$. Thus every operator O_i is applied at a rate λ plus (additionally) a rate $\lambda_i - \lambda > 0$. The extra rate does not improve the results of Theorem 2, but it does not hurt, either. Repeat the proof of Theorem 2 to obtain the result. $\qquad\square$

Thus a "common time base" assumption can be utilized without harm for the slowest rate in a set of rates.

12   Bounded Operators

Suppose we have a set of operators that are not single-step, but instead are guaranteed to find a fixed point in at most L steps, where L is a constant. We can still predict the time at which they will become stable, if any, as follows:

Corollary 3. *Suppose operators $O_1, \ldots, O_n$ achieve fixed points in at most L steps each. Then we can model this system as containing nL operators, and the probability that the operators are consistent, given that consistency has not been observed after time t, is $1 - (1 - e^{-\lambda t/k})^{nkL}$, which approaches 0 as $t \to \infty$.*

Proof. Model each operator that achieves a fixed point in L steps as L separate operators, one per step. Apply Theorem 2 to the resulting set of nL operators to obtain the result. □

Corollary 4. *Suppose every operator O_i has a different constant limit L_i. Let L be the maximum of the K_i. Then the result of Corollary 3 holds for L.*

Proof. Model each operator in the base set as L operators in a new operator set, where some of these are identity operators. The proof above then applies without change. □

Note that these bounds are loose and can be easily tightened. The important point of these corollaries is that these bounds – and even tighter bounds – are easy to compute.

13   Conclusions

In this paper, we turn the problem of analyzing policy consistency somewhat upside-down, viewing consistency as an emergent property of a self-organizing system of operators that try to implement policy. We demonstrate that there are Bayesian hypothesis-testing techniques that aid one in determining whether consistency is present, and discuss their limitations. But this is just the tip of a much larger iceberg.

First, the Bayesian inference techniques we use are just a small part of the true Bayesian lattice of hypotheses for the problem. We are only considering one way of analyzing the hypotheses, based upon one path through the lattice, and are only concentrating upon upper bounds for consistency hypotheses. The theorems in this paper can be thought of as "existence proofs of upper bounds on the probability of hypotheses". These are extremely conservative bounds and ignore much information that might be available. There are many other statistical relationships yet to be explored, and the bounds described herein are not optimal.

Second, it is relatively straightforward (though laborious) to extend these results to test whether a new operator is consistent with an existing fabric of operators. This gives the individual agent the ability to make reasoned choices as to whether it should change its management strategy (by changing the operators that it applies). This requires precisely defining the hypotheses to be tested from an individual agent's point of view, and is left for future work.

One impact of this work is that autonomous agents can use bounds in their reasoning processes that have a reasonable mathematical meaning. This paper shows how – in deciding upon a course of action – an agent can determine when it has waited "long enough" for external events. This is a small first step toward reasoning processes with strong statistical properties.

Acknowledgments

This paper draws its inspiration from the AIMS community, including Mark Burgess, Jan Bergstra, and many others.

References

1. Burgess, M., Couch, A.: Autonomic computing approximated by fixed-point promises. In: Proceedings of the First IEEE International Workshop on Modeling Autonomic Communication Environments (MACE), pp. 197–222. Multicon Verlag (2006)
2. Couch, A.L., Daniels, N.: The maelstrom: Network service debugging via "ineffective procedures". In: LISA, USENIX, pp. 63–78 (2001)
3. Lupu, E., Sloman, M.: Conflicts in policy-based distributed systems management. IEEE Trans. Software Eng. 25(6), 852–869 (1999)
4. Dunlop, N., Indulska, J., Raymond, K.: Dynamic conflict detection in policy-based management systems. In: EDOC, pp. 15–26. IEEE Computer Society, Los Alamitos (2002)
5. Couch, A., Chiarini, M.: A theory of closure operators. In: AIMS (submitted, 2008)
6. Burgess, M., Couch, A.L.: Modeling next generation configuration management tools. In: LISA, USENIX, pp. 131–147 (2006)
7. Anderson, P.: Configuration Management. SAGE Short Topics in System Administration. USENIX (2007)
8. Couch, A.: Configuration management. In: Bergstra, J., Burgess, M. (eds.) Handbook of Network and System Administration, pp. 75–133. Elsevier, Inc., Amsterdam (2007)
9. Couch, A.L., Sun, Y.: On observed reproducibility in network configuration management. Sci. Comput. Program 53(2), 215–253 (2004)
10. Lamport, L.: Time, clocks, and the ordering of events in a distributed system. Communications of the ACM 21(7), 558–565 (1978)
11. Burgess, M.: A site configuration engine. Computing Systems 8(2), 309–337 (1995)
12. Burgess, M., Ralston, R.: Distributed resource administration using cfengine. Softw., Pract. Exper. 27(9), 1083–1101 (1997)
13. Burgess, M.: Theoretical system administration. In: LISA, USENIX, pp. 1–13 (2000)
14. Burgess, M.: Computer immunology. In: LISA, USENIX, pp. 283–298 (1998)
15. Burgess, M.: Cfengine as a component of computer immune-systems. In: Proceedings of the Norwegian Conference on Informatics (1998)

A Theory of Closure Operators

Alva L. Couch and Marc Chiarini

Tufts University, Medford, Massachusetts, USA
`alva.couch@cs.tufts.edu`, `marc.chiarini@tufts.edu`

Abstract. We explore how fixed-point operators can be designed to interact and be composed to form autonomic control mechanisms. We depart from the idea that an operator is idempotent only for the states that it assures, and define a more general concept in which acceptable states are a superset of assurable states. This modified definition permits operators to make arbitrary choices that are later changed by other operators, easing their composition and allowing them to maintain aspects of a configuration. The result is that operators can be used to implement closures, which can in turn be used to build self-managing systems.

1 Introduction

Cfengine[1,2,3,4,5] is a widely used tool for managing computing systems. Cfengine's basic building block is the "convergent operator", an operation that enforces a policy by modifying any non-conforming system state. Operators affect a broad range of system entities, including configuration and dynamic runtime state. Convergent operators *immunize* a system against potential deterioration, by repeatedly repairing any state found to be non-conforming. They are also *idempotent* on properly conforming systems, in the sense that they will do nothing unless nonconformity is discovered. Thus, each operator comprises a tiny autonomic "control-loop" that checks for policy conformity and implements changes if they are needed.

Primitive operators in the current Cfengine-II (and the upcoming Cfengine-III[6]) are simple in structure. It is best to think of Cfengine as an "assembly language" for building convergent operators. Statements in Cfengine's policies affect files, processes, and other entities in straightforward ways, and can be composed to accomplish high-level tasks such as "implementing services". These statements are implemented by local agents running on each managed system.

This paper is about the "next level". While Cfengine embodies Burgess' theories, it does not implement Burgess' more general theoretical definition of convergent operators[7,8]. In that definition, a convergent operator assures that a system attribute has a value in some *set of acceptable values*, while most Cfengine operators assure that a system attribute has *one* value.

The effect of this limitation is that it is difficult for Cfengine to collaborate with other entities in assuring a goal[1]. Cfengine policies are centered around

---

[1] As Q of *Star Trek: the Next Generation* would say, "I don't work well in groups. It's difficult to work in groups when you're omnipotent."

D. Hausheer and J. Schönwälder (Eds.): AIMS 2008, LNCS 5127, pp. 162–174, 2008.
© IFIP International Federation for Information Processing 2008

creating some *specific* state, not an *acceptable* one. Thus, if some other entity creates another *acceptable* state, Cfengine will often detect and revert that state to the one and only state that it considers acceptable.

For example, suppose we set up a web server with Cfengine and then decide to tune its performance (either manually, or via some other software mechanism). Cfengine will – when invoked – revoke the changes we make to tune the server according to its own definition of "health," which is defined in terms of the contents and positions of specific files. To make the tuning "permanent", we have to inform Cfengine itself about the changes we want, and let *it* enforce these rules. This is an extra and potentially costly step if the changes are widespread.

In this paper, we ask the question, "how can convergent operators collaborate?" We explore collaboration as a composition of operators that does not require the step of coding knowledge from one operator (e.g., tuning) into another (e.g., setup). We define a new concept of operator that conforms to Burgess' theoretical definition but is broader than Cfengine's definition, and we explore the effects of composing such operators. We seek a situation in which two operators – one which sets up a web server and another that tunes it – can be composed and efficiently collaborate *without* knowledge of one another. This includes the human kind of operator as well. We explore a concept of convergent operator that encodes *intelligence* without requiring *rigid conformity* to a policy, so that the configuration agent becomes a "partner" rather than a controller. The desirable end result of this work is an autonomic control model that involves a partnership between humans and agents rather than a master-slave relationship in either direction.

How does one construct a well-designed convergent operator for network management? So far, the Cfengine model provides the only answer to this question. In this paper, we look beyond Cfengine's capabilities to a more general definition of convergent operators inspired by the theory of closures. All Cfengine operators comply with this definition, but the definition allows new kinds of operators to be created with desirable properties. Our conclusion is that this broader definition provides kinds of behavior that are otherwise difficult to describe or codify. In particular, while one can translate a policy to an operator, the converse seems intractable for some of the operators in this new class.

In the pages that follow, please keep in mind that fixed-point operators do not abandon the autonomic computing mechanism of closed-loop control; instead, they *encapsulate* control loops into smaller packages called operators. An operator includes a precondition-checking step that decides what control to apply, followed by an implementation step that makes appropriate changes. This can be viewed as a control loop operating *inside* the operator.

For example, consider two approaches to performance tuning of a web server, one based upon fixed-point operators and one based upon traditional control loops. The fixed-point version still contains a control loop, *inside* the operator, which is implemented through multiple invocations of the operator. This includes data collection, planning, and execution phases, but in the context of a single operator, rather than in the context of managing a whole system.

2   Convergent and Closure Operators

All the ideas in this paper presume the existence of a set of convergent operators $\mathcal{O}$ operating on a system that possesses a set of potential states S.

Definition 1. *A convergent operator O over a set of potential states S (that can be present in a network) is a function from S to S that, when applied repeatedly, eventually assures that a subset S^{a} of assurable states of S is present in the network, where O is idempotent over S^{a}, i.e., for $s \in S^{\mathrm{a}}, O(s) = s$.*

In other words, there exists some $k > 0$ such that for $n > k$ and any state $s \in S$, $O^{n}(s) \in S^{\mathrm{a}}$, or, equivalently, $O^{n}(S) = S^{\mathrm{a}}$ (and $O(S^{\mathrm{a}}) = S^{\mathrm{a}}$).

This is fairly close to the Cfengine definition of a convergent operator, but is more limited than Burgess' general definition of convergence, in which k might be infinite. Also, note that the existence of k in a static environment does not assume that there is a k for an environment that is dynamically changing, perhaps in opposition to the goals of the operator. For example, an operator that seeks to limit the number of user processes would never converge if a user attempted consciously to circumvent the operator by creating a steady supply of processes.

We broaden this definition in one fundamental way, inspired by the theory of closures, to admit a new kind of idempotence. A closure[9,10,11] is a domain of semantic predictability in a larger system that may exhibit unpredictability in other ways. Creating a closure requires separating behavior from configuration, so that configuration data can be classed as either *crucial* to behavior or *incidental*. An incidental configuration parameter's value does not affect behavior, while a crucial parameter changes observable behavior. This classification of parameters determines which configuration parameters should be part of the interface to the closure, and which should be internal and unexposed.

In particular, the first definition does not account for the fact that an operator may *accept* (that is, be idempotent over) more states than it *assures*. The *assurable* states of an operator are those that it has the power to create, while the *acceptable* states of an operator are those that it finds acceptable, but might not be able to create itself. More formally,

Definition 2. *A closure operator O over a set S is defined by two sets of states, $S^{\mathrm{a}} \subseteq S^{\mathrm{i}} \subseteq S$, so that O is idempotent over S^{i} but assures a perhaps smaller subset S^{a}.*

For most Cfengine operators, $S^{\mathrm{i}} = S^{\mathrm{a}}$, though there are some advanced operators (e.g., file editing) for which S^{i} is a proper superset of S^{a}.

The fact that assurance is different than acceptance is a core idea in the theory of closures. Many states are "acceptable" simply because they embody *arbitrary* (or "incidental") choices that do not affect the outcome of the goal. Other choices might be *crucial*.

For example, the actual location of the web server document tree has little to do with the basic behavior of a web server, so an operator O_1 that sets up a web server might well make an *arbitrary* choice[10] about those details. But one operator's "arbitrary" might be another operator's "crucial"; consider an

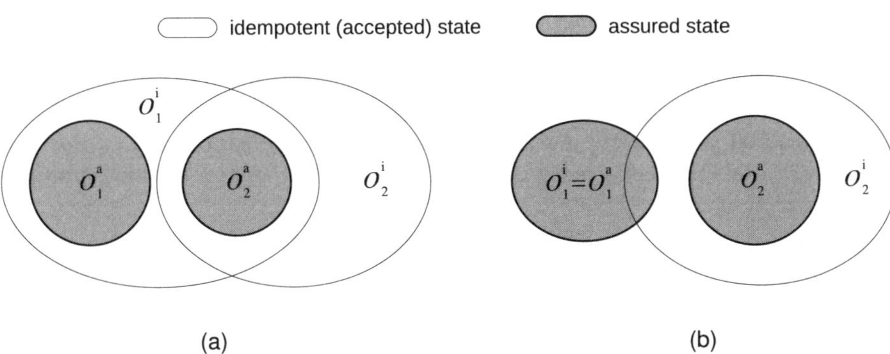

Fig. 1. (a) O_1 accepts some subset of states that are assurable by O_2. (b) O_1 only accepts the states that it assures.

operator O_2 whose goal is to tune the performance of the web server. Then the choice of document root – unimportant to the basic act of setting up the web server – changes from incidental to crucial and is no longer so flexible. However, the first operator O_1 *does not care* about the location, so it should not override the operator O_2's changes to its original design.

The difference between what an operator accepts and what it assures can lead to fixed points that are not readily apparent. If O_1 *assures* that the web service is located on the mounted filesystem, but *accepts* that it could be located anywhere, then the set of operators $\{O_1, O_2\}$ has a fixed point. If O_1 does not accept anything except what it assures, then operators in the set share no fixed point and are not consistent. These two situations are described in Fig. 1. In one case, O_1 accepts states set up by O_2; in the other, it does not.

Thus, the concept of incidental complexity in closures – conceived within a theory based upon syntactic consistency – is reflected in the theory of operators as an acceptance set that allows greater flexibility for incidental choices than those in an assurance set. A third operator O_3 might set up and assure the operation of a particular virtual server, without conflicting with O_1 or O_2.

3   Strategy and Tactics

One way of understanding this new distinction is that the acceptance set reflects a general *strategy* for accomplishing an aim or goal, while the assurance set reflects specific *tactics* for achieving that goal. A strategy is *declarative knowledge*, in the sense that it is about describing acceptable states, while a tactic represents *procedural knowledge* about how to *achieve* one or more assurable states.

In the above example, the strategy of O_1 is to "create a working web server," while the strategy of O_2 is to "create a fast web server." O_1 has a tactic for creating *at least one version* of a "working web server" in which it makes a number of choices that might be incidental to the web server's function. To

O_2, though, some choices (e.g., the locations of particular content) are no longer incidental, because O_2's strategy differs from O_1's strategy. However, a "fast web server" is indeed some subclass of a "working web server", so there is *strategy overlap* between O_1 and O_2. O_1 and O_2 can "collaborate" if O_2's tactic for creating a "fast web server" is *also* consonant with O_1's definition of a "working web server." In this case, we can *compose* O_1 and O_2 to get "a working and fast web server".

The concept of closure operators may seem abstract and unrealistic at first glance, but it is a more direct mimicry of what humans do in administering systems than the actions performed by current configuration tools. We break down installation of a service into multiple steps, each of which requires prerequisites. We tune each step separately, making sure we do not break the function of any prior step. One person might set up a web server, another might populate its content, and a third might tune it. This is exactly what a set of closure operators are meant to do, and one might thus characterize closure operators as "what humans do" to create and then continue to assure a functioning system.

The Cfengine way to construct O_1 and O_2 is to employ assurance sets that equal their acceptance sets. In that case, O_1 must embody all of the complexity of O_2, or the operators are inconsistent. If, instead, we can determine a method that allows O_2 to *embrace* what O_1 has done, without understanding it, and for O_1 to embrace what O_2 will do, then we can compose O_1 and O_2 into a whole greater than the sum of its parts.

4   Operator Consistency

One important question for a set of convergent operators (each of which has a set of fixed points) is whether the *set* shares a fixed point or not.

Definition 3. *A set of convergent operators $\mathcal{O}$ is* consistent *if the set shares a set of fixed points F that is a subset of all states S in the domain of the set of operators.*

Note that this is a set intersection problem: the set of fixed points F for a set of operators $\mathcal{O}$, if it exists, is the intersection of the sets of fixed points $\mathcal{A} = \{A_i\}$ that each individual operator O_i assures. $\mathcal{O}$ is consistent exactly when $\mathcal{A}$ is non-empty[2].

The above definition applies to operators with preconditions in a perhaps unexpected way. Such an operator does nothing until its preconditions are met. For example, one cannot tune a web server (O_2) until it has been installed (O_1). Thus O_2 is idempotent both when its preconditions are not met and after its acceptable states have been achieved.

Definition 4. *Operators with preconditions are consistent only if they exhibit a fixed point after all operator preconditions have been met.*

---

[2] Extended notions of consistency are explored in [12].

In other words, the trivial fixed point for operators that have not become active does not count as a fixed point for the set of operators.

It is often important to know whether consistency is a concrete or abstract property of a set of operators. It is only concrete if it can actually *arise* in practice:

Definition 5. *A set of operators $\mathcal{O}$ is* reachably consistent *(with respect to a set of baseline states B) if they are consistent, and for any state $b \in B$ of the network before the operators, there is some sequence of operator applications that leads to a consistent state.*

We denote the reachable states for a set of operators $\mathcal{O}$ with respect to a set of baseline (initial) states B as $\mathcal{O}^*(B)$.

Reachable consistency of closure operators is *not* a simple set intersection problem unless the acceptance and assurance sets for operators are equal; there are sets of closure operators that are consistent but not reachably consistent, because reachability requires some outside force to be applied. Consider the case where O_1 and O_2 share an *acceptable* point that is not *reachable*. For example suppose that O_1 can locate the web server in */usr/web*, O_2 can locate the web server anywhere in */opt*, and some third operator O_3 can put the web server in */var/www*, which is acceptable to both of the others. The set $\{O_1, O_2\}$ is *consistent* but not *reachably consistent*, because the common acceptable state */var/www* cannot be *reached* by virtue of the knowledge contained in O_1 or O_2. The set $\{O_1, O_2, O_3\}$ is *reachably consistent* (with respect to the set of all states S) because an assurable state of O_3 can satisfy at least one acceptable state of both O_1 and O_2. Thus a set that is not reachably consistent can be made reachably consistent by *adding* operators, a fact that is on the surface quite counter-intuitive and that cannot happen if assurable and acceptable states happen to match (Figure 2).

Reachable consistency depends upon the possible initial states B of a system before operators are applied. This is a rather trivial assertion in the sense that if the baseline states are fixed points of all operators, then the set of operators

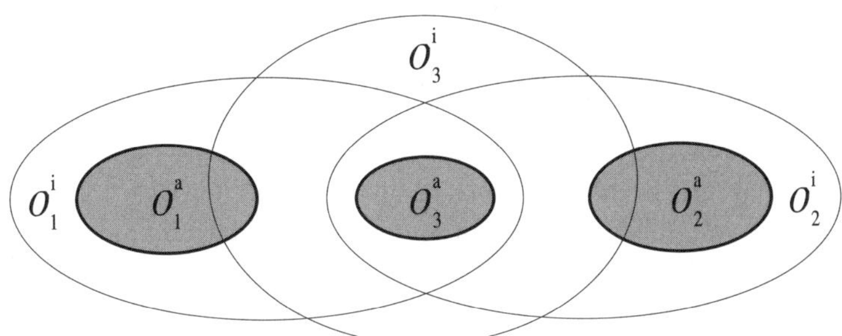

Fig. 2. Operators O_1 and O_2 can never reach a fixed point without O_3, which joins their acceptable states with a common assurable state. An 'i' (idempotent) superscript denotes an operator's set of acceptable states, while an 'a' denotes its assurance set.

is consistent even though they might not be able to assure that particular state themselves. If, for example, the set of operators never moves the system outside a baseline state, then for all practical purposes, the set of all states *is* the baseline set.

In the above example, the result of the three operators is an *emergent* fixed point that is fixed for all three operators, but fixed in *different ways* for each operator. Thus each operator can be thought of as acting on an *aspect* of the network, and the composition of operators into a set can be viewed as similar to *aspect composition* as defined in [13,14,15]. An aspect is one facet of coordination within a configuration; any configuration management tool must *compose aspects* to create a valid configuration.

5   Implementing Closure Operators

One reason that closure operators have not been explored so far is that they are more difficult to implement than simple convergent operators. But there are things that simply cannot be done without them, including management operations that exploit aspect composition. Further, the extra machinery required to implement a closure operator is necessary *anyway*, for other reasons.

Closure operators are more difficult to construct than, e.g., automation scripts that accomplish similar goals. The closure operator, unlike a simple script, must be aware of its surroundings and have knowledge of its preconditions and post-conditions. An ideal closure operator is safe under all conditions, in the sense that it is safe to invoke the operator with the network in any conceivable state, and as a result, the operator will not damage the network through lack of knowledge (though it might not be capable of improving the network either).

Note first that the acceptance set of a closure operator can only be determined by use of a *validation model* that determines what is acceptable. This model is different from the *assurance model* that determines which settings will be changed if the current configuration is not valid. Both of these models could be specified as rulesets.

Consider, for example, how one would implement the operators O_1 and O_2 above. O_1 is straightforward enough; installing the RPM for Apache might do nicely as a first approximation. But O_2 is a much more sophisticated operator than has ever been written before. O_2 must *validate* the install of O_1 and then operate in such a way that this validation is not lost by its changes. This is a matter of *coordinating* settings in files with positions on disk, so that everything one moves is matched with a parameter change in a file. Further, for O_1 to accept this change, it must share with O_2 an underlying validation model that accepts more states than what it can assure. Thus the key to implementing O_1 and O_2 is that *both must agree (at some level) on what constitutes a valid web server, invariant of how that validity was reached*[3].

---

[3] Of course, RPM sets a flag that keeps a web server from being installed on top of another, but this also allows that web server to be manually broken and not repaired. So RPM does not really implement a closure operator.

With this validation model in hand (ostensibly, modeled as a set of "valid web server configurations"), O_1 checks whether this model is satisfied, and takes steps to satisfy it if not. O_2, by contrast, does *nothing* if the web server configuration is invalid, but if it is valid, changes it to perhaps *another* valid state that responds more quickly.

Why would we want to structure operators in this way? One answer is that the monolithic construction of an operator that both installs and tunes a web server is more complex than two operators, each of which handles one aspect, and that there may in fact be different concepts and models of tuning that one might wish to apply. Further, the added complexity of a validation model is desirable whether we implement the tuning as one operator or two, because the alternative is that the web server may be unintentionally rebuilt for no particularly good reason, simply because "incidental" (and meaningless) changes in configuration have occurred out of band. In order to satisfy the spirit of Cfengine, that "if it isn't broken, don't fix it", one must have a model of what it means to be functional or broken.

6   Validation Models

What is a "valid" web server? This is a complex question that has been studied in some detail. First, *inside* the server, there are a set of data relationships that must be preserved. But there is another validation model that depicts how certain data must be present *outside* the web server. These are related via a closure model of web service[10] that expresses external behavior as a set of exterior maps. But in constructing this mapping, many *incidental* choices are made that have nothing to do with the mapping, though they may affect *performance*. These incidental choices must be *coordinated* so that the result is a functional web server. Thus there are two kinds of validation models: an *interior* model that depicts *data* (static) relationships, and an *exterior* model that depicts *behavioral* (dynamic) relationships.

An example of an interior model (reprinted from [10]) is given in Fig. 3. A web server configuration contains many parameters that must agree in order for the webserver to function properly. The directory in which content appears must both be accessible as a directory and mapped to an appropriate virtual server. Likewise, the name of each file must correspond to the appropriate MIME type, etc. Many of these parameters are "incidental" in the sense that choices for internal location of a set of files seldom affects the externally observable behavior of a web server.

The good news is that the internal model of a valid web server is a purely *declarative* description of data relationships, similar to database integrity constraints, and that it is both package-specific and policy-neutral, in the sense that any policy can be enforced while obeying the model. The bad news is that no such model has yet been constructed for many configurable packages in current use. This is a bad thing, because such models are necessary in order to know whether configuration management operators are working properly or not. An instance that does not conform to the basic model for behavior cannot possibly function properly.

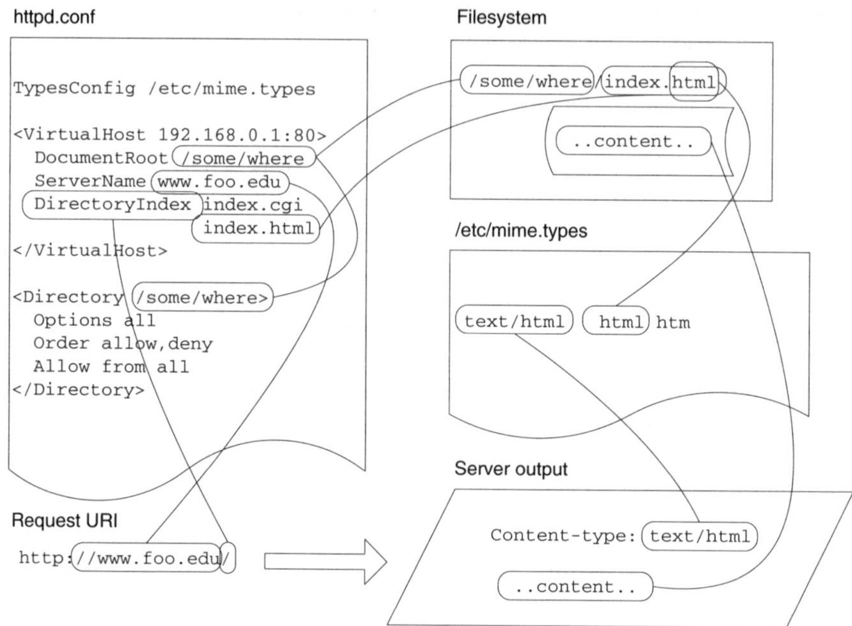

Fig. 3. A relational model of a specific web server's data dependencies (reprinted from [10])

Note that a model of validity is not an *information model* (e.g. CIM), but rather a *relational model*, similar to a set of database constraints or an XML schema. An overall model of a valid web server is (at some level) a version of the server's *user manual*, while a model of a "fast web server" is an embodiment of *best practices* for increasing service speed *while obeying the user manual*.

It might be best to think of each of these models as an XML document conforming to a particular XSchema; this seems to describe the models in the web server example, among others. The O_1 XSchema simply defines what is valid as a configuration according to the user manual, while the O_2 XSchema (which might change over time) eliminates some valid configurations that exhibit poor performance. In the manner of BCFG2 or LCFG, information in an XML configuration file (conforming to the XSchema) corresponds with information stored in package configuration files, wherever they might be located. We do not endorse the use of XML and XSchema for this purpose; we merely remark that they seem powerful enough to serve as a modeling language for this purpose.

To make closure operators practical, we need some form of "strategic schema" for each managed package or unit. This schema serves as a trigger for "tactics" that enforce *one* way to obey the schema. The true purpose of the schema, however, is to allow an operator to leave "well enough" alone. By defining a notion of "health" that is *independent* of the mechanism of assurance, one admits other potentially clever assurance mechanisms that arise from *outside* the operator in question.

7   Properties of Closure Operators

Creating schemas for common packages (or perhaps one might say, "frequently encountered intents") seems a daunting task. Why would one want to do this? In this section, we discuss some of the properties of closure operators as motivation for the work ahead.

First we describe several "composition theorems", that show when a set of closure operators $\mathcal{O} = \{O_1, \ldots, O_k\}$ can be thought of as a single closure operator $\mathcal{O}$, where applying $\mathcal{O}$ consists of randomly choosing and applying one of $O_1, \ldots, O_k$.

First,

Theorem 1. *Suppose we have a set of k closure operators $\mathcal{O} = \{O_1, \ldots, O_k\}$ with the same acceptance set O^i. Then the set of operators, viewed as one operator, is a closure operator.*

Proof. View the set of operators as one operator that randomly chooses which sub-operator to call. The acceptance set of this operator is O^i, while the assurance set is the *union* of the individual assurance sets O_j^a. □

This is just tactic composition in the presence of shared strategy. The most important property of closure operators – as compared to regular Cfengine operators – is *flexibility of response*. Most current operators correspond to "one tactic" for assuring a behavior. "Multiple tactics" can be tried by one closure operator to achieve a coherent aim.

Moreover,

Theorem 2. *Suppose the acceptance sets of $O_1, \ldots, O_k$ intersect in some nonempty set O^i. If O contains the assurance set of one operator O_j, then the set of these operators, viewed as one random operator, is a closure operator.*

Proof. As before, consider the operator O that randomly calls some O_m when invoked. When O_j is invoked, it assures a state inside the acceptance set. Since operators are chosen randomly to be invoked, it is only a matter of time until it *is* invoked, and other operators in $\mathcal{O}$, once it assures an appropriate state, will not modify O_j's tactics. □

Agreement is not always necessary; orthogonality is sufficient:

Theorem 3. *Suppose that two operators O_1, O_2 operate on orthogonal regions S_1, S_2 of a product space $S_1 \otimes S_2$, so that O_1 affects the chosen subset of S_1 and O_2 affects S_2 only. Then $\{O_1, O_2\}$ is a closure operator.*

Proof. Suppose O_1 assures S_1^a, a subset of its acceptance set S_1^i, while O_2 assures S_2^a, a subset of its acceptance set S_2^i. Then $\{O_1, O_2\}$ assures $S_1^a \otimes S_2^a$ and accepts $S_1^i \otimes S_2^i$, so it is a closure operator. □

In other words, closure operators acting on independent entities can be composed into one closure operator.

In general,

Theorem 4. *Suppose that a set of operators $\mathcal{O} = \{O_1, \ldots, O_k\}$ can be factored into subsets of operators, each of which acts on an orthogonal part of configuration, where each subset satisfies the conditions of Theorem 2. Then $\mathcal{O}$ is a closure operator.*

Proof. Apply Theorem 2 to infer that each subset is a closure operator, and then use Theorem 3 inductively to get the result.   □

Conversely,

Theorem 5. *Any set of operators that is reachably consistent can be considered as a single closure operator.*

Proof. If a set of operators is reachably consistent, then it shares an acceptance set that is the intersection of all operators' acceptance sets, and for any initial state, the operators achieve some element of that subset, so that at least one operator in the set must have each state in the intersection in its assurance set.   □

We have shown, thus, that under a variety of conditions, closure operators compose to make a single closure operator. What, then, is inconsistency? We take the approach of [16], that inconsistency indicates that the operators in a set represent two or more distinct strategies, so that sets of operators can be factored into strategic groups.

Two operators O_1 and O_2 are inconsistent if there is some state in O_1's assurance set that is not in O_2's acceptance set, and vice-versa. It is necessary for lack of acceptance to be symmetric, or the operators would settle among themselves upon the more stringent acceptance set and become consistent. Thus inconsistency is a "flip-flop" situation in which two operators feel compelled to undo each other's tactics.

Detecting inconsistency is difficult if not impossible for distributed operators that do not necessarily have knowledge of each others' strategies and/or goals. We study this problem in [12] and conclude that consistency is best considered to be a *statistical* rather than logical property. We demonstrate methods for evaluating the *hypothesis* that a set of operators is consistent, and relate probability of consistency to time of observation.

8   Conclusions

So far, autonomic computing has been asserted by hierarchical means, in which more limited control loops are part of a larger hierarchy of control. In this paper, we propose a boldly different strategy, of composing control loops as *peers* in a control strategy. In this paper, we have explored the structure of such a set of operators, from a practical and an algebraic standpoint. In a second paper[12], we explore notions of operator consistency that are meaningful and useful in this context.

Closure operators are difficult to build, but have some really nice properties. The most significant of these is that they can be composed with other closure operators without tactical agreement, and the results can emerge as a new control strategy that is the composition of several less-general control strategies. It can be extremely difficult to extend a given operator to create a new function, while that function may be added by another consistent operator with less effort, provided that the two operators share the same basic behavioral model. The behavioral model is thus the pivot upon which effective composition is based, and is needed whether composition is desired or not. The result is a compositional model of autonomics in which operators compose simply because they agree on strategy, but not necessarily on tactics.

There are several directions for future work. First, the theory suggests an extension to Cfengine that allows assurance sets to be smaller than acceptance sets. This is a task of significant complexity, however, because Cfengine currently lacks the modeling machinery required to define acceptance as a concept separate from assurance. Using this extension, we can develop practical examples of cooperative management, such as performance tuning. Aside from inspiring new capabilities for Cfengine, this theory allows other autonomic control loops to be composed in like manner – as peers in an operator calculus. It remains to be seen whether this is better, worse, or just different than composing control loops via hierarchy.

But the theory is most powerful in that it offers a method for dealing with open management situations in which there is no way to establish sufficient closed control loops. By expressing management tools and user actions (including intrusions) as operators, we have one coherent theoretical model for everything that can happen in a network. The future promise of closure operators is that we can express mitigating influences for network problems in terms of closure operator activations and deactivations, rather than in terms of selecting features in a monolithic management tool. This enables highly dynamic management strategies, including intelligent operators whose nature evolves with changing conditions, and that can be deployed, erased, recompiled, and redeployed in a live environment. We believe this high level of dynamism will be required to deal with the ubiquitous computing networks of tomorrow.

Acknowledgements

This paper would not exist without the inspiration of the Cfengine community, including Mark Burgess and the many users of Cfengine who have dared to learn a different way of thinking.

References

1. Burgess, M.: A site configuration engine. Computing Systems 8(2), 309–337 (1995)
2. Burgess, M., Ralston, R.: Distributed resource administration using cfengine. Softw., Pract. Exper. 27(9), 1083–1101 (1997)
3. Burgess, M.: Computer immunology. In: LISA, pp. 283–298. USENIX (1998)
4. Burgess, M.: Theoretical system administration. In: LISA, pp. 1–13. USENIX (2000)

5. Burgess, M.: Cfengine as a component of computer immune-systems. In: Proceedings of the Norwegian Conference on Informatics (1998)
6. Burgess, M., Frisch, A.: Promises and cfengine: A working specification for cfengine 3. Technical report, Oslo University College (November 2005)
7. Burgess, M.: An approach to understanding policy based on autonomy and voluntary cooperation. In: Schönwälder, J., Serrat, J. (eds.) DSOM 2005. LNCS, vol. 3775, pp. 97–108. Springer, Heidelberg (2005)
8. Burgess, M., Couch, A.: Autonomic computing approximated by fixed-point promises. In: Proceedings of the First IEEE International Workshop on Modeling Autonomic Communication Environments (MACE), pp. 197–222. Multicon Verlag (2006)
9. Couch, A., Hart, J., Idhaw, E.G., Kallas, D.: Seeking closure in an open world: A behavioral agent approach to configuration management. In: LISA 2003: Proceedings of the 17th USENIX conference on System administration, Berkeley, CA, USA, pp. 125–148. USENIX (2003)
10. Schwartzberg, S., Couch, A.: Experience implementing a web service closure. In: LISA 2004: Proceedings of the 18th USENIX conference on System administration, Berkeley, CA, USA, pp. 213–230. USENIX (2004)
11. Wu, N., Couch, A.: Experience implementing an ip address closure. In: LISA 2006: Proceedings of the 20th USENIX conference on System administration, Berkeley, CA, USA, pp. 119–130. USENIX (2006)
12. Couch, A., Chiarini, M.: Dynamic consistency analysis for convergent operators. In: AIMS (submitted, 2008)
13. Burgess, M., Couch, A.L.: Modeling next generation configuration management tools. In: LISA, pp. 131–147. USENIX (2006)
14. Anderson, P.: Configuration Management. SAGE Short Topics in System Administration. USENIX (2007)
15. Couch, A.: Configuration management. In: Bergstra, J., Burgess, M. (eds.) Handbook of Network and System Administration, pp. 75–133. Elsevier, Inc., Amsterdam (2007)
16. Couch, A., Sun, Y.: On the algebraic structure of convergence. In: Brunner, M., Keller, A. (eds.) DSOM 2003. LNCS, vol. 2867, pp. 28–40. Springer, Berlin (2003)

Entwined Influences of Users' Behaviour and QoS: A Multi-model Approach

Julien Siebert, Vincent Chevrier, and Laurent Ciarletta

LORIA: MADYNES & MAIA teams - Campus Scientifique - BP 239 - 54506
Vandœuvre-lès-Nancy Cedex
{julien.siebert,vincent.chevrier,laurent.ciarletta}@loria.fr

Abstract. In distributed, dynamic networks and applications, such as
Peer-to-Peer (P2P), users' behaviour and quality of service/quality of experiment[1] are known to influence each other. In worst cases, these mutual
influences could lead the system to crash. We propose a novel approach
to model relationships between users and QoS. It is based upon multi-agent systems in order to study the impact of situated behaviours on the
global network and to integrate different levels of representation (users'
behaviour, overlay protocols, network topology). This paper describes
our approach to represent the different models required in such systems
and a first implementation in an existing overlay simulator with the first
results of experimentations.

1 Motivation

For the last couple of years, distributed applications (such as P2P file sharing)
have rapidly expanded. In these applications [1,2], users' behaviour is known
to have a great impact on the quality of service (QoS), as for instance the
problems of free-riding and poisoning (studied in section 3). QoS also impacts the
users' behaviour. For example, a user can stop or defer the use of an application
because of a large bandwidth consumption. Moreover, applications are expected
to become ubiquitous and to be able to guide user's behaviour.

Understanding these mutual influences can help to foresee the behaviours
which can be dangerous/beneficial for the network performance (NP) and the
impact of NP on these behaviours. This work can also be useful to quantify the
dysfunctions based on the frequency/ratio of these behaviours, or to test future
applications.

To do this, we argue that we need to take into account different levels of
representation. Indeed, the users' behaviour depends on the objective QoS and
on the local user's environment (moment, location, stress,...). For the QoS (see
[3]), it depends mostly on NP and on the media environment. In short, we claim
it is needed to study relations between models of (1) *user*, (2) *application* and
(3) *environment* in order to assess the mutual influences (fig. 1).

---

[1] In this article, we use the term QoS to design both quality of service and quality of
experiment.

D. Hausheer and J. Schönwälder (Eds.): AIMS 2008, LNCS 5127, pp. 175–179, 2008.

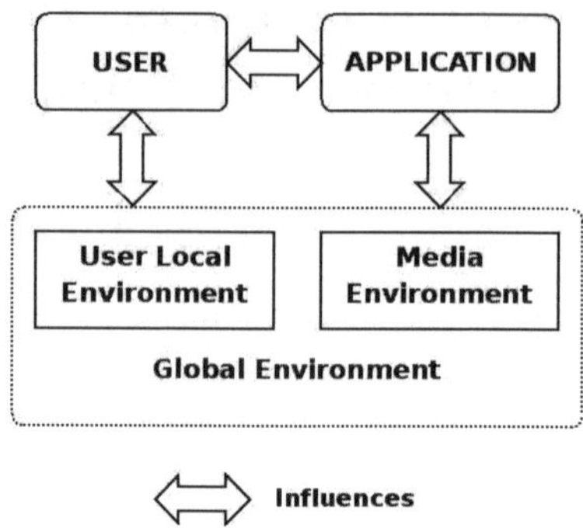

Fig. 1. Relations between the different levels of representation

Models and simulators, in the network domain (such as NS, *etc.* see review [4]), are well fitted to study QoS and network performances. The users' behaviour, if present, is just an input for these models. It is often reduced to a quantity of traffic generated. As a consequence, it seems difficult to model dynamic and heterogeneous users' behaviour, and to take into account the mutual influences of QoS and behaviour with such a limited approach.

Obviously, models and simulators in the field of cognitive sciences (economy, social sciences, game theory,...) are well suited to represent user's behaviours, goals, actions and interactions [5,6]. However, modelling realistic network's parameters is not the primary objective of this field. As a consequence, parameters such as delays, bandwidth or overlay protocols are seldom if ever represented.

After looking at each domain, we conclude that a single point of view does not seem sufficient. Since models already exist for each level, we need to integrate and make them interact.

2   Proposition of Study

We propose to use the multi-agent (MA) paradigm [7] to describe P2P systems and to make interact our different levels of abstraction. MA is appropriate to simulate complex distributed systems such as, for example, societies [8]. It could be defined as a set of organised autonomous entities (the agents) interacting with and within an environment to achieve some goals. In our case, we define *users as agents*[2], *protocols as interactions* and *underlying networks as the (media) environment* (see fig. 2).

Our goal is to implement, to test our multi-agent approach and to compare it with existing models and real data. Then, we want to build a generic framework enabling us to assess the mutual influences of users' behaviour and QoS, not only in P2P but also in other distributed, dynamic networks and applications (ad-hoc, mesh). We wish to test different heterogeneous behaviours and/or different overlay protocols and/or different network topologies. This last point highlights

---

[2] We now use node, agent, user or peer as the same.

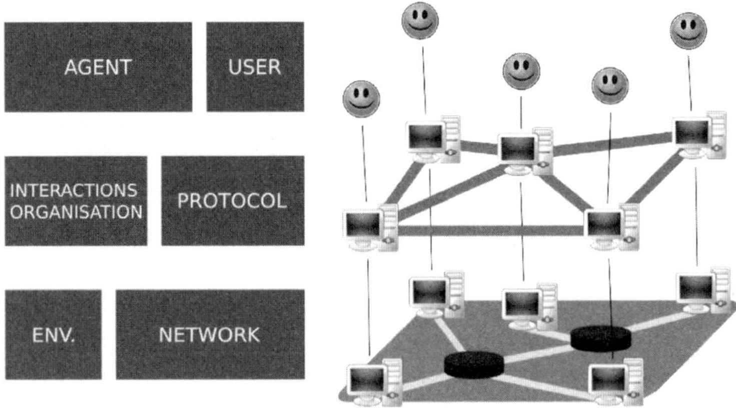

Fig. 2. Multi-agent for P2P [9]

multi-model issues: how several models at different space and time scales can interact ?

3   A First Case Study

As a first case study of our approach, we restrict the domain to P2P file sharing applications (see [9]). We are studying the problems of free-riding: people that do not share their resources; and poisoning: content that differs from the original copy (also called pollution). We would like to assess the impact of sharing and poisoning awareness on the content spreading. These problems are known to be quite hard to solve in decentralised systems and methods to avoid free-riding and poisoning are still an open area (see [10,6,2]).

MA approach enables us to understand the impact of local behaviours on the global state of the system. However, we were firstly interested in its feasibility: we build a simulator and make experiments to answer the questions of realism and scalability of our implementation.

Due to time constraints[3], we chose to adapt an existing overlay simulator: PeerFactSim.KOM[4](PFS). This tool had several advantages for the study of our problematic. The first one is the scalability (up to 10^5 nodes) and the second one is its architecture that separates each level of abstraction and facilitates the implementation of a user model.

We adapted PFS to fit with our approach by explicitly *modelling data* and their *concrete exchanges* (each node has now a list of files which can be shared over the network), by *modelling pollution* within these files and *adding new metrics* such as, for example, number of polluted files per node.

---

[3] This work was done during my Master Thesis.
[4] http://www.peerfact.org

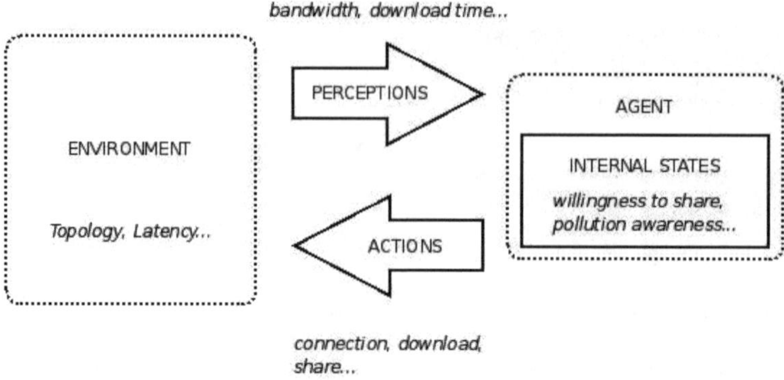

Fig. 3. Perception Decision Action cycle in our model [9]

The user, in our model has a relatively simple behaviour with few internal states and a compact representation of their external environment and neighbours. *It decides which action to undertake considering its local perception and its internal states* (see fig 3).

We establish a first experiment's scenario in order to test our approach: we mainly look at *technical feasibility* (debug), *realism* and *scalability*. We take an initial network of N nodes in which P peers publish each f resources. The scenario is composed of five steps: one agent looks for a file; after a while the agent asks one of the available sources for a download; then it checks the download process; if it gets the file, it can check the pollution and decides to share, otherwise it can decide to restart the whole process.

On scalability: we perform experiments over kademlia networks from $N = 25$ to 50000 nodes (Java 6, 2GbRAM, core duo 2.4GHz). Simulating 50000 nodes with our model of user nearly tooks 15 minutes.

On realism: we studied the impact of the number of initial publishers P in an ideal case (no pollution, no selfish users). The basic idea is that, when P increases, the load per node spreads equally over the networks (ideal P2P behaviour). We measure the number of received messages per nodes as the load carry by each peer. We saw that effectively, in our tool, the more people publish (a greater P), the more equally the load spreads. This means that the modified tool behave correctly.

4   Conclusion and Future Work

We have presented the basis of a multi-model approach to study the entwined influences of user's behaviour and QoS within the field of distributed, dynamic, ubiquitous network and applications. We integrate and make interact an agent-based model with an application and a network one. We implemented this proposal on a kademlia network to build a proof of concept.

Results obtained show that approach enables to study the impact of situated users' behaviours on the global P2P network. We aim now at continuing experiments over P2P file sharing applications. We have recently undertaken experiments to study the impact of poisoning peers: we look at the number of peers that poison the network and how they do it (e.g. number of decoy files they inject). The goal here is to show the conceptual benefits of our approach. We also aim at comparing our results to existing models and real data (in order to validate our model of user).

Currently, underlying network topology and user model are quite simple. However, our long term goal is to build a generic framework to implement and test different models of users and/or different overlay protocols and/or different network topologies. The scientific questions behind is to make interact several models at different time and space scales.

References

1. Hughes, D., Coulson, G., Walkerdine, J.: Free riding on gnutella revisited: The bell tolls? IEEE Distributed Systems Online 6(6), 1 (2005)
2. Lee, U., Choiz, M., Choy, J., Sanadidiy, M.Y., Gerla, M.: Understanding pollution dynamics in p2p file sharing. In: 5th International Workshop on Peer-to-Peer Systems (IPTPS 2006), Santa Babara, CA, USA (2006)
3. Teletraffic engineering handbook. Technical report, ITU-D Study Group 2 Question 16/2 (2006)
4. Naicken, S., Livingston, B., Basu, A., Rodhetbhai, S., Wakeman, I., Chalmers, D.: The State of Peer-to-Peer Simulators and Simulations. Accepted for editorial publication in ACM SIGCOMM journal for Computer Communication Review (2007)
5. Hales, D.: From Selfish Nodes to Cooperative Networks - Emergent Link-Based Incentives in Peer-to-Peer Networks. In: P2P 2004: Proceedings of the Fourth International Conference on Peer-to-Peer Computing (P2P 2004), Washington, DC, USA, pp. 151–158. IEEE Computer Society, Los Alamitos (2004)
6. Feldman, M., Papadimitriou, C., Chuang, J., Stoica, I.: Free-riding and whitewashing in peer-to-peer systems. In: PINS 2004: Proceedings of the ACM SIGCOMM workshop on Practice and theory of incentives in networked systems, pp. 228–236. ACM Press, New York (2004)
7. Ferber, J.: Multi-Agent Systems. In: An Introduction to Distributed Artificial Intelligence. Addison Wesley, Reading (1999)
8. Phan, D., Amblard, F.: Agent-Based Modelling and Simulation in the Social and Human Sciences. Bardwell Press, Oxford (2007)
9. Siebert, J., Chevrier, V., Ciarletta, L.: Modélisation multimodèle des réseaux dynamiques: cas des réseaux pair-à-pair (in french). In: JDIR 2008 - 9èmes Journées Doctorales en Informatique et Réseaux, Villeneuve d'Ascq, France (2008)
10. Thommes, R., Coates, M.: Epidemiological Modelling of Peer-to-Peer Viruses and Pollution. In: IEEE Infocom, Barcelona, Spain (2006)

Business-Driven Management of Policies in DiffServ Networks

Antonio Astorga and Javier Rubio-Loyola

Network Management Group, Departament de Teoria del Senyal i Comunicacions,
Universitat Politècnica de Catalunya
{aastorga, jrubio}@nmg.upc.edu

Abstract. This paper presents a framework to control the life cycle of enforceable policies aligned to business directives. The framework relies on three main aspects: the formalization of measurable business indicators underpinning the management cycle of policies, a holistic approach to conceal Quality of Service delivery with business alignment, and the use of policy-based management as the vehicle to control system behavior accordingly. The core contribution of this research lies in the network management area whose most widespread solutions for QoS delivery have been systematically decoupled from business value, although the research community recognizes business profit as the main motivation for any management solution. The ultimate goal of this research is to develop a management framework that allows exploiting business value in telecommunications infrastructures. As each application domain may have intrinsic peculiarities we propose to validate our approach in the context of DiffServ networks. Simulations will be conducted to evaluate and to optimize the performance of diverse business directives under different patterns of service invocations and patterns of inter-domain traffic exchange between autonomous systems. To the best of our knowledge no other approach has dealt with the above research area in such a holistic view.

Keywords: business driven management, business indicators, policy life cycle, network incidents, profit maximization.

1 Introduction

In networks supporting different classes of services it is expected that users will enjoy different levels of service for the traffic injected into the network. On the one hand, users should be encouraged by service providers to exploit the managed network resources. On the other hand, the allocation of resources to assess the arranged quality of service may need to be adjusted accordingly. The same behavioural pattern applies with inter-domain traffic exchange.

It is widely accepted that without control of any kind like price, admission control, resources limitation, etc, traffic injection would produce resources starvation and consequently network congestion [1]. Statistical phenomena like congestion may eventually cause service degradation which in turn would have some impact on the

D. Hausheer and J. Schönwälder (Eds.): AIMS 2008, LNCS 5127, pp. 180–184, 2008.

business value. From an economical view, SLA violation would have some impact on the profit, reward, and refund strategies of the administrative parties.

In the network management area, the research community has directed some efforts developing mechanisms to deliver end-to-end Quality of Service in the Internet. Mechanisms for network congestion prevention and solving, control of service subscriptions and invocations, and dynamic traffic engineering functions have been the centre of study in potential intra-domain [2] and inter-domain [3] network management solutions. Moreover, although these solutions have been proved to be efficient to guarantee QoS delivery, the requirements, implications and the incremental efforts to elevate their business value have remained almost unexplored.

The ability to carry out business- and QoS-oriented network management introduces several challenging problems addressed in this work. Initially, business strategies must be properly modelled with appropriate business indicators, pivotal for the management of policies. Second, business indicators should be monitored and modelled as functions of measurable parameters of the managed systems. Third, the dynamicity of events occurring in the managed network should be constantly evaluated as to define proactive and corrective management actions enforced through policy. The creation, deployment and modification of policies in runtime should be devoted to optimise business value, all in all under QoS delivery constraints. These problems make this research highly challenging, mainly when we consider a holistic approach to optimise business value under different patterns of resources utilization, patterns of traffic exchange between administrative domains and diverse network topologies. We intend to evaluate the framework in the DiffServ Network Management application domain.

2 Application Domain – Particular Objectives of Our Research

We strongly believe that each application domain should have inherent peculiarities to both maximize business profit and to provide QoS. Developing a bi-directional framework of this kind, valid for any application domain may be very difficult if not impossible. This research lies in the DiffServ Network Management application domain. In principle we propose a framework that exploits the mechanisms of the TEQUILA architecture [2] – Traffic Engineering for Quality of Service for the Internet at Large Scale – which to the best of our knowledge is the only validated network management approach that brings together Service Management and Traffic Engineering functionalities for QoS support in next generation IP Networks. TEQUILA uses policy based management as the key enabler for programmability.

The Service Management part of the TEQUILA architecture has two objectives: to control the traffic entering the network and to commit with the service provider's QoS guarantees. This research deals with the critical nature of achieving these two objectives relying on the dynamic evaluation of business indicators affected by the amount of traffic entering the network. In this sense we propose an overlay approach to dynamically enforce the most optimal admission control settings for service subscriptions and service invocations. Similarly, our proposed overlay approach dynamically enforces the most optimal preventive and corrective actions due to statistical network conditions affecting the business indicators, for example resource starving users (or other service providers), or potential states of network congestion.

The Traffic Engineering functionality of the TEQUILA architecture is concerned with the management of physical network resources. An off-line dimensioning process is responsible for mapping the predicted traffic demand to the physical network resources. In addition, real-time operations are implemented as the means to first, balance the load amongst the established Label Switched Paths (LSPs) in the network, and second, to ensure that link capacities are appropriately distributed among the different Per-Hop-Behaviours (PHBs) sharing each link in the core network. In this functionality our proposed approach dynamically triggers the most suitable policies for the centralized off-line dimensioning process devoted to maximize business value. In addition, our overlay approach dynamically evaluates the business indicators affected by statistical fluctuations of traffic in the core network and enforces real-time operations accordingly.

So far, the policy refinement process in this particular application domain [4] has been carried out taking into account pure QoS-oriented aspects, isolated completely from any business considerations. In summary this research work proposes to introduce a business optimization overlay that dynamically activates the most appropriate set of service management and traffic engineering enforceable policies as a result of a dynamic evaluation of the business indicators.

3 Business Indicators and Management of Policies – Foreseen Technical Approach

The chosen approach to address the research problems of this work is inspired in game theory principles which in turn have enabled recent business-oriented advances in IT Service Management [5], [6]. The proposed solution is an overlay environment in which business strategies are formalised through measurable business indicators. The approach is devoted to prioritise active changes in the managed network in order to prevent negative effects on the business indicators due to statistical changes of the network. The active changes are enforced through policies. More concrete, the framework basically consists in a multi-thread environment that *collects* information from the managed network, *analyses* it against the business indicators and *enforces* changes in the active policies as to maximise the business value due to actual states of the network threatening business value.

Consider for instance a business indicator linked to "the profit generated from a certain type of customers". The overlay framework will produce appropriate sets of policies devoted to maximize the profit obtained from that type of customers under statistical changes in the network utilisation, taking into account Quality of Service constraints. The approach is intended to handle several business indicators.

A critical issue in this research is the modelling that formalises the relationships between the business indicators and pure technological aspects of the DiffServ management domain. Initially, the overlay framework considers the identification of potential *incidents* affecting the business. In the DiffServ domain incidents may be simple ones like a *"service rate threshold crossing"*, or composed like *"a service rate threshold crossing under network congestion state"*. A model establishes formal relationships to link incidents both, simple or composed, with business value threatens. For example, the fact that the network is congested or in normal state may have a measurable impact on service level degradation. Also, traffic injection threshold crossings may imply that users may be starving the network, under-utilising it or injecting traffic according to the pre-signed SLA. In this context the modelling formalises the effects of an incident up to the SLAs. For instance, an incident may affect a set of Per-Hop-Behaviours (PHBs) in a network link. Each PHB affected by an incident may in turn affect a set of services and finally, a service may have some effect on a given SLA. SLAs may eventually be linked with user information or with other service provider's information. Incident effect trees are the source of information to carry out the *analysis* and consequently this information should be modelled properly.

The complexity of the *analysis* stage of the framework lies in the generation of policies aimed at minimising the negative effect of the above incidents on the business indicators throughout system execution. The central part of the *analysis* deals with the formalisation of the effect, from now on referred to as *impact*, of incidents over the *business indicators*. The total impact of an incident i should consider all the business indicators affected by such incident. As an incident may have different impact on different business indicators, the chosen approach considers the formalisation of this situation by means of weights [6], [7]. Weights represent the degree of importance ω that an incident i has on a business indicator j.

The analysis stage evaluates the total impact of incidents occurring on the network affecting all the business indicators and defines priority actions *enforced* with QoS policies. An automatic policy refinement approach [4] deploys QoS-oriented policies for this last *enforcement* step.

The evaluation of priority actions is by no means a trivial task. The DiffServ application domain is a multi-service environment with shared resources. Priority actions committed to some user's (or administrative domains) may have some influence on other business indicators, most probably linked to other users of the network. A trade-off processing step committed to stability is mandatory at this stage of this work. As priority actions are enforced through policy, stability passes through the management cycle of policies. An event handler enables the communication amongst the monitoring sub-systems of the managed network and the overlay system itself. This way the incidents affecting our business indicators are correlated dynamically and in case of further priority actions are needed those can be effectively scheduled.

4 Concluding Remarks

This paper has described our ongoing research work towards controlling the life cycle of enforceable policies aligned to business directives for the DiffServ network management area. We rely on game theory principles applied to the business area in which business indicators underpin the prioritization of corrective actions through policy once threatening incidents affecting the business are detected. The approach is to be validated with an overlay framework embedded to the network management functions of the described application domain.

So far we have built a strong knowledge in the DiffServ network management application domain, in particular the QoS-oriented policy refinement process [4] with a validated methodology and appropriate tools. We are currently defining the model to bring QoS DiffServ Network Management and business alignment into a unified framework.

Our immediate future work will be the definition of a holistic scenario in which we demonstrate our approach with realistic business indicators. Implementing our overlay framework and integrate it with our existing functional refinement solution is also part of our future work. Our intentions are to validate and refine our solution through OPNET simulations. We intend to execute scenarios to analyze different patterns of user's utilization and patterns of traffic exchange between different administrative domains. The ultimate objective of our research is to define patterns of policy management procedures to minimize profit losses and possibly to maximize profit due to patterns of behavior from users and eventually from other service providers e.g. for inter-domain issues. The results of this research can be further validated in real life scenarios in which traffic traces collected from real-life capturing process may be used to prove the effectiveness of the patterns induced in this holistic study.

We strongly believe that the management of policies constrained to business perspectives is an issue that is tightly coupled to application domains. With this regard, our contribution lies in the network management area in which to the best of our knowledge, not a single approach to manage policy in this context has been proposed so far as agreed by the research community.

Acknowledgments. This paper is supported in part by the IST-EMANICS Network of Excellence (#26854).

References

1. Chang, X., Petr, D.W.: A survey of pricing for integrated service networks. Elsevier Computer Communications 24(18) (December 1, 2001)
2. EU IST TEQUILA – Traffic Engineering for the Internet at Large Scale, http://www.ist-tequila.org
3. EU IST MESCAL – Management of End-to-End Quality of Service Across the Internet at Large Scale, http://www.mescal.org
4. Loyola, J.R., et al.: A Methodological Approach towards the Refinement Problem in Policy-based Management Systems. IEEE Communications Magazine (October 2006)
5. Aib, I.: A business-driven approach to policy optimization. University Pierre & Marie Curie (July 2007)
6. Bartolini, C., Salle, M.: Business Driven Prioritization of Service Incidents. In: Sahai, A., Wu, F. (eds.) DSOM 2004. LNCS, vol. 3278, pp. 64–75. Springer, Heidelberg (2004)
7. Buco, M.J., Chang, R.N., Luan, L.Z., Ward, C., Wolf, J.L., Yu, P.S.: Utility computing SLA management based upon business objectives. IBM Systems Journal 43(1) (2004)

Token-Based Payment in Dynamic SAML-Based Federations

David J. Lutz[1] and Burkhard Stiller[2]

[1] Rechenzentrum Universitaet Stuttgart
Allmandring 30, 70550 Stuttgart, Germany
`David.Lutz@rus.uni-stuttgart.de`
[2] University of Zurich, Department of Informatics (IFI)
Binzmühlestr. 14, CH-8050 Zürich, Switzerland
`stiller@ifi.uzh.ch`

Abstract. The newly developed approach on token-based payments introduces an integration of payments with current schemes for Identity Federations based on SAML. This new design utilizes an established federation infrastructure as well as its protocols. Only relevant mechanisms to support the payment on the federation infrastructure level are extended.

Keywords: Payment Token, Payment Assertion, Identity Federation, Payment.

1   Introduction

The concept of Identity Federation is quite well known and understood in the academic [8] as well as in the business area [4]. Within such a federation, several service providers agree on accepting user authentication not at their systems, but on the user's home institution, e.g., the user's universtity or his/her telecom operator. This leads to a reduced efford regarding the administration of credentials on both the user's side (only one account at the idenity provider and not several at each service provider) and the service provider's side (only simple account management needed). Almost all of these federations focus on authentication and authorization[1], an essential aspect is missing today: payment. Currently, payment is build on top of the federation structure using specific payment protocols, which means additional work and security concerns for the implementation itself. It is quite obvious that an implementation of payment solutions on the federation level would allow for an easy setup of business federations without considering payment solutions separately. Therefore, this work, partly developed in the SWIFT [7] project, focuses on the development of a payment scheme for identity federations without touching the federation structure itself to allow for an easy use of payment structures without the need of rebuilding the federation. This means that the former high-level payment could now be done by using the

---

[1] For both purposes mainly the Security Assertion Markup Language (SAML) is used.

D. Hausheer and J. Schonwalder (Eds.): AIMS 2008, LNCS 5127, pp. 185–189, 2008.

federation language (SAML [2], XACML [6]), its protocols (e.g., HTTP, SOAP) and its structure (service provider, identity provider, user), whereas the original federation concept should be kept unchanged as far as possible.

2   Related Work

Since the token-based payment approach builds on Identity Federations and the payment for electronic business, this section briefly introduces Identity Federations and discusses possible electronic payment mechanisms.

Many different Identity Federation approaches have been developed over the last years, like CAS, PERMIS, VOMS, all related to the Grid area, and Shibboleth [8], Liberty Alliance [4] and Web Service Federation [5] from within the web community. The key concept of such an Identity Federation is the Single Sign-on (SSO) principle, which means that a user has to log in only once. To do so, the user's profile is stored at a component called Identity Provider (IdP). Whenever a user wants to access a service, he authenticates himself at his IdP and receives after a successfully login an assertion or a token that is used as an identifier inside this federation. If a user requests a service at a Service Provider (SP), he presents the token/assertion from the IdP to claim his identity. Since all IdPs and SPs in such a federation have a contractually established trust relationship, the SP can trust the token/assertion based on the IdP's signature. If the SP needs specific user attributes, he requests them directly from the user's IdP, which releases them based on the release policy the user has chosen. Afterwards, the SP evaluates submitted attributes to decide on the access.

In electronic commerce, three different schemes of handling electronic payments exist: the transmission of payment-related information, the transmission of exchange information, and the transmission of digital cash. Although the implementation of the two firstly mentioned approaches in a federation infrastructure would also show some improvement regarding the convenience of payment, our work applies the third scheme. The transmitted information can be used as cash within the federation. Early approaches like NetCash and Digital Cash [1] covered ideas that a piece of information may be interpreted and used like money. These ideas of digital cash determine the foundation for the payment-enabled Identity Federation.

3   Payment-Enabled Identity Federation

The key idea of this work is to enable a payment within an Identity Federation and without changing the federation's infrastructure, protocols, or languages. Since most important federations today are based on SAML and an architecture including an Identity Provider, a Service Provider, and the User, it is straightforward that the new payment-enabled federation is also based on SAML and supports this common infrastructure.

The concept of the **Identity Provider** (IdP) does not have to be changed compared to its functions in usual SAML-based federations. It authenticates the user based on contracts as well as credentials and sends after a successfully login a token or assertion for further authentication to the consumer. It also sends attribute information for authorization purposes to the Service Provider.

The **Service Provider** (SP) has to be extended, because it needs the possibility to use additional hardware and software. Besides this, policy decision functions have to be changed in a way that a request for payment is sent to the user and upon the reception of a valid payment it has to be evaluated.

The **Payment Provider** (PP) determines the new component that enables the payment within an Identity Federation. It hosts the user's account, thus, it may become part of a banking institute, but it could also be integrated into the administrative structure of an IdP. The PP issues SAML Payment Assertions [3] for validating payment transactions and SAML Payment Tokens that are handled like cash within the federation.

Besides the contractual binding with his IdP, the **Consumer** needs additionally an account at a PP and possibly special hardware or software that has to be used for the token handling and other payment procedures.

The **Payment Token** can be considered to be like a banknote or a coin within the federation. It contains information about the identity of payer, payee and the PP as well as information on currency and the payment's amount. Also, related to security aspects, a lifetime, an identification number, and an issuer's signature are added. The token is issued by the PP on request of a consumer and send by the consumer to the SP for paying requested service access. The SP, in turn, can use the token for other business purposes. Due to the crucial nature of the token, a sufficient security level has to be achieved.

A scenario within such a payment-enabled identity federation can be split up into three different steps: the authentication, the authorization, and the payment. Since authentication and authorization are already established within usual federations, those processes are reused. When the authorization was successful, the SP sends a payment offer back to the consumer, who, in turn, contacts his PP requesting a payment token. After being authorized at the PP, the consumer receives his token, which he may now present to the SP. The SP checks the validity of the token, stores it for further purposes in his database, and allows the user to consume the resource protected.

4   Security Analysis

This chapter considers key security issues for the token-based payment scheme, since a high security level is required for productive uses of the new approach.

The **Identity Provider** cannot start any attack related to the payment, which has not been avoided by standard federation techniques, since the IdP has not been extended with respect to its functionality regarding a non-payment federation.

The **Consumer** shows the weakest piece of the chain in this concept, since he can copy the token and try to double-spend it. Therefore, two approaches can deal with this threat: Detect a misuse or prevent it. If only the detection of misuse is required, it provides for a sufficient security level to ensure that the token is signed correctly to identify the consumer, if he tampered with the token. If the SP wants to exchange the token into money, the PP is able to detect the double-spending. He will hand over the money to the SP, but will charge the consumer for this misbehavior. The prevention of misuse requires hardware-related security such as a Trusted Platform Module or Smart Cards. These systems are able to protect tokens and the application that is used for payment against any attacks from the user. It is an interesting research topic, which of both solutions may fit best.

The **Payment Provider** could try to issue invalid tokens or to refuse exchanging valid tokens. The PP's signature determines the protection against both attacks. If the PP issues an invalid token, this misbehavior will be detected due to its signature. And a valid token must be exchanged by the issuing PP, who can also be detected by its signature on the token.

The **Service Provider** can try to violate the contract. This attack is not specific to the approach of payment in a federation and would invoke penalties. But besides this, the SP can try to attack the infrastructure in the same way as a consumer may do. Thus, further research is needed here as well.

Eavesdropping and the man-in-the-middle attacks are not specific to the payment scenario and may be prevented by using common underlying security technologies, such as X.509 certificates in a trustful Public Key Infrastructure.

A **hardware theft** or **data loss** on consumer's side would be problematic, if the thief is able to pay with the stolen hardware or a data loss would lead to money loss. Basic security ideas like an additional check with a PIN and the revocation of amount reservation if a token is not presented for exchange at the PP within the stated lifetime can avoid that. If the hardware is stolen at SP's side, the thief is not able to reuse the tokens, since they contain information about the payee's identity. But the SP will lose its money because of theft or data loss, if he has no other proof about a transaction, because he cannot claim for exchanging the tokens.

5   Conclusions and Outlook

This paper describes the idea of integrating payment mechanisms into currently established SAML-based federations, which can be done by including the component of a Payment Provider into the federation architecture. Since only few changes in language, protocols, and infrastructure have to be made, this idea is a viable solution to resolve the lack of functionality detected in current identity federations. Apart from the normal payment usage in a federation without having the need to trust an add-on software solution, another important use-case for this approach is the possibility of using micro-payment within the academic Shibboleth-Federations (e.g., [10], [9]). This provides an incentive for many small commercial service providers to join such a federation.

Since the federation architecture and its infrastructure is already sketched above and designed, the three main topics of further work include the analysis of the exact information that has to be transmitted inside of the Payment Token, a security validation on a high level, and due to the business impact of the idea a cost and acceptance estimation. The analysis of exact information deals with the problem, which information is needed in the token to allow a secure payment process without violating privacy aspects. Security validation is very important within this approach, since a successful attack may lead directly to a loss of money. Regarding the business view, a cost and acceptance estimation should predict, whether the idea could be implemented in practice. Apart from those analytic steps, the approach will also be implemented within a prototype to prove its practicability as well as to take measurements in a validation scenario.

Acknowledgement

The approach published in this paper was partly developed in the project SWIFT [7], funded by the EC under the FP7-ICT programme. The authors thank all partners involved in that project.

References

1. Chaum, D., Fiat, A., Naor, M.: Untraceable electronic cash. In: Goldwasser, S. (ed.) CRYPTO 1988. LNCS, vol. 403, pp. 319–327. Springer, Heidelberg (1990)
2. Hughes, J., Maler, E.: Security Assertion Markup Language (SAML) V2.0 Technical Overview (October 2006) (2008), http://www.oasis-open.org/committees/download.php/14361/sstc-saml-tech-overview-2.0-draft-08.pdf
3. Jennings, C., Fischl, J., Tschofening, H., Jun, G.: Payment for Services in Session Initiation Protocol (SIP), 2007: Document ID draft-jennings-sipping-pay-05 (2008), http://www.ietf.org/ID.html
4. Liberty Alliance Project: Liberty Alliance Project Whitepaper: Personal Identity (2006) (2008), http://www.projectliberty.org/liberty/content/download/395/2744/file/Per-sonal_Identity.pdf
5. Lockhart, H., et al.: Web Services Federation Language (WS-Federation). Version 1.1, IBM Corporation (December 2006) (2008), http://www.ibm.com/developerworks/library/specification/ws-fed/
6. OASIS eXtensible Access Control Markup Language (XACML) TC (2008), http://www.oasis-open.org/committees/tc_home.php?wg_abbrev=xacml
7. Secure Widespread Identities for Federated Telecommunications (SWIFT). Funded by the EC under the FP7-IST programme (2008), http://ist-swift.org/
8. Shibboleth (2008) Website, http://shibboleth.internet2.edu/
9. Switch, The Swiss Education & Research Network: AAI Introductory Tutorial (2008), http://www.switch.ch/proxy/aai/support/presentations/infoday-2006/AAI-ID06-20-Intro.pdf
10. Verein zur Foerderung eines Deutschen Forschungsnetzes e. V.: DFN-AAI - Authentifikation Autorisierungs Infrastruktur (2008), https://www.aai.dfn.de/

Conceptual Integration of Flow-Based and Packet-Based Network Intrusion Detection

Gregor Schaffrath and Burkhard Stiller

Department of Informatics IFI, University of Zürich
Communication Systems Group CSG
Binzmühlestrasse 14, CH—8050, Zürich, Switzerland
schaffrath@ifi.uzh.ch, stiller@ifi.uzh.ch

Abstract. Network-based Intrusion Detection Systems aim at the detection of malicious activities by an inspection of network traffic. Since network link speeds and traffic volume grew over the last years, payload-based analysis became difficult, leading to the development of alternative approaches for flow-based analysis. Although each approach alone suffers a set of drawbacks, a few experiments with hybrid approaches show potential for synergies. This work analyses these drawbacks in order to develop a conceptual framework for hybrid approaches, integrating the two concepts in a fashion to compensate for their respective weaknesses proposed.

1 Introduction, Motivation, and Goals

Network-based Intrusion Detection Systems (NIDS) aim at the detection of malicious activities by inspection of network traffic. As network link speeds and traffic volume continued to grow, the traditional approach of Packet-based (or Payload-based) NIDS (PNIDS) became difficult [2]. Alternate Flow-based NIDS (FNIDS) approaches were developed, but while the development of evaluation methods are still ongoing [6], they are generally recognized as featuring a reduced confidence level expressed by higher false positive rates and do not allow for a fine grained labelling, as PNIDS concepts do.

Although few experiments with hybrid approaches indicate synergy potential [4], PNIDS and FNIDS seem to be rarely considered in combination in current research literature and seem to be perceived rather as competing than complementary concepts.

The goal of this work is the development of a conceptual framework for hybrid approaches. Strengths and weaknesses of both PNIDS and FNIDS are analyzed. Sample scenarios are developed, in which characteristics of PNIDS and FNIDS may be mapped onto requirements in order to compensate for respective drawbacks. These are generalized into abstract use templates based on a conceptional understanding of common issues and requirements, enabling easier design of security concepts by instantiation rather than complete redesign for each scenario.

2 Analysis

In an ideal world without any resource constraints, the set of attacks detectable by FNIDS, both on suspicion as well as on certainty level, are a full subset of attacks

D. Hausheer and J. Schönwälder (Eds.): AIMS 2008, LNCS 5127, pp. 190–194, 2008.

detectable by PNIDS. This is the consequence of FNIDS operating on a subset of information available to PNIDS. However, in real world environments, PNIDS is confronted with several problems reducing its effectiveness, resulting in a separation the of sets of detectable attacks for both approaches, as presented in Figure 1. These problems can be summarized in two categories:

- **Resources:** Packet-based inspection in high volume networks requires many resources in terms of memory and usually also CPU time. This is due to the low level of abstraction of the data basis in combination with the high frequency of data arrival and possible large data quantities per information instance.
- **Availability:** The placement of monitoring devices is crucial. However, if analysis requires transfer of monitored packets to a remote location, availability easily becomes an issue to several respects. Examples are bandwidth constraints for these transfers or privacy concerns on the transmission of actual payload information from production systems.

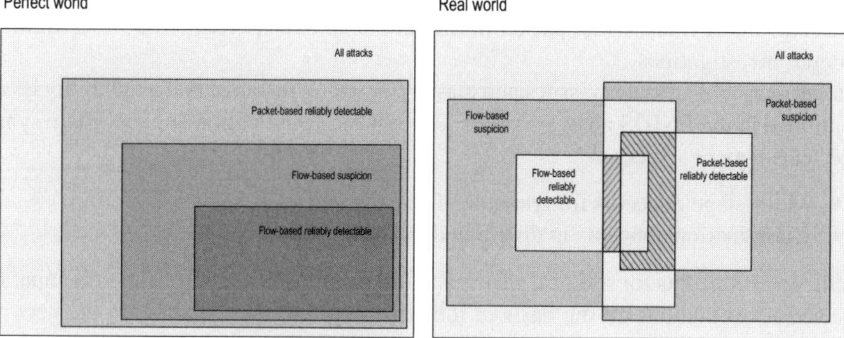

Fig. 1. Detection Coverage [3]

While the resource issue has been recognized by the research community, attempts to solve it (*e.g.*, [6]) have been largely focused on the OS and tool level. No work addressing it by a conceptual combination with other approaches has been established on the analysis level.

FNIDS is in a better position to handle large traffic volumes, since it processes a smaller amount of information and allows for the delegation of assembly work of input data even to regular network devices like switches. These two characteristics also increase their potential w.r.t. data availability, since device installation is less of a problem, data transfer is easier to handle and privacy concerns are less important. Nonetheless, it suffers a set of problems as well, which can be summarized by the following three categories:

- **Confidence:** In a complex context like security, where every arbitrary detail may by crucial to accurate analysis, the reduced amount of information can be expected to result in the experienced drop of confidence (resulting in higher false positive rates) or alert expressiveness (*e.g.*, allowing statements only about activity categories, instead of concise attack labelling)

- **Underdeveloped understanding:** Attack characteristics on the flow level are not yet thoroughly analyzed. This is also reflected by the fact that available research documentation shows a trend to visualization concepts (*e.g.*, [5]) and almost all work in FNIDS remains anomaly-based. Misuse model-based concepts remain underdeveloped and are the exception in FNIDS research.
- **Real-time:** When information assembly is delegated to the network infrastructure delivering, *e.g.*, NetFlow records in order to take full advantage of the resource requirement reduction advantage, reports will be delayed after flow's end w.r.t. reported activities, severely reducing FNIDS usability for real-time intrusion detection.

3   Proposed Combination Angles

Since flow information reflects a high level view on the interaction behavior of network nodes with each other, but seldomly allow for statements about specific instances of these interactions, they can be deemed predestined for high level characterizations of host behavior or roles, while packet information can be expected to be fit for directed in-depth investigations.

Considering distribution issues and classifying along resource and availability issues mentioned in the PNIDS analysis yields to two basic combination angles, where synergy effects may be expected:

- Multi-stage concepts for resource efficiency and
- Coordination concepts in distributed environments.

Multi-stage concepts for resource efficiency use results of one approach as the input for directed investigations on the basis of the other approach. Depending on the network environment and specific protection goals determined in advance, this can be beneficial in both directions:

FNIDS may be used as a selection filter for PNIDS activities for CPU or memory requirement reasons. Example use cases (to be evaluated) for this include the isolation of P2P traffic, recognized by flow level characteristics, for packet level inspection of suspicious flows, in order to tell regular P2P traffic apart from P2P botnet traffic, or the use of PNIDS for labelling purposes upon FNIDS based worm recognition. Depending on scenario requirements and available capacities to capture and cache all relevant packet data, the follow-up inspection may either be restricted to the subsequent communication of hosts involved or be performed on the actual data that triggered the flow-based alert.

Critical assets may be protected by PNIDS for real-time reasons, whose alert confidence upon a signature trigger could be increased by judgement on the overall behaviour of hosts involved. Example use cases for this include (a) the search for repetitive host behavior upon a alert triggered from a generic payload signature indicating worm activities, or (b) the flow-based search for control streams upon botnet detection, where flows of hosts involved are checked for common communication partners and properties. This is exemplified in [4], while the analysis encompasses possibly the communication between different administrative zones and additional subsequent PNIDS.

In some scenarios, coordination concepts in distributed environments are related to multi-stage concepts. This may be based on network resource-related problems, where efficiency depends on which information is analyzed locally w.r.t. each site and which information is forwarded to another site. An example of this is a scenario, in which a customer is connected to the Internet via two different Internet service providers, for load balancing or redundancy reasons, and parts of attacks are distributed over uplinks. In this case, flow information could be exchanged in order to correlate flows on both links and start packet transfers for PNIDS-based inspection of suspicious traffic. *E.g.*, upon the detection of flows with equal endpoints, these flows might be checked locally for packet-level fragmentation, followed by a potential packet data exchange for reassembly.

However, in many scenarios, coordination concepts involve additional concerns and issues not covered by scenarios for multi-stage concepts: While the transfer of information may not be a technical issue, payload transfer from one site to another may be impossible and even the transfer of flow-based information may be restricted, *e.g.*, by policies. This shift of focus w.r.t. concerns can be expected to result in shifted use concepts of PNIDS and FNIDS. An example for this is a scenario, where an administrative domain A registers an anomaly triggered by a host in domain B, and suspects a correlation to the activity registered from domain C. Since the domains are prohibited to exchange payload information, they are restricted to tentative correlation via FNIDS or delegation of PNIDS tasks to individual sites.

4   Evaluation

While evaluation of the effectiveness of the hybrid approaches may be relatively straightforward for experimentation w.r.t. resource efficiency, at the time of writing, it is yet an open point, how to evaluate the quality of distributed scenarios and their respective templates and solutions.

Resource efficiency of multi-stage concepts may be determined by running both a simple packet-based IDS and the combined approach simultaneously in the same environment on equal infrastructure and measuring respective resource consumption, as well as altert, false positive and false negative rates. If the processed traffic is reduced to an amount manageable by both approaches, the direct correlation of overall resource consumption with achieved results concerning alert correctness may serve as quality measure.

However, while quality in distributed environments may be measurable by similiar metrics to some extend, several aspects are yet unaddressed and, therefore, still open in terms of the evaluation. *E.g.*, the scenario choice, especially in terms of environments, detection goals, and attack scopes, needs to be validated for realism. Solutions need to be validated w.r.t. policy compatibility (and, therefore, applicability), and real world evaluation will depend on the availability of cooperation partners.

As these scenarios are potentially arbitrarily numerous and complex, it is intended to start by isolating motivations for distributed Intrusion Detection and mapping them to real world instances of distributed systems. Thereby, a break down of the problem into a manageable complexity will follow a practical track of solutions.

5   Preliminary Conclusions, Tasks, and Issues

Following the two combination angles, the work will be split into two parts. The investigation into the resource effectiveness of multi-stage approaches consists of:

- the definition of use scenarios for comparative evaluation of resource and detection efficiency in a real world test environments,
- the generalization into use templates, if results confirm the efficiency hypothesis,
- re-instantiation of templates into different use scenarios for validation of the generalization.

Investigations of coordination concepts in distributed environments consist of:

- generation of realistic prototypical cooperation scenarios,
- development of approaches to handle political, legal, and operational issues,
- integration of concepts into use templates based on respective scenarios

Investigations and evaluations w.r.t. multi-stage approaches for resource efficiency are currently ongoing in the context of [3].

Acknowledgements. The work of Fabian Hensel in support of first steps for developing the evaluation scenarios and implementation environments is acknowledged.

References

[1] Brauckhoff, D., May, M., Plattner, B.: Flow-Level Anomaly Detection - Blessing or Curse? In: IEEE INFOCOM 2007, Student Workshop, Anchorage, Alaska, U.S.A (May 2007)

[2] Dreger, H., Feldmann, A., Paxson, V., Sommer, R.: Operational experiences with high-volume network intrusion detection. In: 11th ACM Conference on Computer and Communications Security, Washington, U.S.A (2001)

[3] Hensel, F.: Flow-based and Packet level-based Intrusion Detection as Complementary Concepts, Diploma Thesis, University of Zurich, Department of Informatics IFI, Switzerland (April 2008)

[4] Karasaridis, A., Rexroad, B., Hoeflin, D.: Wide-scale Botnet Detection and Characterization. In: HotBots 2007, Usenix Workshop on Hot Topics in Understanding Botnets, Cambridge, Massachusetts, U.S.A (April 2007)

[5] Lakkaraju, K., Yurcik, W., Lee, A.J.: NVisionIP: netflow visualizations of system state for security situational awareness. In: 2004 ACM Workshop on Visualization and Data Mining for Computer Security, Washington D.C., U.S.A (2004)

[6] Schneider, F.: Performance evaluation of packet capturing systems for high-speed networks, Diploma Thesis, Technische Universität München, Munich, Germany (November 2005)

Towards Resilient
Community Wireless Mesh Networks

Sara Bury and Nicholas J.P. Race

Computing Department, Lancaster University, Lancaster LA1 4WA, UK
{sara.bury,race}@comp.lancs.ac.uk

Abstract. Wireless Mesh Networks are an increasingly common technology providing connectivity in many communities, particularly where Internet access is unavailable or restricted via more conventional means. Their comparative ease of installation and relatively low cost makes this especially true for communities which might previously have lacked the technical knowledge or skill to attempt such an endeavour. In such a situation it is important that the operation of the network should be easily manageable; to this end the overall resiliency of the network is a key factor, enabling the network to resolve and remediate problems as they arise without requiring external technical understanding or input. This research aims to improve the resilience of community mesh networks by improving their security, initially examining the use of risk analysis techniques in this environment to identify potential attack vectors. This understanding will then be used to investigate intrusion detection techniques for operation specifically in a community environment.

1   Introduction

Wireless mesh networks (WMNs) are becoming increasingly common, particularly to provide network connectivity to communities where wired deployment strategies are either not possible or are prohibitively expensive. The proliferation of 'off the shelf' mesh hardware and software [1,2] has resulted in communities creating wireless mesh networking installations themselves where previously they might not have possessed the understanding or technical skill. These factors combined with the many potential issues which might occur throughout the operation of a wireless mesh have led to a requirement for increased resiliency, enabling the network to resolve and remediate against problems as and when they arise without the need for external technical understanding or input.

Resilience in this context can be thought of as the aim to provide an acceptable level of service when challenges to network operation occur, whatever the adverse event or condition might be [3]. A resilience strategy to address potential problems has been developed as part of the EU FP6 ANA Project – D^2R^2+DR. This consists of two ongoing phases, firstly (D^2R^2) Defence against potential challenges and Detection of their presence as and when they occur, Remediation of the effects and eventual Recovery of the system back to normal operation.

D. Hausheer and J. Schönwälder (Eds.): AIMS 2008, LNCS 5127, pp. 195–199, 2008.

Secondly, (DR) consists of Diagnosis and Refinement of the system based on the results of previous first phase iterations.

WMNs are intended to be resilient by design. Their infrastructure is created using a combination of wireless networking technology and ad-hoc routing protocols to create a self-managing network in which all nodes act as routers [5], able to route traffic either directly or via a multi-hop path. Unfortunately, whilst WMNs are considered to be functional the technology and protocols behind these mechanisms are still relatively new and research is ongoing to improve their dependability and efficiency [4]. Security is a necessary facet of resiliency in wireless mesh networking; resilient routing protocols and autonomous configuration can only go so far if these processes can be abused by attackers. Due to this security has been chosen as the main focus of this research.

2   The Research Problem

The specific scenario being investigated is that of community wireless mesh networking – situations where mesh networking technology has been introduced into a community environment, rather than through any commercial application, and where it is operated by the users themselves. An example of this is the situation at Wray, a small rural village in the North West of England. In 2003, members of the community approached academics at Lancaster University searching for a solution to their lack of broadband Internet access. The result was the deployment of a WMN throughout the village with nodes owned and hosted by individual members of the community, making available an Internet connection fed into the local school via a 5.8Ghz radio link [6]. In this situation, though the University has access to use the network for research purposes, the villagers themselves oversee and operate the network on a daily basis and users with a range of expertise and computer literacy have responsibility and control over how the network runs. The resilience of the network is incredibly important. In many cases the users rely on the network as their sole method of access to the Internet, but they lack the technical experience and knowledge of computer networking to manually fix problems if they arise.

For generic network security there are goals which applications aim to achieve: confidentiality, integrity, availability, authentication, authorisation and accountability - in a WMN there are specific challenges to these goals over and above those found in more conventional wired networks. The shared wireless medium exists such that any one with suitable wireless hardware has the ability to listen to traffic on the network, launch jamming attacks to deny network functionality, or even to send out malicious control traffic to other routing nodes [7]. Also, a lack of physical protection for the mesh nodes themselves could result in legitimate mesh infrastructure becoming compromised; this is emphasised by the nature of ubiquitous access within a community mesh, all members of the community are offered network access, but with no specific assurance that attackers won't come from within the community group, potentially hosting the infrastructure they have compromised. In a community WMN scenario, attack vectors can occur externally and internally to the network infrastructure and this results in an extremely wide scope of potential attacks to combat. Another factor alongside this is the diversity of needs, requirements and backgrounds within the community. A single community group may contain home users, small businesses, people making use of the network for educational purposes and so on, all with different understandings of what the network provides and what functionality is most important to them. Also each of these users may have particular security requirements, for stored data or important communications.

Without a clear idea of these requirements, the security needs for the network are both vague and wide in scope. This makes the development of a security strategy for use in this scenario incredibly difficult. An understanding of the uses, priorities, and necessary services would substantially aid the creation of security systems, procedures, and policies by narrowing the problem space involved.

3   Chosen Approach

In order to gain an insight into the utilisation of the network and the requirements of individual users, we need to understand from the perspective of the users themselves what they consider to be their most important assets and what they feel are most vulnerable to attack. The concept of risk analysis within computer networking is not new; there are many tried and tested frameworks for the assessment of such factors, particularly within enterprise scale networks used for businesses or academia. Examples include the OCTAVE risk based strategic assessment process [8], or STRIDE, a practice for computer security threat modelling [9]. Unfortunately due to the distinct operational nature and requirements of community mesh networks, such proven formalised methods are not directly applicable, even in scenarios for which the processes were designed each individual method has strengths and weaknesses for it's application depending on the exact circumstance, as shown by Vorster and Labuschagne [10].

Other work in the area of mesh network resilience has often focussed on specific perceived threats, from low level control and management improvements [11] to multiple radio hardware and protocol solutions for increased throughput [12] [13]; little work has been carried out which takes the opinions and concerns of the mesh users into account when identifying threats to resilience. This research intends to apply risk analysis techniques in a community wireless mesh network setting, with the aim identifying the most important risks for the users from their own perspective, what assets exist and are most appealing to an attacker, and the weighted probability of the occurrence of types of attack aimed at specific assets.

This approach has been chosen firstly because of the benefits of being able to narrow down the attack vectors present in a WMN, but secondly to investigate whether risk analysis techniques can be formalised for use in similar situations. Such a formalised process would enable community users of mesh networks to perform risk analysis themselves, looking for ways to improve their security without involving external consultants. The process of consulting members of the community about their own security concerns also fits well with the way that community WMNs operate – everyone having a hand in their continued functionality and contributing to the project as a whole.

Before involving network users in the project, certain decisions must be made regarding the suitability of particular risk analysis techniques and assumptions within this community scenario. For example, the concept of an 'asset' is likely to be different when compared with an enterprise setting – users may consider the safety of their children on the Internet of the utmost importance, whereas within a company employees would be expected to in many respects look after themselves. The community risk analysis will be carried out through small focus groups and discussion sessions with real world users, using carefully selected scenarios and lines of questioning to help explain the project. The research is in its preliminary stages and over the course of the next year sessions are planned with members of the community at Wray.

4   Conclusion

Resiliency in WMNs is a complex area and security is a critical factor. This research aims to improve the resilience of WMNs by examining improvements in the area of security. Firstly by reducing the problem space involved, then leading to the development of a security strategy with relevant and appropriate security systems for use in community WMNs. In order to reduce the problem space, a breakdown of assets and risks from the perspective of community WMN users will be produced; the process of creating which should indicate the feasibility of formalising this risk analysis procedure for users themselves to carry out as a community project. This information will be used to narrow down the number of attack vectors necessary to anticipate, prevent and detect in the target development of an IDS to demonstrate the functionality in a community WMN environment.

Acknowledgements

The authors are grateful to the resilient networking group for their work in developing the D^2R^2+DR resilience strategy, which will guide this work. More information available from: `http://www.comp.lancs.ac.uk/resilinets`

References

1. LocustWorld, `http://www.locustworld.com/`
2. Kiyon Autonomic Networks, `http://www.kiyon.com/`
3. Sterbenz, J.P.G., Schller, M., Jabbar, A., Hutchison, D.: Resiliency and Security Framework, First Draft. ANA - Autonomic Network Architecture, Deliverable FP6-IST-27489/WP3/D3.2 (2007)
4. Lee, M.J., Zheng, J., Ko, Y.-B., Shrestha, D.M.: Emerging Standards for Wireless Mesh Technology. IEEE Wireless Communications 13, 56–63 (2006)

5. Akyildiz, I.F., Wang, X., Wang, W.: Wireless Mesh Networks: A Survey. Computer Networks 47, 445–487 (2005)
6. Ishmael, J., Race, N.J.P.: Building a Rural Community Mesh Network. In: IST Broadband Europe Conference, Geneva, Switzerland (2006)
7. Zhang, W., Wang, Z., Das, S.K., Hassan, M.: Security Issues in Wireless Mesh Networks. In: Houssain, E., Leung, K. (eds.) Wireless Mesh Networks: Architecture and Protocols. Springer, Heidelberg (2008)
8. Alberts, C., Dorofee, A., Stevens, J., Woody, C.: Introduction to the OCTAVE Approach (2003), http://www.cert.org/octave/approach_intro.pdf
9. Hernam, S., Lambert, S., Ostwald, T., Shostack, A.: Uncover Security Design Flaws Using The STRIDE Approach. MSDN Magazine (2006), http://msdn.microsoft.com/msdnmag/issues/06/11/ThreatModeling/default.aspx
10. Vorster, A., Labuschagne, L.: A framework for comparing different Information security risk analysis methodologies. In: SAICSIT 2005: Proceedings of the 2005 annual research conference of the South African institute of computer scientists and information technologists on IT research in developing countries, Republic of South Africa, pp. 95–103 (2005)
11. Quercia, D., Lad, M., Hailes, S., Capra, L., Bhatti, S.: Survivable Wireless Networking - Autonomic Bandwidth Sharing in Mesh Networks. BT Technology Journal 24(3), 99–107 (2006)
12. Kyasanur, P., So, J., Chereddi, C., Vaidya, N.H.: Multichannel Mesh Networks: Challenges and Protocols. IEEE Wireless Communications 13(2), 30–36 (2006)
13. Draves, R., Padhye, J., Zill, B.: Routing in Multi-Radio Multi-Hop Wireless Mesh Networks. In: ACM Annual Conference of the Special Interest Group on Data Communication (SIGCOMM), pp. 133–144 (2004)

Resource Management of Disruption Tolerant Networks

Iyad Tumar and Jürgen Schönwälder

Computer Science, Jacobs University Bremen, Germany
{i.tumar,j.schoenwaelder}@jacobs-university.de

Abstract. Disruption tolerant networks (DTNs) differ from traditional networks due to their special characteristics such as frequent partitions, intermittent connectivity, and message delivery delay. This paper presents a new idea for the resource management of sparse disruption tolerant networks where the density of nodes is insufficient to support direct end-to-end communications. The idea combines an asynchronous approach, where nodes work on their own wake up schedules without synchronized clocks, with an on-demand scheme, where a low power radio (LPR) is used to search about contacts and a high power radio (HPR) undertakes the actual data transmission.

Keywords: Disruption Tolerant Networks, Power Management.

1 Introduction

Disruption tolerant networks (DTNs) is a research area aiming at developing network communication when connectivity is intermittent and prone to disruptions. In general, DTNs are applicable in remote and hazardous areas where the energy sources are constrained. They are also assumed to operate over a long period of time. Therefore, several research efforts have been started to develop power management schemes for disruption tolerant networks.

In DTNs, nodes need to discover neighbors to establish communication. Searching for neighbors in sparse DTNs can consume a large amount of power compared to the power consumed by infrequent data transfers. Banerjee et al. [1] show that using an 802.11 radio to search for contacts consumes 99.5% of the total energy. Therefore, novel power management schemes are needed to address this problem and to save energy in the neighbor searching mode. Designing such power management schemes is challenging because nodes need to know when to sleep to save power and when to wake up to search for neighbors. Ideally, power management schemes should not reduce network connectivity opportunities, which would negatively affect the overall performance of the network.

There are three categories for wake-up based power management approaches. The first category are scheduled rendezvous, in which sleeping nodes wake up at the same time based on deterministic wake-up patterns (assuming synchronized nodes). The second category are asynchronous approaches with overlapping active periods within a specific number of sleep cycles for any two neighbor nodes.

D. Hausheer and J. Schönwälder (Eds.): AIMS 2008, LNCS 5127, pp. 200–204, 2008.

The third category are on-demand approaches where nodes can be awakened on-demand at any point of time. For example, an additional low power radio can be used to trigger a high power radio.

A new power management scheme is developed in this proposal. This scheme tries to save energy in searching mode with a minimum degradation of the overall network performance. It is based on the context aware power management (CAPM) scheme [2], and it also uses an additional low power radio interface (LPR) [3]. The rest of this paper is structured as follows: Section 2 details the research questions and outlines the proposed power management scheme and how it is being evaluated. Related work is discussed in Section 3 before we conclude the paper in Section 4.

2 Research Questions and Proposed Approach

The goal of this work is to develop a new power management scheme for sparse disruption tolerant networks that saves energy and extends the network life time with minimum reduction of the network connectivity opportunities. The specific research questions are:

1. *What are efficient approaches to save energy in sparse DTNs?*
2. *Can we design power management schemes without affecting the network performance?*
3. *More precisely what are efficient approaches to save the maximum amount of energy in sparse DTNs with the minimum degradation of network performance?*
4. *What is the impact of traffic load and node speed on power management scheme in DTNs?*

Our approach combines the on-demand scheme and the asynchronous scheme. It uses an additional low power radio to search about contacts and it allows each node to work on its own wake up schedule without synchronized clocks. Each node uses a fixed duty cycle. Within this duty cycle, each node wakes up for a fixed or adaptive period and sleeps for the rest of the time. When a node wakes up, it broadcasts a beacon that includes its identifier and the time it will stay active. If this node has data to deliver, it will piggyback a notification delivery (destination identifier) to the beacon. We assume that there will be overlapping active periods between nodes within a certain number of duty cycles.

We do not consider the energy consumption of computations; we only consider the energy consumption of wireless interfaces in searching mode when nodes search about each other to communicate. Two alternative operations are considered in this scheme: neighbor discovery in which a node wakes up to search about neighbor nodes for data forwarding, and data delivery in which data is exchanged among nodes. Data delivery uses the HPR to transfer the data, while neighbor discovery is based on both radios to find contacts.

There are two scenarios when using LPR and HPR radios to search about contacts. The first one is based on the LPR waking up once each duty cycle to

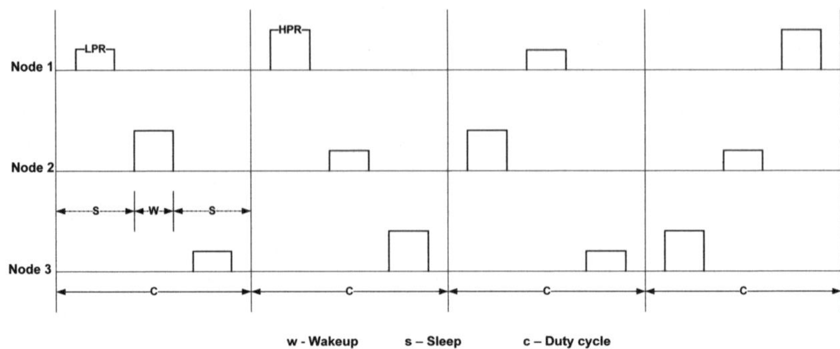

Fig. 1. Low and high power radios random wake up

search about contacts and uses the HPR on demand to transfer data after a communication link between two nodes has been established. The second scenario alters between LPR and HPR to search about contacts. In this scenario, the LPR wakes up once each two duty cycles, and the HPR wakes up each two duty cycles or when it is triggered by the LPR to undertake the data transmission after a connection is established between two nodes (see Fig. 1). Using an additional low power radio in an asynchronous manner to search about contacts leads to overlapping periods between HPR and LPR. In order to enable both radios to communicate with each other, we assume that both radios use the same MAC layer and the same frequency (only one radio will be active at any point of time). By allowing both radios to communicate with each other and by utilizing both radios to search about contacts, we expect that a significant amount of power can be saved in searching mode.

The proposed power management scheme will be implemented and evaluated by simulation. In order to evaluate our power management scheme, two DTN routing protocols will be implemented (Epidemic [4], PRoPHET [5]). We will first evaluate the performance of Epidemic and PRoPHET in the absence of power management based on the delivery ratio and the delivery delay. Then, we will investigate the impact of our power management scheme on the delivery ratio and the delivery delay for both routing schemes under different traffic loads, and node movement speeds. The following metrics will be considered:

- The *Delivery Ratio* is the amount of successfully received data over the total amount of delivered data.
- The *Delivery Delay* is the average delay per delivered message.
- The *Energy Cost* is the total energy consumption over the number of delivered messages (the average energy consumption to deliver a message).
- The *Normalized Energy Consumption* is the ratio of the energy consumption with power management over the energy consumption without power management.

We will use the network scenario that has already been used to evaluate CAPM [2]. This scenario consists of 40 nodes that are distributed over a square of size $1km \times 1km$. These nodes move according to the random waypoint model with a maximum speed of $5m/s$ and a pause time in each waypoint of 10 seconds. The communication range for HPR is 250 m with data rate 2 Mbps, while the communication range for LPR is 100 m with data rate 76.8 Kbps. To be sure that simulation results are correct, they will be compared with published results in [2].

3   Related Work

Several power management schemes have been proposed for ad hoc networks. These schemes allow nodes to disable their radios when they are not used to save energy and to prolong the network life time while keeping network connectivity [6, 7]. Unlike our work, these schemes assume that a node has another node within its communication range most of time.

There have been several efforts to develop energy efficient medium access control (MAC) protocols [8, 9]. These efforts are motivated by the observation that transmissions of multiple nodes in a wireless network may interfere with each other. To avoid this interference, only two nodes can communicate with each other at any point in time. Therefore, significant energy can be saved if a node sleeps while others communicate, thereby in many cases improving overall network performance. These MAC protocols propose mechanisms to increase sleeping time based on the traffic in the neighborhood. However, these MAC protocols are designed for dense networks rather than sparse networks.

There are three approaches for power management of sparse disruption toler- ant networks. These approaches focus on saving energy in searching mode when nodes search about each other to communicate. The first approach presented by Jun et al. [10] assumes synchronized clocks and allows nodes to be in one of three modes, dormant (sleep) mode, search mode, and contact mode based on knowledge of future contacts. There are three levels of knowledge: (i) complete knowledge in which nodes know everything about their future contacts so they know exactly when to wake up and when to sleep, (ii) zero knowledge in which nodes have no information about each other and so they need to search about each others, (iii) partial knowledge in which nodes wake up and sleep based on probability metrics derived from statistical information. The second approach described by Jun et al. [3] tries to minimize the power consumed in searching mode by using an additional low power radio to discover contacts and to awake the high power radio to undertake the data transmission. The third approach introduced by Chuah et al. [2] is an asynchronous mechanism in which each node works on its own wake-up schedule independently. It has a fixed duty cycle which consists of a wake-up and a sleep period. Each node wakes up for a fixed or adaptive period and sleeps for the remaining time.

4   Conclusion

This paper presents a new power management scheme for sparse disruption toler- ant networks (DTNs) where the density of nodes is insufficient to support direct end-to-end communication. We formulate the research questions, outline a novel power management scheme approach combining on-demand and asynchronous schemes, and we describe how this new scheme will be evaluated.

Acknowledgement

The work reported in this paper is supported by the EC IST-EMANICS Network of Excellence (#26854).

References

1. Banerjee, N., Corner, M., Levine, B.: An Energy-Efficient Architecture for DTN Throwboxes. In: Proceeding of IEEE INFOCOM 2007, Anchorage, Alaska, USA, May 6-12 (2007)
2. Chuah, M., Xi, Y., Chang, K.: Performance Evaluation of a Power Management Scheme for DTNs. In: Proceedings of IEEE QShine, Vancouver, British Columbia, Canada, August 14-17 (2007)
3. Jun, H., Ammar, M.H., Corner, M.D., Zegura, E.W.: Hierarchical Power Management in Disruption Tolerant Networks with Traffic-Aware Optimization. In: Proceedings of the 2006 SIGCOMM Workshop on Challenged Networks (CHANTS 2006), pp. 245–252. ACM Press, New York (2006)
4. Vahdat, A., Becker, D.: Epidemic Routing for Partially Connected Ad Hoc Networks. Technical Report CS-200006, Duke University (April 2000)
5. Lindgren, A., Doria, A., Schelen, O.: Probabilistic routing in intermittently connected networks, pp. 239–254 (August 2004)
6. Tseng, Y.C., Hsu, C.S., Hsieh, T.Y.: Power-Saving Protocols for IEEE 802.11-Based Multi-Hop Ad Hoc Networks. In: Proceedings of the Twenty-First Annual Joint Conference of the IEEE Computer and Communications Societies (INFO-COM 2002), June 23-27, 2002, vol. 1, pp. 200–209 (2002)
7. Zheng, R., Hou, J.C., Sha, L.: Asynchronous Wakeup for Ad Hoc Networks. In: Proceedings of the 4th ACM International Symposium on Mobile Ad Hoc Networking and Computing (MobiHoc 2003), pp. 35–45. ACM Press, New York (2003)
8. Singh, S., Raghavendra, C.S.: PAMAS: Power Aware Multi-Access protocol with Signalling for Ad Hoc Networks. ACM Computer Communication Review 28(3), 5–26 (1998)
9. Ye, W., Heidemann, J., Estrin, D.: An Energy-Efficient MAC protocol for Wireless Sensor Networks. In: Proceedings of the IEEE INFOCOM, New York, NY, USA, June 2002, pp. 1567–1576 (2002)
10. Jun, H., Ammar, M., Zegura, E.: Power Management in Delay Tolerant Networks: A Framework and Knowledge-Based Mechanisms. In: IEEE SECON 2005 Second Annual IEEE Communications Society Conference on Sensor and Ad Hoc Communications and Networks, pp. 418–429 (September 2005)

Design of an IP Flow Record Query Language

Vladislav Marinov and Jürgen Schönwälder

Computer Science, Jacobs University Bremen, Germany
{v.marinov,j.schoenwaelder}@jacobs-university.de

Abstract. Internet traffic is often summarized by collecting Net-Flow/IPFIX flow records. Several tools exist to filter or to search for specific flows in a collection of flow records. However, there is a need for a framework (filter language) which allows certain types of traffic patterns to be defined and matched in a collection of flow records. The goal of this project is to research the various filter/query languages used by tools or proposed in the literature and to extract a common basis for a new orthogonal flow record query language. We present research motivation and state of the art in this paper.

Keywords: NetFlow, IPFIX, network traffic analysis, query language.

1   Introduction

The analysis of network traffic and more specifically Internet traffic has become an important area of research. Cisco has designed the Netflow/IPFIX protocol [1,2], which allows to create a summary for the traffic flows that traverse a router. A network flow is defined as an unidirectional sequence of packets between given source and destination endpoints. Flow records include details such as IP addresses, packet and byte counts, timestamps, Type of Service (ToS), application ports, input and output interfaces, etc. Network elements (routers and switches) gather flow data and export it to collectors for analysis.

Although the flow records carried by NetFlow/IPFIX provide aggregated information about the packets traversing a specific router, this information still contains too many details for network administrators and is not useful unless processed by network analysis tools. Most of the existent tools provide mechanisms for selecting specific flows in a collection of flow records. This makes possible some simple tasks like filtering by an IP address or port number or generating Top N talkers reports. However, identifying more complex flow patterns resembles a search for a pin in a haystack. In order to describe complex traffic patterns and match a collection of flow records against the description, one needs a useful flow record query language.

The rest of this paper is structured as follows: Section 2 presents the state of the art in query languages used by network analysis tools. In Section 3, we present the research motivation for a new filter/query language and we conclude in Section 4.

D. Hausheer and J. Schönwälder (Eds.): AIMS 2008, LNCS 5127, pp. 205–210, 2008.
© IFIP International Federation for Information Processing 2008

2   State of the Art in Query/Filter Languages

Several early implementations of network analysis tools used a Relational Database Management System (RDBMS) to store the data contained in flow records and therefore they use SQL-based query languages for selecting flows.

B.Nickless [3] describes a system which uses standard MySQL and Oracle DBMS for storing the attributes from NetFlow records. Using powerful SQL queries, the tool was able to provide good support for basic intrusion detection and usage statistics. With the advance of high-speed links, however, network managers could not rely on pure DBMS anymore because of performance issues. There was also a semantic mismatch between the traffic analysis operations and the operations supported by the commercial DBMS. The data used by network analysis applications can be best modeled as transient data streams as opposed to the persistent relational data model used by traditional DBMS. It is recognized that continuous queries, approximation and adaptivity are some key features that are common for such stream applications. However, none of these is supported by standard DBMS. Based on these requirements B.Babcock et al. [4] propose the design of a Data Stream Management System (DSMS). Together with the model the authors also extend the SQL query language so that the DSMS can be queried over time and provide examples of network traffic reports that are generated based on flow data that is stored in such a DSMS. *Gigascope* [5] is another stream database for network monitoring applications. It uses GSQL for query and filtering which is yet another modification of the SQL query language adopted in a way so that time windows can be defined inside the query. *Tribeca* [6] is another extensible, stream-oriented DBMS designed to support network traffic analysis. It is optimized to analyze streams coming from the network in real time as well as offline traces. It defines its own stream query language which supports operations such as projection, selection, aggregation, multiplexing and demultiplexing of streams based on stream attributes. The query language also defines a windowing mechanism to select a timeframe for the analysis.

The *Berkeley Packet Filter (BPF)* [7] specifies simple rules which are widely used among network analysis tools to filter a stream of packets. BPF allows users to construct simple logical expressions for filtering network traces by IP address, port number, protocol etc. and translates them into a small program executed by a generic packet filtering engine. One popular use of the BPF is in the `tcpdump` utility. The BPF rules for constructing filter expressions are also used in `nfdump` [8], which is a powerful and fast filter engine used to analyze network flow records. `nfdump` is currently one of the *de facto* standard tools for analyzing NetFlow data and generating reports. BPF expressions are also used in the *CoralReef* network analysis tool described in [9,10] in order to generate traffic reports from collected trace files. The *Time Machine* tool described in [11] uses BPF expressions to define classes of traffic and BPF is also part of the query language used by the engine for retrieval of interesting traffic.

The `flow-tools` package [12] is another widely-used collection of applications for collecting and analyzing NetFlow data. Two of the flow-tools applications are responsible for filtering flows and generating reports: `flow-filter` and `flow-report`. The former application uses the Cisco Access Control List (ACL) format to specify a filter for IP addresses and command line arguments for specifying other filtering parameters such as port numbers, ASes etc. The latter uses a configuration file where reports can be defined by using a number of primitives.

FlowScan described in [13] is a collection of perl scripts which glues together a flow-collection engine such as the `flow-capture` application from `flow-tools`, a high performance RRD database, which is specifically designed for time series data [14], and a visualization tool. FlowScan has the capability of generating powerful high-level traffic reports, which might help operators to detect interesting traffic patterns. However, reports must be specified as separate perl modules, which is not trivial and might involve some heavy scripting.

C.Estan et al. [15] proposes an approach for detecting high-level traffic patterns by aggregating NetFlow records in clusters based on the flow record attributes. Aggregation on several flow attributes results in a multidimensional cluster. Initially all possible multidimensional clusters are constructed. Then an algorithm is executed which selects only clusters that are interesting to the network administrator. It aims at retaining clusters with the least degree of aggregation (so that a bigger number of flow attributes is contained). Interesting activities are considered to be exceeding a certain threshold of traffic volume of a cluster or significant change of the traffic volume inside the cluster. Finally, all clusters are prioritized by being tagged with a degree of *unexpectedness* and presented to the network administrator as a traffic report.

The *SiLK* Analysis Suite [16] is another script-based collection of command-line tools for querying NetFlow data. It provides its own primitives for defining filtering expressions. Unlike other network analysis tools, *SiLK* contains

Table 1. Query languages used by network traffic analysis tools

Tool	Query Language	Input Data Format
B.Nickless et. al. [3]	SQL	RDBMS
B.Babcock et. al. [4]	extended SQL	DSMS
Gigascope	GSQL	DSMS
Tribeca	proprietary	DSMS
`tcpdump`	BPF	`pcap` files
`nfdump`	BPF	`nfcapd` raw NetFlow files
CoralReef	BPF	`pcap` and `crl` files
Time Machine	BPF	indexed `pcap` files
Flow-Tools	ACL/proprietary	`flow-capture` raw NetFlow files
FlowScan	perl script	`flow-capture` raw NetFlow files
AutoFocus	proprietary	packet header traces/raw NetFlow files
SiLK	proprietary	raw NetFlow files

two applications that allow an analyst to label a set of flows sharing common attributes with an identifier. The `rwgroup` tool walks through a file of flow records and groups records that have common attributes, such as source/destination IP pairs. This tool allows an analyst to group together all flows in a long lived session such as a FTP connection. `rwmatch` creates matched groups, which consist of an initial record (a query) followed by one or more responses. Its most basic use is to group records into both sides of a bidirectional session, such as a HTTP request. From the huge collection of tools that we have surveyed *SiLK* is the only one, which is capable of declaring some correlation between flows. Therefore, we believe that it might serve as a good basis for a new flow query language.

A summary of the query languages used by the various network traffic analysis tools is presented in Table 1.

3   Research Issues

Given the large number of flow records collected on high-speed networks, it is necessary to reduce their number to a comprehensible scale using filtering and aggregation mechanisms. Each flow or aggregated flow has a set of properties attached to it that characterize the flow. It is to be expected that flows that correspond to similar network activities (certain applications or certain attacks) have similar properties. In addition to the properties recorded in flow records, one can derive further properties that are even more suitable to characterize the behavior of a flows. One objective when investigating traces is to detect regularities such as repeating patterns. These patterns typically spread over several flows. For example, if an intensity peak in flow X always occurs after an intensity peak in flow Y with a fixed delay, they form a pattern describing a certain network behavior. The goal of network administrators is to detect such patterns of correlated flows.

For example, one would be interested in finding out where, when, and how often a certain Internet service is used. A concrete scenario is a network administrator who wants to detect VoIP applications by finding STUN flows generated by VoIP applications when they try to discover whether they are located behind a Network Address Translator (NAT). If one knew the pattern that is created when a service is trying to establish a connection, one could search for this specific pattern in the selected flows.

The goal of this project is to design a flow record query language, which allows to describe patterns in a declarative and easy to understand way. The language should be able to define filter expressions (needed to select relevant flows) and relationships (needed to relate selected flows). Another requirement is that it should be possible to express causal dependencies between flows as well as timing and concurrency constraints. Existent query languages as discussed in Section 2 are not suitable for detecting complex traffic patterns because of either performance issues (SQL-based query languages) or because they lack a time and concurrency dimension (BPF expressions and the other query languages we discussed). Furthermore, the new query language should provide support for network specific aggregation functions, such as IP address prefix aggregation, IP address suffix aggregation, port number range aggregations, etc. which are not part of many standard query languages.

4 Conclusions

We presented the state of the art in query languages used by network traffic analysis tools and motivated the need for developing a new declarative language that allows to define and identify high level traffic patterns in a collection of network flow records. We plan to collect a comprehensive set of interesting traffic patterns from network operators and base our new query language on the needs to express these patterns.

Acknowledgement

The work reported in this paper is supported by the EC IST-EMANICS Network of Excellence (#26854).

References

1. Claise, B.: Cisco Systems NetFlow Services Export Version 9. RFC 3954 (October 2004)
2. Claise, B.: Specification of the IP Flow Information Export (IPFIX) Protocol for the Exchange of IP Traffic Flow Information. RFC 5101 (January 2008)
3. Nickless, B.: Combining Cisco NetFlow Exports with Relational Database Technology for Usage Statistics, Intrusion Detection, and Network Forensics. In: Proc. of LISA 2000, pp. 285–290. USENIX Association (2000)
4. Babcock, B., Babu, S., Datar, M., Motwani, R., Widom, J.: Models and issues in Data Stream Systems. In: Proc. of PODS 2002, pp. 1–16. ACM, New York (2002)
5. Cranor, C., Johnson, T., Spataschek, O., Shkapenyuk, V.: Gigascope: A Stream Database for Network Applications. In: Proc. of SIGMOD 2003, pp. 647–651. ACM, New York (2003)
6. Sullivan, M., Heybey, A.: Tribeca: a System for Managing Large Databases of Network Traffic. In: Proc. of ATEC 1998, pp. 13–24. USENIX Association (1998)
7. McCanne, S., Jacobson, V.: The BSD Packet Filter: A New Architecture for User-level Packet Capture. In: Proc. of USENIX 1993, pp. 259–270. USENIX Association (1993)
8. Nfdump, `http://nfdump.sourceforge.net/`
9. Moore, D., Keys, K., Koga, R., Lagache, E., Claffy, K.: The Coral Reef Software Suite as a Tool for System and Network Administration. In: Proc. of LISA XV, pp. 133–144. USENIX Association (2001)
10. Keys, K., Moore, D., Koga, R., Lagache, E., Tesch, M., Claffy, K.: The Architecture of CoralReef: an Internet Traffic Monitoring Software Suite. In: Proc. of PAM 2001, CAIDA, RIPE NCC (April 2001)

11. Kornexl, S., Paxson, V., Dreger, H., Feldmann, A., Sommer, R.: Building a Time Machine for Efficient Recording and Retrieval of High-Volume Network Traffic. In: Proc. of IMC 2005, USENIX Association (2005)
12. Flow-tools, `http://www.splintered.net/sw/flow-tools/`
13. Plonka, D.: FlowScan: A Network Traffic Flow Reporting and Visualization Tool. In: Proc. of LISA 2000, pp. 305–318. USENIX Association (2000)
14. Rrdtool, `http://oss.oetiker.ch/rrdtool/`
15. Estan, C., Savage, S., Varghese, G.: Automatically Inferring Patterns of Resource Consumption in Network Traffic. In: Proc. of SIGCOMM 2003, pp. 137–148. ACM, New York (2003)
16. Collins, M., Kompanek, A., Shimeall, T.: Analysts Handbook: Using SiLK for Network Traffic Analysis. CERT. 0.10.3 edn. (November 2006)

Enabling Next Generation Peer-to-Peer Services

Fabio Victora Hecht and Burkhard Stiller

Department of Informatics IFI, University of Zurich
Binzmühlestrasse 14, CH—8050 Zürich, Switzerland
{hecht,stiller}@ifi.uzh.ch

Abstract. Peer-to-peer (P2P) applications have the potential to improve network scalability and create a community in which resources are under the shared responsibility of its members. Current popular solutions target specific applications, such as file sharing and VoIP (Voice-over-IP), but important challenges prevent P2P technology from having wider acceptance in other services. Overwhelmed by interdomain traffic generated by P2P applications that build overlays asymmetric to the network topology, ISPs offer at a home user level only connections with asymmetric bandwidth. This measure efficiently hinders P2P applications. This paper introduces a new incentive model for overlay applications and ISPs to collaborate and to create at the same time a win-win situation. The approach combines two principles: (1) ISPs and P2P applications communicate to correct overlay asymmetry and (2) ISPs diminish bandwidth asymmetry by providing users additional bandwidth reserved for intradomain traffic.

1 Introduction, Motivation, Goal

Peer-to-peer (P2P) applications, such as [2], have emerged in the last decade providing many technical advantages over the client/server model; for instance, scalability in respect to resources, fault tolerance, and load balance. Recent surveys show that P2P traffic is currently responsible for more than 50% of Internet Traffic [7]. Applications that use the Peer-to-peer paradigm provide, for instance, file sharing, Voice-over-IP (VoIP), and real-time video distribution, relying on resources from the end-user to form an overlay network without necessary presence of central servers. The success of those applications causes reactions from Internet Service Providers (ISP). Alleging traffic excess, ISPs take several measures to reduce the use of P2P.

From the user point of view, however, the use of P2P applications brings many advantages. Besides these technical advantages listed above, there are other reasons for its popularity, *e.g.*, anonymity, lack of censorship, vast content variety, performance, forming of communities, and lower (usually zero) price.

Typically, ISPs differentiate between two types of customers: (1) end-users, who receive unreliable downstream bandwidth for a low price, and (2) content or service providers, who pay more for a more reliable connection with large upstream capacity. In a P2P model, end-users also become providers, thus negatively affecting ISP revenue. Additionally, traffic costs increase, since P2P applications offer content and services not available through other means. Nevertheless, the popularity of P2P suggest

D. Hausheer and J. Schönwälder (Eds.): AIMS 2008, LNCS 5127, pp. 211–215, 2008.

that services and content offered by it is a strong factor for users to contract the ISP in the first place.

Taking those conflicting factors into account, ISPs currently take measures to diminish peer-to-peer traffic [5], while not blocking it. Measures include closing certain client ports, using ISP-level Network Address Translation, shaping traffic, and offering only low upstream bandwidth. P2P applications can, at a certain level, work around those measures, except the latter one. For example, Swisscom [9] — market leader in Switzerland — offers for home users ADSL (asymmetric) connections through which end-users may only upload at rates 5% to 33% of their download bandwidth, efficiently hindering peer-to-peer applications. This is due to the fact that P2P applications have mechanisms to enforce that a peer is only able to downloads at rates it can upload [4]. Facing those limits imposed, some users are migrating to centralized alternatives [7] in order to explore all their download link capacity. ISPs usually do offer an option for symmetric access, but it is aimed at corporate clients and the relevant market price is much higher. At Swisscom, while prices per month currently start at 390 CHF for a 1.200 kbit/s symmetric connection, an asymmetric connection costs only 49 CHF, with 3.500 kbit/s download and 300 kbit/s upload capacities.

Analyzing these arguments outlined in this introductory chapter, the imbalance of incentives at the ISP level is clear. It is crucial, in order to see P2P applications being used at their full potential, that incentives are in equilibrium. The main question is on how ISPs and end users can cooperate to create a win-win situation.

2   Approach

Connections between ISPs are usually established through commercial agreements [6]. Traffic leaving ISP boundaries (interdomain) represents costs for the ISP. intradomain traffic is expected to cost less for ISPs and to be faster for users, since it does not leave the ISP, travels a smaller distance and has less chance of congestion.

One of the major factors that contributes to high cost of ISPs [8] with P2P application regards the latter's method of establishing an overlay network oblivious to the network topology. This situation can be referred to as overlay asymmetry. By building an overlay asymmetrical to the underlay topology, P2P applications waste resources by establishing a high number of interdomain connections. Optimizing overlay would, in this case, be an incentive for both end users and ISPs.

In order to manage this issue, many papers propose optimization on the peer side, not taking the ISP side into consideration [8]. Peers should establish connections preferentially with peers that are closer to them, from a network point of view, according to different metrics. Some papers suggest peers to make measurements — for example, ping, traceroute, a geographical database or IP prefix matching. The use of those techniques causes, however, a significant overhead and can be inaccurate.

[1] proposes an interesting model in which peers query ISPs to check for peers that are located within the same provider. The algorithm improves overall download speed of peers, while lowering ISP cost by reducing interdomain traffic. The work, however, addresses overlay asymmetry without considering bandwidth asymmetry. The

incentive for an ADSL end-user to prefer P2P applications instead of client/server ones is still missing.

ISPs must have an incentive to reduce bandwidth asymmetry without raising price, to allow home users to benefit from P2P. By coping with P2P applications, ISPs will enable users to benefit from new cutting-edge services, for example Internet TV and online gaming, possibly increasing number of customers.

The ideal method for users and ISPs to cooperate for locality exploitation requires actions on both parties. The new newly developed approach combines two principles:

1. Peers explore locality, with the cooperation of the ISP, favouring intradomain connections, and
2. ISPs provide end users with additional reserved upload bandwidth for intradomain traffic only; ideally, the total upload bandwidth is equivalent to the total download bandwidth.

ISPs must provide a helper service for P2P applications to communicate with, obtaining information about peer locality (whether intradomain or interdomain), which can be coupled with useful information, like delay, jitter, packet loss, hop count, and available bandwidth, since applications might have different requirements. For instance, in a file transfer, applications ambition maximization of bandwidth, while, for application layer multicast or voice over IP, low delay and jitter is required, while a constant bandwidth is enough. In this sense, a protocol must be designed for the communication, and P2P applications would have to be modified to use such service.

The P2P helper service can be implemented as an XML-based (eXtended Mark-up Language) Web Service in a fully decentralized and redundant manner. This technology allows for an easier development over different platforms. The protocol works as follows: the P2P application sends a request message to the helper service, containing the desired application class, and a list of IP addresses from possible peers the application may choose to connect to. Application classes are predefined as part of the designed protocol, and contain a set of characteristics that influence the decisions of the helper service; they may include, for example, different quality levels. The helper service responds with a list containing every peer in the request and a 0-100 integer number, representing a grade for each peer, according to the specified class. Peers from the same ISP will naturally receive a high grade. It is up to the application to use that information in its own benefit.

In general, peers with a higher grade should be preferred, although some randomness may be beneficial for the application to keep its P2P network well connected and more robust. It is important that the grade be an absolute value so peers can cache the value for some time, saving the effort of reevaluating the whole candidate set every time a new peer is discovered. Some metrics might be too volatile to make caching useful, but such inconsistent metrics have very limited usability and should be avoided. Exactly what metrics benefit most each P2P application is an interesting and open research question, together with the method for the ISP to gather such information from its own network.

Technical realization of additional bandwidth for intradomain traffic is trivial. Since ISPs already throttle bandwidth according to several factors, it would be necessary only to add the appropriate rules at the bandwidth broker. By reserving upload bandwidth for intradomain traffic, impact on ISP's costs are foreseen to be minimal, since intradomain traffic has much lower cost if compared to interdomain. Users of mobile phones are already familiar with this scheme, since calls to users within the same company usually cost less. It can also be used as a marketing tool, since users that have several Internet connections are likely to keep loyal to the same ISP and to convince friends to join the same. Further studies in a socioeconomic environment may become necessary at this point.

3   Challenges

Setting up such new service raises important questions and challenges on both sides. One concern regards customer and strategic data protection by the ISP. The helper service does not need to provide information on a detailed level, but instead general application classes are present in the request, and only an absolute grade is part of the reply. The right trade off must be found not to reveal information that are sensitive about customers, but that are still useful for applications.

By supporting P2P traffic, it is also feared that total traffic could increase. Although preference will be given to intradomain traffic, it is possible to reach a point that interdomain traffic will also increase. Further investigation is required to find this exact point.

What is considered a major issue regards legality of content. Anonymity, provided by some P2P applications to support censorship free information, is also used by some to offer a range of illegal content — mostly due to copyright infringement. Yet, anonymized networks are not necessarily the focus of P2P networks, as it is possible to use authentication methods as in a client/server approach if wanted.

4   Simulation Scenario

In order to validate the proposed approach, it is imperative to define a realistic scenario and perform simulations and measurements. Ideally, the solution should be deployed in an ISP and implemented on one or more popular P2P applications. Results must include several measurements. On the user side, quality of experience (QoE) is a key metric — depending on the application chosen, it may include start-up or buffering time, delay, and total bandwidth. On the helper service, the overhead created by introduction of the proposed protocol, together with its scalability and fault-tolerance can be measured. Benefits to the ISP must also be accounted, comparing volume of intradomain and interdomain traffic, preferentially from a cost perspective.

In addition to making measurements on a P2P application with and without the proposed mechanisms, it would be useful to also compare it to classical client/server (C/S) distribution paradigm. The results could be an incentive for ISPs to actually support P2P, assuming that a customer has the choice of obtaining content from either a P2P or C/S system. Possibly, it can be shown that, with locality aware mechanisms in place, hindering P2P traffic may not be a good decision.

5   Preliminary Conclusions

Although it is believed that the approach presented in this paper represents a major improvement over the state of the art due to the combined approach, extensive and realistic simulations must be done to prove its assertions. A more detailed protocol specification must be developed, with predefined service classes. Although there are different P2P applications, they share similar concepts. Since there are marketing issues involved with the approach as well, research on their evaluation must be performed.

Acknowledgment. The authors appreciate many discussions with Dr. David Hausheer on this paper's topic.

References

1. Aggarwal, V., Feldmann, A., Scheideler, C.: Can ISPS and P2P users cooperate for improved performance? ACM SIGCOMM Computer Communication Review 37(3), 29–40 (2007)
2. Bit Torrent (last visited: February 22, 2008), http://www.bittorrent.com
3. Brecht, S., Racz, P., Stiller, B. (eds.): Investigation of Application-level Routing, University of Federal Armed Forces Munich (UniBwM), Information Systems Laboratory IIS, Master Thesis (2003)
4. Cohen, B.: Incentives build robustness in BitTorrent. In: First Workshop on the Economics of Peer-to-Peer Systems, Berkeley, California, U.S.A (June 2003)
5. Constantinou, F., Mavrommatis, P.: Identifying Known and Unknown Peer-to-Peer Traffic. In: Fifth IEEE International Symposium on Network Computing and Applications (NCA 2006), Cambridge, Massachusetts, U.S.A, pp. 93–102 (2006)
6. Huston, G.: Interconnection, Peering, and Settlements. The Internet Protocol Journal 2(1), 2–16 (1999)
7. Karagiannis, T., Broido, A., Brownlee, N., Claffy, K.C., Faloutsos, M.: Is P2P dying or just hiding? In: IEEE Global Telecommunications Conference, 2004 (GLOBECOM 2004), Dallas, Texas, U.S.A, December 2004, vol. 3, pp. 1532–1538 (2004)
8. Le, H., Hong, D., Simmonds, A.: A self-organising model for topology-aware overlay formation. In: 2005 IEEE International Conference on Communications (ICC 2005), Seuol, Korea, May 2005, vol. 3, pp. 1566–1571 (2005)
9. Swisscom (last visited: February 22, 2008), http://www.swisscom.com
10. Zink, M., Mauthe, A.: P2P streaming using multiple description coded video. In: 16th Euromicro Conference, Sicily, Italy, August/September 2004, pp. 240–247 (2004)

Author Index

Printing: Mercedes-Druck, Berlin
Binding: Stein+Lehmann, Berlin

Lecture Notes in Computer Science

Sublibrary 5: Computer Communication Networks and Telecommunications

Vol. 5127: D. Hausheer, J. Schönwälder (Eds.), Resilient Networks and Services. XII, 217 pages. 2008.

Vol. 5067: S.E. Nikoletseas, B.S. Chlebus, D.B. Johnson, B. Krishnamachari (Eds.), Distributed Computing in Sensor Systems. XVIII, 552 pages. 2008.

Vol. 5031: J. Harju, G. Heijenk, P. Langendörfer, V.A. Siris (Eds.), Wired/Wireless Internet Communications. XII, 225 pages. 2008.

Vol. 4982: A. Das, H.K. Pung, F.B.S. Lee, L.W.C. Wong (Eds.), NETWORKING 2008 Ad Hoc and Sensor Networks, Wireless Networks, Next Generation Internet. XXII, 945 pages. 2008.

Vol. 4979: M. Claypool, S. Uhlig (Eds.), Passive and Active Network Measurement. XI, 234 pages. 2008.

Vol. 4913: R. Verdone (Ed.), Wireless Sensor Networks. XIII, 388 pages. 2008.

Vol. 4866: S. Fdida, K. Sugiura (Eds.), Sustainable Internet. XIII, 257 pages. 2007.

Vol. 4864: H. Zhang, S. Olariu, J. Cao, D.B. Johnson (Eds.), Mobile Ad-Hoc and Sensor Networks. XVII, 869 pages. 2007.

Vol. 4852: J. Janssen, P. Prałat (Eds.), Combinatorial and Algorithmic Aspects of Networking. VIII, 149 pages. 2007.

Vol. 4837: M. Kutyłowski, J. Cichoń, P. Kubiak (Eds.), Algorithmic Aspects of Wireless Sensor Networks. X, 163 pages. 2008.

Vol. 4793: G. Kortuem, J. Finney, R. Lea, V. Sundramoorthy (Eds.), Smart Sensing and Context. X, 301 pages. 2007.

Vol. 4787: D. Krishnaswamy, T. Pfeifer, D. Raz (Eds.), Real-Time Mobile Multimedia Services. XII, 197 pages. 2007.

Vol. 4786: D. Medhi, J.M. Nogueira, T. Pfeifer, S.F. Wu (Eds.), IP Operations and Management. XII, 201 pages. 2007.

Vol. 4785: A. Clemm, L.Z. Granville, R. Stadler (Eds.), Managing Virtualization of Networks and Services. XIII, 269 pages. 2007.

Vol. 4773: S. Ata, C.S. Hong (Eds.), Managing Next Generation Networks and Services. XIX, 619 pages. 2007.

Vol. 4745: E. Gaudin, E. Najm, R. Reed (Eds.), SDL 2007: Design for Dependable Systems. XII, 289 pages. 2007.

Vol. 4725: D. Hutchison, R.H. Katz (Eds.), Self-Organizing Systems. XI, 295 pages. 2007.

Vol. 4712: Y. Koucheryavy, J. Harju, A. Sayenko (Eds.), Next Generation Teletraffic and Wired/Wireless Advanced Networking. XV, 482 pages. 2007.

Vol. 4686: E. Kranakis, J. Opatrny (Eds.), Ad-Hoc, Mobile, and Wireless Networks. X, 285 pages. 2007.

Vol. 4685: D.J. Veit, J. Altmann (Eds.), Grid Economics and Business Models. XII, 201 pages. 2007.

Vol. 4581: A. Petrenko, M. Veanes, J. Tretmans, W. Grieskamp (Eds.), Testing of Software and Communicating Systems. XII, 379 pages. 2007.

Vol. 4572: F. Stajano, C. Meadows, S. Capkun, T. Moore (Eds.), Security and Privacy in Ad-hoc and Sensor Networks. X, 247 pages. 2007.

Vol. 4549: J. Aspnes, C. Scheideler, A. Arora, S. Madden (Eds.), Distributed Computing in Sensor Systems. XIII, 417 pages. 2007.

Vol. 4543: A.K. Bandara, M. Burgess (Eds.), Inter-Domain Management. XII, 237 pages. 2007.

Vol. 4534: I. Tomkos, F. Neri, J. Solé Pareta, X. Masip Bruin, S. Sánchez Lopez (Eds.), Optical Network Design and Modeling. XI, 460 pages. 2007.

Vol. 4517: F. Boavida, E. Monteiro, S. Mascolo, Y. Koucheryavy (Eds.), Wired/Wireless Internet Communications. XIV, 382 pages. 2007.

Vol. 4516: L.G. Mason, T. Drwiega, J. Yan (Eds.), Managing Traffic Performance in Converged Networks. XXIII, 1191 pages. 2007.

Vol. 4503: E.M. Airoldi, D.M. Blei, S.E. Fienberg, A. Goldenberg, E.P. Xing, A.X. Zheng (Eds.), Statistical Network Analysis: Models, Issues, and New Directions. VIII, 197 pages. 2007.

Vol. 4479: I.F. Akyildiz, R. Sivakumar, E. Ekici, J.C.d. Oliveira, J. McNair (Eds.), NETWORKING 2007. Ad Hoc and Sensor Networks, Wireless Networks, Next Generation Internet. XXVII, 1252 pages. 2007.

Vol. 4465: T. Chahed, B. Tuffin (Eds.), Network Control and Optimization. XIII, 305 pages. 2007.

Vol. 4458: J. Löffler, M. Klann (Eds.), Mobile Response. X, 163 pages. 2007.

Vol. 4427: S. Uhlig, K. Papagiannaki, O. Bonaventure (Eds.), Passive and Active Network Measurement. XI, 274 pages. 2007.

Vol. 4396: J. García-Vidal, L. Cerdà-Alabern (Eds.), Wireless Systems and Mobility in Next Generation Internet. IX, 271 pages. 2007.

Vol. 4373: K.G. Langendoen, T. Voigt (Eds.), Wireless Sensor Networks. XIII, 358 pages. 2007.

Vol. 4357: L. Buttyán, V.D. Gligor, D. Westhoff (Eds.), Security and Privacy in Ad-Hoc and Sensor Networks. X, 193 pages. 2006.

Vol. 4347: J. López (Ed.), Critical Information Infrastructures Security. X, 286 pages. 2006.

Vol. 4325: J. Cao, I. Stojmenovic, X. Jia, S.K. Das (Eds.), Mobile Ad-hoc and Sensor Networks. XIX, 887 pages. 2006.

Vol. 4320: R. Gotzhein, R. Reed (Eds.), System Analysis and Modeling: Language Profiles. X, 229 pages. 2006.

Vol. 4311: K. Cho, P. Jacquet (Eds.), Technologies for Advanced Heterogeneous Networks II. XI, 253 pages. 2006.

Vol. 4272: P. Havinga, M. Lijding, N. Meratnia, M. Wegdam (Eds.), Smart Sensing and Context. XI, 267 pages. 2006.

Vol. 4269: R. State, S. van der Meer, D. O'Sullivan, T. Pfeifer (Eds.), Large Scale Management of Distributed Systems. XIII, 282 pages. 2006.

Vol. 4268: G. Parr, D. Malone, M. Ó Foghlú (Eds.), Autonomic Principles of IP Operations and Management. XIII, 237 pages. 2006.

Vol. 4267: A. Helmy, B. Jennings, L. Murphy, T. Pfeifer (Eds.), Autonomic Management of Mobile Multimedia Services. XIII, 257 pages. 2006.

Vol. 4240: S.E. Nikoletseas, J. Rolim (Eds.), Algorithmic Aspects of Wireless Sensor Networks. X, 217 pages. 2006.

Vol. 4238: Y.-T. Kim, M. Takano (Eds.), Management of Convergence Networks and Services. XVIII, 605 pages. 2006.

Vol. 4235: T. Erlebach (Ed.), Combinatorial and Algorithmic Aspects of Networking. VIII, 135 pages. 2006.

Vol. 4217: P. Cuenca, L. Orozco-Barbosa (Eds.), Personal Wireless Communications. XV, 532 pages. 2006.

Vol. 4195: D. Gaiti, G. Pujolle, E.S. Al-Shaer, K.L. Calvert, S. Dobson, G. Leduc, O. Martikainen (Eds.), Autonomic Networking. IX, 316 pages. 2006.

Vol. 4124: H. de Meer, J.P.G. Sterbenz (Eds.), Self-Organizing Systems. XIV, 261 pages. 2006.

Vol. 4104: T. Kunz, S.S. Ravi (Eds.), Ad-Hoc, Mobile, and Wireless Networks. XII, 474 pages. 2006.

Vol. 4074: M. Burmester, A. Yasinsac (Eds.), Secure Mobile Ad-hoc Networks and Sensors. X, 193 pages. 2006.

Vol. 4033: B. Stiller, P. Reichl, B. Tuffin (Eds.), Performability Has its Price. X, 103 pages. 2006.

Vol. 4026: P.B. Gibbons, T. Abdelzaher, J. Aspnes, R. Rao (Eds.), Distributed Computing in Sensor Systems. XIV, 566 pages. 2006.

Vol. 4003: Y. Koucheryavy, J. Harju, V.B. Iversen (Eds.), Next Generation Teletraffic and Wired/Wireless Advanced Networking. XVI, 582 pages. 2006.

Vol. 3996: A. Keller, J.-P. Martin-Flatin (Eds.), Self-Managed Networks, Systems, and Services. X, 185 pages. 2006.

Vol. 3976: F. Boavida, T. Plagemann, B. Stiller, C. Westphal, E. Monteiro (Eds.), NETWORKING 2006. Networking Technologies, Services, and Protocols; Performance of Computer and Communication Networks; Mobile and Wireless Communications Systems. XXVI, 1276 pages. 2006.

Vol. 3970: T. Braun, G. Carle, S. Fahmy, Y. Koucheryavy (Eds.), Wired/Wireless Internet Communications. XIV, 350 pages. 2006.

Vol. 3964: M.Ü. Uyar, A.Y. Duale, M.A. Fecko (Eds.), Testing of Communicating Systems. XI, 373 pages. 2006.

Vol. 3961: I. Chong, K. Kawahara (Eds.), Information Networking. XV, 998 pages. 2006.

Vol. 3912: G.J. Minden, K.L. Calvert, M. Solarski, M. Yamamoto (Eds.), Active Networks. VIII, 217 pages. 2007.

Vol. 3883: M. Cesana, L. Fratta (Eds.), Wireless Systems and Network Architectures in Next Generation Internet. IX, 281 pages. 2006.

Vol. 3868: K. Römer, H. Karl, F. Mattern (Eds.), Wireless Sensor Networks. XI, 342 pages. 2006.

Vol. 3854: I. Stavrakakis, M. Smirnov (Eds.), Autonomic Communication. XIII, 303 pages. 2006.

Vol. 3813: R. Molva, G. Tsudik, D. Westhoff (Eds.), Security and Privacy in Ad-hoc and Sensor Networks. VIII, 219 pages. 2005.

Vol. 3462: R. Boutaba, K.C. Almeroth, R. Puigjaner, S. Shen, J.P. Black (Eds.), NETWORKING 2005. XXX, 1483 pages. 2005.